RICE

RICE

Maria Luisa Scott &
Jack Denton Scott

𝕿imes BOOKS

*For Antoine Gilly, our friend
and mentor, the most talented of the chefs.*

Copyright © 1985
by Maria Luisa Scott and Jack Denton Scott

All rights reserved under International and Pan-American
Copyright Conventions. Published in the United States by
Times Books, a division of Random House, Inc., New York,
and simultaneously in Canada by Random House of Canada
Limited, Toronto.

Library of Congress Cataloging in Publication Data

Scott, Maria Luisa.
  Rice.

  Includes index.
  1. Cookery (Rice)   I. Scott, Jack Denton, 1915–
II. Title.
TX809.R5S34   1985   641.6'318   85-40265
ISBN 0-8129-1254-3

Coordinating Editor: Rosalyn T. Badalamenti
Designed by Barbara M. Marks
Manufactured in the United States of America
9 8 7 6 5 4 3 2
First Edition

CONTENTS

ACKNOWLEDGMENTS

We are grateful for the assistance and generosity of The Rice Council, Houston, Texas; Madeline Altman (United States). Fung-Chan and Wah Chin (United States); Mary Neville and Alberto Wirth (Rome, Italy); Leela Nadhan (Madras, India); Motisingh (camp cook, Madhya Pradesh, India); Joakium Cleamanto Rodriguis (Goa, India); Sobham Sotara (Bangkok, Thailand); Denzil Wirasinha (Colombo, Sri Lanka); Marcelino Arias Artola (Hostal de los Reyes Católicos, Santiago de Compostela, Spain); Antonio Gonzalez (Restaurant Antigua Casa Sobrino de Botin, Madrid, Spain); Johannes Jensen (Copenhagen, Denmark); Nuyam Yigit (Istanbul, Turkey); and other helpful friends and chefs in the United States, Asia, and Europe.

RICE

Of all books produced since the most remote ages by human talents and industry, those only that treat of cooking are, from a moral point of view, above suspicion.

The intention of every other piece of prose may be discussed and even mistrusted; but the purpose of a cookery book is one and unmistakable. Its object can conceivably be no other than to increase the happiness of mankind.

—JOSEPH CONRAD

INTRODUCTION

THE WORLD'S MOST IMPORTANT FOOD

A meal without rice," the Chinese say, "is like a beautiful woman with only one eye." They should know; they've been cooking rice for 7,000 years. In fact, their word for culture is the same as their word for rice.

Do the Chinese know something we don't? Probably. They've long been aware of the remarkable energy it provides, which enables a Chinese coolie, who eats mainly rice, to work at dockside all day unloading ships and handling three times his weight with every load he carries. The rice-eating rickshaw coolie can pull two passengers for hours, running at the speed of a trotting horse.

For those of us with less strenuous pursuits, it'll probably come as a surprise to know that rice can actually supply 80 percent of our daily food requirements, one pound delivering four times the food energy of an equal weight of potatoes.

We hasten to add that rice is also delicious, a recipe rage, a menu classic in most countries, and the main ingredient in countless extraordinary dishes.

Yet a serving of rice costs just pennies, less than five cents, even in the United States. With all of its other assets, rice also is considered by professional chefs to be the most versatile of all foods, even more so than pasta, which may be the most pampered food of our time.

Speaking of pasta, some of you may know that we authored the first complete book on that subject, published in the United States. *The Complete Book of Pasta* appeared in 1968 and the critics have been kind enough to call it a classic. In fact, before we wrote the book, "pasta" was literally an unknown word in America. That remarkable food was unexplored, largely undiscovered, and simply called "spaghetti" or "macaroni." In that book we published many unique recipes for the first time: *carbonara, pesto,* nine *fettuccine,* and introduced the public to "angel's hair," that delicate fine pasta, and the first techniques which teamed pasta with vegetables.

When that first man of food, Craig Claiborne, visited our home in Washington, Connecticut, we introduced him to hot pasta with a cold sauce, *estivi.* He wrote that the flavor was reminiscent of *gazpacho.* We hadn't thought of that, but that's why he's Craig Claiborne.

What we hope to do with this book is place rice where it belongs, on a par with pasta, and also prove what a truly amazing food rice is.

Exactly what is this remarkable, prolific grain that is responsible for the survival of over two billion people and has such a magical way with world menus?

Oryza sativa is a cereal said to have 40,000 varieties in all. It is a member of the grass family, which grows on a slender stalk two to four feet high. It originally came from wild plants found in Asia, India, and Indo-China. Some archeologists believe that it was cultivated in Southeast Asia and Southern China 5,000 years before Christ; then it spread to India, Indonesia, the Philippines, the remainder of China, Japan, and Korea. Other historians say that rice originated in India in 3000 B.C. They relate it to a wild plant, "newaree," which grew at that time.

Wherever it originated, credit for its first cultivation came out of China in 2800 B.C., when Emperor Shen Nung wrote of yearly rice-planting ceremonies he created, during which he himself planted the first choice seeds.

Archeological excavations in China, in 1974, unearthed rice more than 6,960 years old; in India, rice was uncovered which dated back to 4530 B.C.; and in northern Thailand, rice was found that was grown in 4000 B.C.

It isn't surprising that in Asia rice is considered much more than food. In Indonesia, it is the gift of the goddess Dewie Srie; there no girl can be considered ready for marriage until she can skillfully prepare rice. The Javanese believe that rice has a soul and must never be stolen. In Madagascar, throwing rice, or playing a flute while rice is growing is certain to bring a harmful hailstorm. An old Chinese cure for aching bones, stomach upsets, and colds involved combining toasted brown rice and minced gingerroot, which had been simmered in whiskey, in a cloth. The compress was then rubbed on the joints or stomach. Alternately, it could also be inhaled.

Rice fields in Japan are given names as if they were people. Throughout Japan there are thousands of miniature shrines of Inari, the rice god. For centuries, Japan's standard of wealth was rice; feudal lands were valued according to their rice yield, and the famous *samurai,* or warriors, were paid in rice.

In China, an entire day of the New Year is set aside in memory of the first planting of rice, 7,000 years ago. Quitting or losing a job in China is called "breaking the rice bowl." It is considered very bad luck to upset a bowl of rice, and the deadliest insult of all is to pick up a bowl of someone else's rice and spill it on the ground. Chinese parents admonish their children to eat all of a serving of rice. For every grain of rice not eaten, they point out, there will be a pockmark on the face of their future husband or wife.

The custom of pelting newlyweds with rice originated in China and India as a fertility rite. The thrown grains are supposed to grant young couples many children and prosperity.

The story of how this greatest of grains came to America began in 1685, with a storm off the coast of South Carolina. Blown off course, a British brigantine en route from Madagascar put in to port at Charleston. As one token of his gratitude for the hospitality of the colonists, the ship's captain, James Thurber, presented a leading South Carolina citizen, Henry Woodward, with a bag of rough rice ready for planting.

Some historians disagree with this romantic version, claiming that the introduction of rice to America was neither an accident nor a single historical event, but that it was gradually developed by English colonists whose African slaves knew how to grow rice. It is a fact that many of the slaves in the Carolinas came from the West African coast south of the Sahara, where rice had been grown for centuries.

The rice-from-the-ship supporters claim that the single gift bag of rice soon supplied not only both Carolinas but Georgia as well. That could be within the realm of probability, as 100 pounds of seed planted per acre yield 5,000 pounds.

For a long time in the United States we probably threw more rice at weddings than we ate. Disgruntled rice farmers claimed that Northerners only made pudding out of it and Southerners just put gravy on it. Today, however, 84 percent of our households use rice often, and it is important as a health food, in cereal, and in a rapidly growing number of unique recipes. Finally, we are discovering rice!

Ninety-nine percent of the rice we eat in the United States is grown in the southern "rice belt" and in California, where the farming relocated when it petered out in the Carolinas after the Civil War. Established in Louisiana in 1888, it soon spread to Arkansas, California, Mississippi, Missouri, and Texas, where 18.5 billion pounds are raised each year on 3.3 million acres.

Our gourmet president, Thomas Jefferson, risked his life to smuggle a pocketful of seed out of Italy. Impressed with the quality of the rice grown in the Po Valley, and knowing that smuggling it out of the country was a crime punishable by death, Jefferson took the chance and brought Italian rice back to Monticello.

Less distinguished mortals all over the world are also taken with rice, not because it supplies more food for the money, but more taste for the food. It has such a remarkable way with other foods that it not only imparts its own flavor but seems to accentuate the flavors of the foods with which it is combined.

The Italians have made their *risotti* minor masterpieces, and in some areas they replace pasta. Spain's *paella* with seafood, sausage, and chicken, baked with saffron rice, is so outstanding that it is regarded as the national dish. The French *riz pilafs* and India's *pulaus* are classics, served with all kinds of seafoods and meats. The Creoles in Louisiana create poetry with rice, their gumbos and jambalayas making seafood sing. South Americans and other Latins consider it ridiculous to serve chicken without rice. The Indonesians, old hands with rice, set an entire table with rice and assorted savory dishes to serve with it. Called *rijsttafel,* it is such a spectacular offering that it has been adopted by the Dutch as one of Holland's major culinary attractions. The Chinese and the Japanese are the rice-eating champs of the world: The Chinese polish off at least a pound a day; the Japanese (who eat half a pound daily) word for meal is the same as their word for rice.

But some United States rice-eaters rank right up there with the Orientals. In Louisiana, rice is often eaten three times a day, and it is included in most Creole dishes. It is said that the Cajuns of that state can look at a field of growing rice and rattle off the number of gallons of gravy needed to serve with that amount of cooked rice.

We could have saved reading time and summed up the foregoing by simply saying that rice is the world's most popular food—but we're too enthusiastic for that. We had to prove it by writing a book in which we recount some of the experiences we had in discovering rice recipes in a dozen trips around the world.

We were fortunate in signing a contract with a major book publisher and a major airline to write a travel book in which we would record our adventures in as many off-the-beaten-track places of the world that we could find. We were given plenty of time and could wander anywhere that we thought would be rewarding.

Not only did we collect sights, sounds, and experiences (for example, searching for tigers on the backs of trained elephants in the foothills of the Himalayas), but we filled pages of notebooks with recipes of the various dishes we had. Most important, we made friends everywhere: Africa, India, the Philippines, Spitzbergen (above the Arctic circle), all of Europe, Sri Lanka (then Ceylon), Hong Kong, Cambodia, Thailand, and other places in the Near and Far East. Everywhere we went we found color and adventure, and rice—the world's common food denominator, served in many uncommon ways.

Along with some of these unique rice recipes, we also offer a few of the adventures associated with rice.

1

The
REWARDS
of
RICE

The food world today is full of fads that flare and then fizzle out like fireworks on the Fourth of July. For a while, the favorite was the exotic but bland fruit, kiwi, which appeared in ridiculous ways in all manner of recipes. As this is written, palate-dominating peppers, large and small, sweet and hot, are overwhelming many recipes in silly combinations. But this fad, too, will disappear.

Rice is no fad. The Orientals first discovered its rewards many years ago: Each pound triples in volume when cooked, so that you can get about 18 servings from a pound of raw rice. The same amount of potatoes yields only three servings. Uncooked, rice needs no refrigeration, stores on a shelf indefinitely, doesn't spoil, sprout, shrivel, or lose nutritional value. Cooked, rice holds its personality well for up to four hours, which, compared to pasta or potatoes, is a unique convenience.

At this time in the United States, rice is being hailed by the majority of households as the new American staple that can be used in all courses. We're also discovering that it adds appeal to most dishes, especially curries, stews, vegetables, and even salads. Rice dramatically gets the host or hostess out of the meat-and-potato rut and also is superb for meatless meals: Many of us have discovered the old Chinese favorite, fried rice with eggs and vegetables, and we're adopting the Middle Eastern technique of stuffing vegetables (eggplants, peppers, tomatoes, and zucchini) with rice. Rice also is excellent as a stuffing for pork chops, poultry, or game birds.

Rice rejuvenates all kinds of leftovers, and is unbeatable as a flavorful extender, making a little chicken, meat, or seafood look and taste like a lot. It is so compatible with seafood that crab, scallops, and shrimp with rice have become international favorites.

Although it is not native to America, and most of the classic dishes using rice did not originate here, one fact is clear: American rice is the world's best. Research and scientific farming here (seeding by airplane, harvesting with the assistance of laser beams, and the creation of hardy, prolific new types) have produced rice that is superior to any other in flavor, in cooking and storing qualities, and in cleanliness. Most other rices have to be washed, drained, and then washed again, but not ours. In fact, we are advised not to do this with American rice, as vitamins, its abundant food value, can be washed away.

Nutritional Value

We are trying to become an "eat light" society. Rice not only ranks at the top of the light foods, but it is the dream food for weight-worriers and health fans: Low in calories (just 84 in ½ cup, supplying enough energy to dance for 18 minutes, or walk for 35), rice is free of cholesterol, has all of the body-building essential amino acids, and is very low in sodium. It also is the most digestible of the important complex carbohydrates. Most food requires 2 to 4 hours to digest; rice requires just 1. It is also gluten-free and non-allergenic.

Like bread, most of the rice we buy in supermarkets is enriched, which means it also contains calcium, iron, and B complex vitamins in addition to its other assets. It also is the answer for natural food devotees—if they eat brown rice, it has all of the nutrients naturally, without enrichment. The bran layer in brown rice (removed in white rice) also has beneficial fiber and oil and another bonus, vitamin E.

Varieties of Rice

Although other types of rice are available here, the United States mainly produces twenty types, which are classified by length into just three categories: long grain, medium grain, and short grain.

Long-grain rice is about five times as long as it is wide. The cooked grains are usually separate and fluffy. It is the popular rice in the United States. Although it is excellent for general use, long-grain rice is especially good in curries, pilafs, *risotti*, and salads.

Medium- or short-grain rice are much shorter and plumper and cook much the same: moist and tender, clinging together more than long-grain rice does. They are used best in desserts, molds, meat loaves and croquettes, where their "cling" is advantageous. Short grain is raised only in California and sometimes is difficult to find, so you can substitute medium grain for recipes which call for short grain.

The three types of rice are also found in different forms, or different degrees of processing.

Regular milled white rice is sometimes called *white* or *polished* rice. This is probably the most widely used form of rice. The outer husk of the grain is removed, and the bran layers are then milled until the grain is white.

Brown rice is the whole, unpolished grain that still retains most of its bran layer. That bran gives a "nutty" flavor and slightly chewy texture to the rice.

Parboiled rice (or "Converted® rice") has extra-fluffy, separate grains, which hold after cooking for a longer period of time without "clumping." The fluffy characteristic results from the steam-pressure process the rice goes through before it is milled.

Precooked (so-called "minute rice") is the fastest, and, for us, the least satisfying of all rices to prepare or eat. Already fully cooked and dehydrated, this type simply needs to be rehydrated and it is ready to be eaten.

There are also a growing number of premixed *specialty rices* on the market, designed for those who'd rather eat fast than eat well. Just follow package directions. These dehydrated mixtures do not compare in flavor, aroma, and presentation with freshly cooked rice combined with fresh ingredients.

In doing research for this book, with the assistance of the Rice Council in Houston, Texas, spokesman for the rice industry, we collected all of the American and foreign rices we could find and tested them.

We tried Boil-in-Bag precooked long-grain rice; the Texas long-grain *basmati;* and a regular milled medium grain, much like a Japanese rice that was "coated with an edible cereal."

Even though this was American-grown rice, the cooking directions advised us to wash it in water (Japanese style) until the water ran clear; then soak in water for 30 minutes before draining and cooking. A California medium-grain brown rice, *Tsuru Mai,* had similar complicated directions.

Four regular milled long grains were excellent, but a California pearl short grain needed washing first. We didn't care for the results of three long-grain precooked rices that cooked in 5 minutes. We liked the ten brown rices we tried, long grain, medium grain, and short grain, and were very taken with a "Wild Pecan Rice" from Louisiana, a long grain with a lovely nutty, slight pecan-like flavor and aroma. That rice isn't wild rice, and there are no pecans in it, but it is an exceptional aromatic rice, grown only in the Evangeline farmland of south Louisiana.

We also tried a glutinous, "sweet," or "sticky" rice, which costs more than twice the amount of other American rices. It sure was sticky! Despite recommendations from friends who had eaten it in numerous ways in China, we didn't find it worth the effort. It required washing four times, or until the water ran clear; then it had to be soaked for at least one hour and then strained for two hours. After all this, it had to be steamed.

We also sampled imported "bagged" Chinese long-grain, Japanese medium-grain, Italian *Arborio,* and Indian *basmati.* Rices we tried from Latin America were usually broken, and all needed washing. The Italian rice (which was difficult to find and expensive) required special attention, constant stirring (18 minutes), and frequent additions of hot water or broth until it was absorbed and *al dente,* slightly moist, *risotto* style. It was good, but it was not superior to our long-grain rice. No foreign variety had the fluffy, firm separation of grains of American rice.

Besides finding the foreign rices at least twice as expensive (sometimes more) as ours, slow retail movement of those rices produced some that we found rancid. And some were contaminated with insects.

All this testing sounds complicated—and confusing. It was. India alone has seven kinds of rices, all with different cooking techniques. Our recommendation is to stay with American rice in the American styles, regular milled long grain, medium grain, or short grain, or the parboiled or converted rice in the same grains. Or use long-grain or medium-grain brown rice. These rices will do for any recipe in this book, and they will be easy to cook, reasonable in price, and excellent in taste.

Ingredients

Rice keeps coming up with rewards: Unlike many foods, it absorbs and magnifies flavors while it is cooking and usually is not drained. Although it may also be dressed with various sauces and cheeses, it's right in the pot that the cook should begin adding taste-making ingredients.

Onions add flavor to about anything except ice cream and chocolate cake. They work taste wonders with rice. The Italians, when preparing a *risotto,* generally sauté onions in butter and then stir in the rice. We learned our technique from them. But briefly sautéing rice in butter before adding the liquid does more than add flavor to the rice-flour coating. It also helps prevent the rice from getting sticky.

Broths and stocks: It is always preferable to make your own. For example, we make a basic stock in our Old-Fashioned Chicken and Rice Soup (page 32). But today many of us are pressed for time, so cans and cubes are helpful. We like College Inn beef and chicken broth, and Knorr beef, chicken, and fish bouillon cubes.

Using these liquids (beef or chicken stocks) instead of water add new taste textures. It's also interesting to experiment with tomato, V-8, lemon, and orange juices diluted with water (1 cup of juice to 1 cup of water). With pork, we've had rice simmered in apple or pineapple juice, mixed with water. We've found it rewarding and very different.

Rice cookery also encourages the use of imagination. Try

tossing hot rice with crumbled bacon and sour cream, a mixture of chopped scallions and fresh mushrooms sautéed in butter, a medley of cooked fresh vegetables, chopped pimiento, and chopped broadleaf (Italian) parsley leaves, even chopped mixed nuts. Rice is delicious mixed with the pan drippings and gravies from roasts, and we like plain white rice tossed with chutney when we serve a curry.

Cheeses

We've found that we use almost as much cheese in cooking rice as we do in preparing pasta. Readers will note that in the recipes (although several other kinds of cheese are used) we mainly recommend two cheeses: Asiago and Parmesan. Parmesan is widely known, but Asiago we discovered only a few years ago. Like Parmesan, it is a Grana type, a grating cheese that originated in Italy's province of Vicenza. Properly aged (it should be golden, hard, nutty, and two or three years old), it has, in our opinion, more flavor than Parmesan—at about half the price.

The best Asiago we've found is produced by the Frigo family, which has been working with Asiago in Italy for six generations. Today, they produce an excellent Asiago in Wisconsin. Frigo's is superior to the small amounts of the imported Italian Asiago that are found in some stores, because only the Frigo family in Connecticut properly ages (the Italians do not) it in special vaults. We get it quickly by mail order from Frigo Food Products Co., Inc., 46 Summer Street, P. O. Box 446, Torrington, Connecticut 06790. We prefer the *stravecchio* (very old), but *vecchio* (old) is also excellent.

Equipment

Not much equipment is involved in rice cookery. For such an exotic food, it's requirements are simple. We, however, like the cast iron, enameled heavy pots, with tight-fitting covers, made in France, Belgium, or The Netherlands. Not only are they excellent utensils, they are also colorful additions to your kitchen. We have the orange-red Le Creuset hanging from our racks. These pots are perfect conductors of heat, cooking evenly (rice will not burn or stick on the heavy bottoms, and the tops fit snugly for the perfect simmering of rice), and are easy to clean, good for storing in the refrigerator, or serving from stove to table.

Our Le Creuset pots (we are collectors; we have ten) range in size from 1¼ quarts to 11 quarts; they are what the French call round *cocottes,* casseroles with tight-fitting covers.

We also like the Le Creuset oval au gratin dishes. We have five, ranging in size from 7¾ to 14 inches. These go from oven to table with rice dishes that have cream and cheese, so-called casserole dinners.

We also hasten to add that all this equipment isn't necessary for rice cookery. For us, having these handsome pots and dishes enhances the whole idea of cooking and brightens the kitchen, but you can use whatever you have. Just make sure the pot or dish is large enough to handle the amount of rice you are cooking or serving.

We use a wooden fork for stirring the rice in its pot, and a metal fork for tossing up to mix and for fluffing the rice with butter for serving.

Molds

Depending upon what you're serving with it, it can be creative and dramatic to present rice in molds. Numerous of our tests proved that short- or medium-grain rice molds best. It clings, and that is important if you are trying to achieve various shapes. But all rice—long grain, brown, wild—can be molded if you're careful. The rice should not be cooked *al dente;* longer cooking is advised. Molded rice also needs lots of butter stirred in before it is molded to help it stay in the desired shape. Also, the mold itself should be well buttered.

The molds can be in any form (there are many sizes and shapes on the market, mainly for various pastries, hearts, flowers, balls, loaves, etc.); dainty *espresso* cups make neat little molds. For example, unmold a quartet beside an offering of curried shrimp. The presentation opportunities are limitless. But that's another rice reward: eye appeal.

Ring Molds

For example, consider the piece of equipment that we think is the most important and use most often when we are entertaining: ring molds. We have several recipes that illustrate how they dramatize and decorate a dinner table. The rice is usually cooked, placed in a buttered mold, and then briefly baked in the oven. Unmolded on a hot platter, it then can be filled with any number of creamed dishes, chicken, fish, shrimp, chipped beef, or chicken livers in a sauce. The possibilities are plentiful. Or if you're having a roast or a broiled chicken, the ring can be filled with creamed (or plain) vegetables. Even serving from a ring mold is interesting: A large spoonful of rice is placed on each guest's or diner's warm plate; then the creamed offering is spooned on top of the rice. Or it can be placed beside the rice, with diners handling it the way they prefer. We have ring molds in several sizes, ranging from 7¼ to 9½ inches in diameter.

Storage

White rice will keep indefinitely on the shelf. Once opened, however, it should be placed in containers that keep it clean and free from moisture. However, because of the oil in the bran, brown rice has a shelf life of just six months. Refrigeration will retard spoilage. Wild rice may be stored in a tightly covered container in a cool, dry place. It will keep indefinitely.

All cooked rice can be refrigerated for a week or ten days, or frozen for four months. A dish of leftover rice should be covered tightly with plastic wrap so that it won't pick up any refrigerator flavors or odors. It is a hypersensitive food that latches onto other flavors quickly.

Leftover rice "reheats" perfectly, coming back to a flavor as good as when it was first prepared. Simply add 2 tablespoons of hot liquid to each cup of cooked rice and heat on top of the stove for 5 minutes, stirring and fluffing the rice with a metal fork.

2

HOW TO COOK
RICE

As we do in all matters pertaining to cooking, we sought advice while writing this book from our mentor, Antoine Gilly, one of the greatest of French chefs. We spent nearly two decades working with and learning from this talented man, probably the longest cooking course on record. Antoine has been the chef for a king of England, a Prince of Wales, and a prime minister; he created the cuisine for France's famous Blue Train, and he was master chef for several of France's most distinguished restaurants.

Antoine Gilly's recommendations and suggestions are important to us, so we put the question to him: What American rice should we use for most dishes? What does he use?

Antoine went right to the point. "American Converted® rice is fail-proof," he said, "cooking just right every time. It is parboiled by a special process, but not precooked. It is not an 'instant rice.' Some people are put off or confused by the word 'converted.' This rice has been prepared by the processors to cook easily and perfectly and retain its natural vitamins and flavor. Most chefs I know use it because it holds on a steam table, on top of the range, or in an oven without becoming sticky."

We do use other types of rice, and we give explicit cooking directions in every recipe in this book, but cooking Converted® rice, which has also become our favorite, is as simple as reading the directions on the box. Here are our directions (which differ from those on the box only slightly) for cooking 1 cup of raw Converted® rice, which yields about 3 cups or five ⅔-cup servings.

1. In a pot (with a heavy lid and heavy bottom, large enough to handle 2½ cups of liquid and the eventual expanded 3 cups of cooked rice), over medium heat, melt 1 tablespoon of butter. Add 1 small onion, chopped, and cook for 2 minutes, stirring. (We don't always add the onion. It depends upon how the rice will be used.) Stir in 1 teaspoon of salt (if using broth, taste before adding the salt) and 1 cup of rice, blending well.

2. Pour 2½ cups of liquid (broth, water, etc.) into the rice

pot, stirring into the rice with a wooden fork. Raise the heat and bring to a boil.

3. Cover tightly, lower the heat, and simmer for 20 minutes, or until the liquid has been absorbed and the rice is tender.

Note: For firmer rice, use less liquid (2 cups) and simmer 5 minutes less, 15 rather than 20 minutes. For softer rice, use more liquid (¼ cup more) and simmer 5 minutes longer, 25 minutes, rather than 20.

- Directions on some boxes of rice suggest bringing the liquid to a boil first, then adding it to the rice that has been briefly sautéed with butter, salt, and onion. Bringing the liquid to a boil first is a step that we discovered isn't necessary. We found that adding the liquid to the sautéed rice, then bringing it to a boil worked just as well. Either way, the choice is yours. Rice cooperates.
- Some directions suggest that the pot be removed from the heat after 20 minutes and allowed to sit, covered, for 5 minutes, while the absorption is taking place. We have not found this necessary, but it does result in a somewhat drier rice.
- For regular milled rice, use 2 cups (2½ for Converted®) of liquid for 1 cup of rice.
- If using water, always add salt and butter.
- Stir the rice with a wooden fork only *after* the liquid comes to a boil. Then lower the heat and simmer the rice with the pot covered.
- *Keep* the lid *on* the pot. After the rice is simmering do *not* peek to see how it is doing.
- The heat must be low, but constant, so the simmer is even.

Some Questions and Answers

Why does rice become gritty? The cover has been frequently removed during the cooking period. It's like lifting your head to watch where the golf ball will go after the swing. Bad technique. Keep your head down, and keep the lid on the rice pot down on top of the pot, not lifted so you can watch the progress of the rice cooking.

Why does long-grain rice sometimes become "chalky" and hard when refrigerated? A chemical change takes place with some rices when they become cold. It's a starch change called "retrogradation." It can be corrected by adding small amounts of boiling water or broth to the hard refrigerated rice, stirring gently with a metal fork and reheating slowly. Also, if rice is going to be refrigerated, cooking it in more liquid than usual will soften it and retard that hardening process. For 1 cup of Converted® rice, use 3 cups of liquid rather than 2½ cups; for 1 cup of regular milled rice, use 2½ cups of liquid rather than 2 cups.

Why is rice sometimes sticky? Rice gets sticky if you stir it while it's cooking or if you cook it for too long a time.

What do I do if the rice isn't dry enough? Simply remove the cover and place over low heat for about 3 or 4 minutes, or until the rice is as dry as desired.

Most American rices seem to take about 20 minutes, covered, to cook. Is there an American rice that takes longer? Yes, brown rice. There are many brand names on the market, but all brown rices are natural and have had less milling than white rice. All need about 45 minutes of cooking, covered, and some directions also state, "After simmering in 2½ cups of water for 45 minutes, turn off the heat and let the rice pot sit on the hot burner for 10 minutes. Do not remove the cover until ready to serve." We found that this was good advice. It is also wise to check the directions carefully on the boxes of brown rice. Different processors vary procedure, some increasing the liquid and cooking time.

After cooking all rices (not dessert rice), we add room-temperature butter to the hot rice just before serving. We then "fluff" the rice with a metal fork, lifting it up with the fork rather than stirring. This not only increases the fluffiness but helps separate the grains. We use "sweet" butter; added at the last minute, it also gives additional flavor.

You'll note that we use the Italian term *al dente* in some recipes. By that we mean that the rice should be slightly chewy, slightly underdone. We suggest that the rice be *al dente* when it will be cooked further, such as baking in a casserole with other ingredients. We also recommend it for *risotti*.

Other Cooking Methods

OVEN

In order to save energy we often use this method (it's also the method of many French chefs) when we have a roast or other dishes in the oven.

Place 1 cup of rice in a baking dish, add 1 tablespoon of butter and 1 teaspoon of salt. Pour in 2½ cups of boiling liquid. Stir with a fork. Cover tightly and bake in a preheated 350-degree oven for 25 to 30 minutes, or until the rice is tender and the liquid has been absorbed. (Brown rice needs 1 hour.)

MICROWAVE

For regular milled, parboiled, or brown rice: In a 2-quart microwave baking dish (Corningware is excellent) place 1 cup of rice, 1 tablespoon of butter and 1 teaspoon of salt. Add 2 cups of liquid (not boiling) and stir well with a fork. Cover tightly and cook on HIGH (maximum power) for 5 minutes, or until boiling. Reduce setting to MEDIUM, or 50 percent power, and cook for 15 minutes, or until the rice is tender and the liquid has been absorbed. For brown rice, reduce the setting to 30 percent power and cook for 30 minutes, or until the rice is tender.

RICE COOKERS AND STEAMERS

There are a number of automatic and non-automatic rice cookers available. We don't use one (or a steamer either), as we are partial to the simple never-fail, top-of-the-stove method. If you choose to use one, it is important to follow the manufacturer's directions carefully. Generally, about ½ cup less liquid is required with the rice cookers. We offer the same advice for steamers, which are becoming popular: Follow the manufacturer's directions.

DOUBLE BOILER

Sometimes when rice is cooked in milk for dessert recipes, it is simmered over boiling water. Place 1 cup of uncooked regular milled medium- or short-grain rice in the top of a double boiler with 3½ cups of milk and 1 teaspoon of salt. Heat the mixture to boiling. Place over the boiling water in the bottom of the double boiler and cook, covered, for 40 minutes, or until the rice is tender and the milk has been absorbed.

Before reading the recipes, we again remind you that in all recipes where we use long-grain rice, that rice is Converted® or parboiled, for the reasons that we have detailed. If another type of rice is called for, we state that in the recipe.

For example, another type of rice may be the Rolls Royce of rices, wild rice, which is not a rice at all. It is *Zinzania Aquatica,* the seed of a grass plant that grows in shallow fresh water, primarily in lakes in Minnesota, which produces 80 percent of the world's crop. But we all call this luxury (more than $10 a pound) "rice," so we include it here.

Preparation of Wild Rice

Wash by running cold water over the wild rice in a wire strainer until the water runs clear.

Use 3 to 1 as the rule of thumb for the amount of liquid to use, i.e., for 1 cup of uncooked wild rice, boil 3 cups of water salted to taste. When the water boils add the rice. Return to the boil, stir, and lower the heat until the water slowly simmers. Cover and cook until the rice puffs open and reveals a white interior. The degree of doneness is a matter of personal taste. Some prefer a nutty, chewy texture; others prefer soft wild rice.

If the wild rice is to be cooked again, such as in a casserole or stuffing, it should be cooked only to the point where it puffs but does not open.

YIELD

One cup of wild rice yields 3 to 4 cups when cooked.

Other Methods

OVEN

Wash 1 cup of wild rice thoroughly in cold running water until the water runs clear. Combine with 3 cups of water in a 2-quart casserole. Stir, cover, and bake in a preheated 350-degree oven for 1 hour. Check the wild rice. Add more water, if needed, and fluff with a fork. Continue cooking for 30 minutes. Wild rice should be moist, not dry.

MICROWAVE

Wash 1 cup of wild rice thoroughly in cold running water until the water runs clear. Combine with 3 cups of water in a 2-quart microwave baking dish. Stir well. Cover and microwave on HIGH for 5 minutes. Microwave on MEDIUM (50 percent power) for 30 minutes. Let stand for 15 minutes; then drain.

3

RICE

with

SOUPS

Among other adventurous ambitions, we had always wanted to travel to the North Pole. Finally, a few years ago we decided that, if we were ever going to do it, we had better get the plan into motion. So we chartered a special ice-breaking 57-foot diesel ketch, *Havella,* with a five-man Norwegian crew. It broke ice all right, some of which we used in our predinner cocktails.

The steward (read "cook"), Aage Rutwold, proved to be somewhat of a genius, producing excellent meals on seas sometimes so rough that we often could not stand upright. Often all we could get down was a delicious soup, always rice in a rich broth, sometimes floating bright green specks (parsley, chives?).

We had, of course, brought along provisions—beef, pork, poultry—and several times we had bagged eider ducks to give the menu variety. But that rice soup was on the table almost every other day, and we always looked forward to it. We asked Aage for the recipe—several times. He always bobbed his head and said that he wouldn't forget to give it to us. But he never did. We wondered what meat or poultry (wild duck?) made the broth so rich, so consistently delicious.

As we were about to leave *Havella* for the last time, Maria Luisa said to Aage, "You haven't forgotten that you were going to give us the recipe for the rice soup?"

He shook his head, went to his galley, and came back with three items. Abashed, he held out a package of Knorr chicken bouillon cubes and one of beef.

The last item he gave us was a box of American long-grain rice.

"This is the secret," he said. "I couldn't make a pot of decent soup without it."

Savoia Rice and Cabbage Soup

SERVES 4 TO 6

1 1½-inch cube of fatback, blanched in boiling water
    for 5 minutes, drained, and cut into ¼-inch cubes
2 tablespoons butter
3 large ripe tomatoes, peeled, seeded, and finely
    chopped
1 1-pound firm head Savoy cabbage, cored and
    shredded
1 medium-sized onion, minced
1 garlic clove, minced
Salt and freshly ground black pepper
6 cups beef broth
½ cup long-grain rice
½ cup grated Asiago or Parmesan cheese

1. In a large pot, over medium heat, cook the fatback in the butter until it is golden and crisp but not brown. Add the tomatoes, cabbage, onion, and garlic and simmer for 10 minutes. Lightly season with salt and pepper.

2. Add the broth and bring to a simmer. Stir in the rice, cover, and simmer for 15 minutes, or until the rice and cabbage are tender. Taste for seasoning, adding salt and pepper, if needed. Serve with the cheese sprinkled on top.

Cream of Carrot-Rice Soup

SERVES 4 TO 6

2 tablespoons butter
3 large leeks (white part only), trimmed, well washed,
    and thinly sliced
3 carrots, scraped and thinly sliced
¼ teaspoon ground mace
Salt and freshly ground black pepper to taste
6 cups chicken broth
¾ cup cooked long-grain rice
About ¾ cup heavy cream
½ carrot, scraped and finely grated

1. In a large pot, over medium heat, melt the butter. Add the leeks and cook for 1 minute, stirring. Do not brown. Add the sliced carrots and cook, stirring, for 1 minute. Stir in the mace, salt, and pepper. Add the broth and half of the rice. Cover and simmer for 30 minutes, or until the carrots and rice can be mashed against the side of the pot.

2. Cool slightly and pour into the container of a blender and blend into a smooth liquid.

3. Before serving, stir in 2 tablespoons of cream for each cup of soup. Heat just to a simmer. Taste for seasoning, adding salt and pepper, if needed. With a metal fork, mix the remaining rice with the grated carrot and sprinkle over the top of each serving.

Bolognese Chicken Liver Soup

SERVES 4 TO 6

We enjoyed this in Bologna, where Thomas Jefferson risked his life to smuggle out that short-grain, nutty Italian rice. He needn't have bothered: U. S. rice is superb. But it took time and Jefferson was in a hurry.

> 2 tablespoons butter
> ½ pound chicken livers, trimmed
> 2½ cups water
> 1 teaspoon salt
> 1 cup long-grain rice
> 7 cups chicken broth
> ⅓ teaspoon leaf sage, crumbled
> Salt and freshly ground black pepper to taste
> ½ cup grated Asiago or Parmesan cheese
> 2 tablespoons chopped broadleaf (Italian) parsley
>   leaves

1. In a frying pan, over medium heat, melt the butter and cook the livers for 4 minutes, or until they are brown outside and slightly pink inside. Remove from the heat and cut into ¼-inch pieces.

2. In a saucepan, bring the water to a boil. Stir in the salt and rice. Lower the heat, cover, and simmer for 20 minutes, or until the rice is tender and the liquid has been absorbed.

3. In a large pot, bring the chicken broth to a boil. Stir in the chicken livers, rice, and sage. Heat for 1 minute. Taste before seasoning with salt and pepper; the broth may have supplied enough. Serve piping hot, sprinkled with the cheese and parsley.

Old-Fashioned
Chicken and Rice Soup

SERVES 6

This is a classic, that many processors try to reproduce in cans, but can't quite master. Rice doesn't like cans.

> 1¼ cups water
> 1 teaspoon salt
> ½ cup long-grain rice
> 6 meaty chicken backs
> 2 large onions, halved and each half nailed with a
>   whole clove
> 2 celery stalks, coarsely chopped
> 2 medium-sized carrots, scraped and coarsely chopped
> 1½ teaspoons salt
> ½ teaspoon freshly ground black pepper
> 1 bay leaf
> ½ teaspoon dried thyme
> 3 quarts water
> 4 chicken thighs

1. In a saucepan, bring the 1¼ cups of water to a boil. Stir in the 1 teaspoon of salt and the rice. Lower the heat, cover, and simmer for 15 minutes, or until the rice is tender and the liquid has been absorbed. Reserve.

2. Put the chicken backs, onions, celery, carrots, 1½ teaspoons of salt, pepper, bay leaf, and thyme into a large pot. Pour on the 3 quarts of water. Bring to a boil, cover, lower the heat, and simmer for 45 minutes, or until the chicken is tender, skimming the scum from the top as necessary. Remove the cover and reduce the stock by one-third over high heat. Strain the stock, discarding the vegetables and bay leaf.

3. Discard the skin and bones from the chicken backs, reserving the good pieces of meat.

4. Pour the strained stock back into the pot and add the chicken thighs. Bring to a boil. Lower the heat and simmer, partially covered, for 25 minutes, or until the thighs are tender. Remove the thighs to cool. Discard the skin and bones and cut the meat from the backs and thighs into bite-sized pieces.

5. Add all of the chicken meat to the stock. Stir in the rice and taste for seasoning, adding salt and pepper, if needed. Bring to a boil and serve piping hot.

Note: If the stock is not as rich as you would like after it has reduced, add 2 or 3 Knorr chicken bouillon cubes.

Greek Rice and Lemon Soup

SERVES 6

The Greeks sometimes vary this soup by adding small pieces of cooked meat or poultry during the last, simmering stage.

> *7 cups rich chicken broth*
> *6 tablespoons long-grain rice*
> *3 eggs*
> *¼ cup fresh lemon juice*
> *Salt to taste*

1. In a pot large enough to hold all the ingredients, bring the broth to a boil. Add the rice, cover, lower the heat, and simmer for 15 minutes, or until the rice is tender. Remove the pot from the heat and let stand for 5 minutes.

2. Beat the eggs and lemon juice together. Then stir the egg-lemon mixture into the soup. Taste and add salt, if needed. The broth may have supplied enough seasoning. Heat just to a simmer and serve immediately in hot soup bowls.

Chicken Gumbo Soup

SERVES 6 TO 8

1 3- to 3½-pound chicken
1 celery stalk, including leaves, coarsely chopped
2 carrots, scraped and coarsely chopped
1 large onion, nailed with 2 whole cloves
1 bay leaf
½ teaspoon dried oregano
1½ teaspoons salt
½ teaspoon freshly ground black pepper
3 quarts water
½ cup long-grain rice
1 1-pound can plum tomatoes with liquid (Pour into a
     bowl and break up the tomatoes with your
     hands.)
1 small sweet green pepper, cored, seeded, and
     chopped
1 medium-sized onion, chopped
½ cup corn kernels, preferably fresh (or use frozen,
     defrosted)
1 cup thinly sliced fresh okra

1. Put the chicken, celery, carrots, onion with the cloves, bay leaf, oregano, salt, and pepper into a large pot. Pour in the water. Bring to a boil, lower the heat, and simmer, partially covered, for 1 hour, or until the chicken is tender and the liquid is reduced by one-third. (If the chicken is tender before the liquid has reduced, remove the chicken, raise the heat, and reduce the liquid.) Remove the chicken and strain the stock.

2. Return the stock to the pot and stir in the rice, tomatoes, green pepper, and chopped onion. Simmer, covered for 20 minutes; then stir in the corn and okra and simmer, uncovered, for 10 minutes, or until the rice and vegetables are tender.

3. Remove and discard the skin and bones from the chicken and cut the meat into small cubes. Stir the chicken into the soup pot. Taste for seasoning, adding salt and pepper, if needed. Bring to a boil and serve.

Note: If the stock is not as rich as you would like after it has reduced, add 2 or 3 Knorr chicken bouillon cubes.

Consommé with Rice

SERVES 6

Rice is classic with simple soups, because it adds character and flavor.

> *1 cup water*
> *½ cup long-grain rice*
> *9 cups beef broth*
> *1 bunch watercress, washed and stems removed*

1. In a small saucepan, bring the water to a boil. Stir in the rice, cover, lower the heat, and simmer for 5 minutes. Drain if any liquid remains in the pan.

2. Pour the broth into a pot and bring to a boil. Stir in the rice, cover, lower the heat, and simmer for about 15 minutes, or until the rice is tender. Taste for seasoning, adding salt and pepper, if needed. The broth may supply enough seasoning. Serve in hot bowls with watercress leaves floating on top.

Cock-a-Leekie Soup

Brown Rice with Chicken and Leeks

SERVES 6

*8 leeks, including all of the white part and 1 inch of
    the light green part
1 3½- to 4-pound whole chicken with its giblets
2 teaspoons salt
½ teaspoon freshly ground black pepper
Water to cover (about 3½ quarts)
6 pitted prunes (optional)
½ cup long-grain brown rice
2 tablespoons chopped broadleaf (Italian) parsley
    leaves*

1. Remove and discard the root end of the leeks. Cut the
leeks into halves lengthwise. Wash well under cool running
water and cut into ½-inch-long pieces. Set aside.

2. Put the chicken, its giblets, salt, and pepper into a large
pot. Pour in the water and bring to a boil. Lower the heat,
cover, and simmer for 40 minutes, skimming the scum from
the top as necessary.

3. Add the leeks and prunes and simmer, uncovered, for
20 minutes, or until the chicken is tender.

4. Remove the chicken from the pot. When cool enough
to handle, separate the breast and thighs and reserve them for
another meal. Remove the skin and bones from the rest of the
bird and cut the meat, along with the giblets, into small, bite-
sized pieces. Reserve this cut up chicken.

5. With a slotted spoon, remove the leeks and prunes and
reserve them.

6. Raise the heat under the stock pot and reduce the liquid by half. Stir in the rice. Bring to a boil, lower the heat,

cover, and simmer for 30 minutes, or until the rice is tender but not too soft.

7. Return the cut up chicken, leeks, and prunes to the pot with the rice. Bring to a boil. Taste for seasoning, adding salt and pepper, if needed. Sprinkle with the parsley.

Note: If the stock is not as rich as you would like after it has reduced, add 2 or 3 Knorr chicken bouillon cubes.

Genovese Rice and Egg Soup

SERVES 6

8 cups rich chicken broth
¾ cup long-grain rice
1 tablespoon chopped fresh thyme, or ½ teaspoon
*   dried thyme*
3 eggs
¼ cup chopped broadleaf (Italian) parsley leaves
1½ cups grated Asiago or Parmesan cheese
Salt and freshly ground black pepper to taste

1. In a pot, bring the broth to a boil. Stir in the rice and thyme. Cover the pot, lower the heat, and simmer for 15 minutes, or until the rice is almost tender (*al dente*).

2. In a bowl, beat the eggs with the parsley and half of the cheese, blending well. Stir 1 cup of the broth into the egg-cheese mixture. Quickly stir this mixture into the pot with the rice. Simmer for 5 minutes, stirring constantly. Taste and season with salt and pepper. Serve immediately. Pass the remaining cheese at the table to be sprinkled on each bowl of soup.

Porro Brodo

Leek, Prosciutto, Rice, and Spinach Soup

SERVES 6

8 cups chicken broth
6 medium-sized leeks (white part only), trimmed, well
    washed, and cut into ¼-inch-long pieces
½ cup long-grain rice
10-ounce package fresh spinach, trimmed, washed,
    and coarsely chopped, or 1 10-ounce package
    frozen leaf spinach, defrosted and coarsely
    chopped
2 tablespoons butter
½ cup small prosciutto slivers
Salt and freshly ground black pepper to taste
1 cup grated Asiago or Parmesan cheese

1. Pour the broth into a large saucepan. Add the leeks and
bring to a simmer over medium heat. Cover and cook for 10
minutes.

2. Stir in the rice and cook, covered, for 12 minutes, or
until the rice is tender but still a little *al dente*.

3. Add the spinach (if using fresh) and cook for 5 minutes. Add the butter and prosciutto and the spinach (if using
frozen) and cook for 3 minutes. Taste for seasoning, adding salt
and pepper, if needed. The broth may have supplied enough. If
the soup is too thick for your taste, add more hot broth. Serve
the cheese on the side.

Athenian Fish Soup

SERVES 6

2 pounds firm white fish fillets (haddock, cod, etc.)
Cheesecloth, sufficient to completely wrap the fish
1 quart water
1 cup clam juice or fish stock (page 51)
1 cup dry white wine
1½ teaspoons salt
½ teaspoon freshly ground black pepper
6 whole scallions, trimmed and diced
2 celery stalks, scraped and chopped
1 small turnip, peeled and diced
1 1-pound can plum tomatoes (Chop the tomatoes and
reserve the liquid.)
¾ cup long-grain rice

1. Wrap the fish in the cheesecloth; then put it into a large pot. Add the water, clam juice, wine, salt, and pepper. Bring to a boil, cover, lower the heat, and simmer for 15 minutes, or until the fish begins to separate. Remove and flake the fish, discarding any skin and bones. Reserve. Strain the stock.

2. Return the stock to the pot. Add the scallions, celery, turnip, tomatoes and their liquid, and the rice. Bring to a boil, cover, lower the heat, and simmer for 20 minutes, or until the rice is tender.

3. Stir in the flaked fish and simmer until the soup is very hot. Taste for seasoning, adding salt and pepper, if needed. Serve in warm deep soup bowls, with hot, crisp buttered French or Italian bread.

Zuppa alla Abruzzese

Rice, Anchovy, Lentil, and Tomato Soup

SERVES 6 TO 8

1 cup dry lentils, picked over, rinsed, and soaked in
　water to cover for 3 hours, and then drained
1 teaspoon salt
½ cup long-grain rice
1¼ cups water
1 tablespoon butter
2 tablespoons olive oil
2 large celery stalks, scraped and chopped
2 garlic cloves, minced
4 large ripe tomatoes, peeled, seeded, and diced
8 cups chicken broth
8 anchovy fillets, drained of oil and mashed
3 tablespoons chopped broadleaf (Italian) parsley
　leaves
Freshly ground black pepper to taste
Salt to taste
1 cup grated Asiago or Parmesan cheese

1. Put the lentils and salt into a saucepan. Pour in enough
water to cover and bring to a boil. Cover the pan, lower the
heat, and simmer for 45 minutes, or until the lentils are tender.
Do not overcook. Reserve the lentils and the liquid in which
they cooked.

2. In another saucepan, combine the rice and the 1¼ cups
of water. Bring to a boil, cover, lower the heat, and simmer for
20 minutes, or until the rice is tender and the liquid has been
absorbed. Reserve the rice.

3. In a large pot, over medium heat, heat the butter and
oil. Stir in the celery and garlic. Cook for 5 minutes. Do not

brown. Add the tomatoes and cook for 5 minutes. Pour in the chicken broth. Stir in the anchovies and bring to a boil. Then lower the heat and simmer, uncovered, for 20 minutes.

4. Add the lentils with their liquid, the rice, parsley, and black pepper. Taste before adding more salt as the broth and anchovies may have supplied enough. Heat through. Sprinkle cheese on each serving.

Cream of Rice Soup

SERVES 4 TO 6

6 cups beef broth
1 cup long-grain rice
2 cups hot milk
3 egg yolks, beaten in a medium-sized bowl
2 tablespoons butter, cut into small pieces
Salt and freshly ground black pepper to taste
2 tablespoons finely chopped fresh chives
1 cup unseasoned croutons

1. In a pot, bring the broth to a boil. Stir in the rice, cover, lower the heat, and simmer for 20 minutes, or until the rice is tender. Drain the rice, returning the broth to the pot. Rub the rice through a fine sieve and return it to the pot with the broth.

2. Gradually beat the milk into the egg yolks. Stir into the pot with the broth and rice, along with the butter, blending well. Heat thoroughly, but do not boil.

3. Taste before adding salt and pepper; the broth may have supplied enough. Sprinkle with the chives and float the croutons on top of each serving.

Mulligatawny Soup

SERVES 4 TO 6

1¼ cups water
1 teaspoon salt
½ cup long-grain rice
1 large whole chicken breast
6 cups chicken broth
1 onion, quartered
1 carrot, scraped and quartered
4 tablespoons butter
6 whole scallions, trimmed and minced
2 celery stalks, scraped and minced
1 green apple, peeled, cored, and finely chopped
1 tablespoon curry powder, or to taste (page 86)
1½ tablespoons all-purpose flour
½ teaspoon dried thyme
2 medium-sized ripe tomatoes, peeled, seeded, and
    finely chopped
Salt and freshly ground black pepper to taste
½ cup heavy cream

1. In a saucepan, bring the water to a boil. Stir in the salt and rice. Lower the heat, cover, and simmer for 20 minutes, or until the rice is tender and the liquid has been absorbed. Reserve the rice.

2. Put the chicken in a pot with the broth, onion, and carrot. Bring to a boil, lower the heat, cover, and cook for 30 minutes, or until the chicken is tender, skimming the scum from the top as necessary. Remove and cool the chicken. Discard the skin and bones and cut the meat into slivers. Strain and reserve the broth.

3. In a large deep pot, over medium heat, melt 2 tablespoons of the butter. Add the scallions, celery, and apple and cook for 5 minutes. Do not brown. Stir in the curry powder, flour, and thyme. Add the tomatoes and cook off most of the liquid, about 7 minutes. Gradually add the broth, stirring. Simmer for 10 minutes. Taste for seasoning, adding salt and pepper, if needed. Stir in the chicken, rice, cream, and the remaining butter and bring just to a boil. Serve immediately.

Turkey-Yogurt-Rice Soup

SERVES 6 TO 8

9 cups chicken broth
⅔ cup long-grain rice
2 cups diced cooked turkey
2 tablespoons butter
1½ tablespoons all-purpose flour
1 cup plain yogurt
½ teaspoon ground cumin
Salt and freshly ground black pepper to taste
2 tablespoons chopped fresh dill

1. In a large pot, bring the broth to a boil. Stir in the rice, cover, lower the heat, and simmer for 20 minutes, or until the rice is tender. Stir in the turkey and remove from the heat.

2. In a saucepan, over medium heat, melt the butter. Stir in the flour, blending it into a smooth paste. Add the yogurt and cumin and simmer, stirring, for 1 minute.

3. Stir the yogurt mixture into the pot with the rice and turkey and simmer, uncovered, for 5 minutes, or until the soup thickens. Taste for seasoning before adding salt and pepper, as the broth may have supplied enough. Sprinkle dill on each serving.

Pork Balls and Rice Soup

SERVES 6

Serve this soup in deep bowls, accompanied by warm, crusty, buttered French or Italian bread. We also like a glass of cold ale with this lusty soup.

Vegetable Soup Base

*3 large leeks, including all of the white part and half
  of the green*
9 cups chicken broth
2 garlic cloves, minced
2 large celery stalks, scraped and chopped
2 medium-sized carrots, scraped and chopped
*1 1-pound can tomatoes with their liquid (Pour into a
  bowl and finely break up the tomatoes with your
  hands.)*
1 teaspoon salt
½ teaspoon freshly ground black pepper

Pork Balls and Rice

¾ pound ground lean pork
1 medium-sized onion, finely chopped
1 garlic clove, minced
½ teaspoon salt
⅛ teaspoon hot red pepper flakes
1 teaspoon ground allspice
*3 tablespoons finely chopped broadleaf (Italian)
  parsley leaves*
1 egg, beaten
⅔ cup long-grain rice

1. To make the soup base, cut off and discard the root end of the leeks. Cut the leeks in half lengthwise and wash them well under cool running water; then chop them.

2. In a large pot, bring the broth to a boil. Lower the heat and simmer, stirring in the leeks, garlic, celery, carrots, tomatoes with their liquid, salt, and pepper. Stir, cover, and simmer for 30 minutes. Taste for seasoning, adding salt and pepper, if needed.

3. To make the pork balls, combine all the ingredients but the rice in a large bowl. Blend well.

4. Moisten your hands with cold water and form the pork mixture into compact balls ½ to ¾ inch in diameter. With a slotted spoon, lower the balls into the simmering vegetable-chicken broth. Stir in the rice, cover, and simmer for 25 minutes. Taste for seasoning, adding salt and pepper, if needed.

Rice and Potato Soup

SERVES 6

1 1-inch cube salt pork, blanched in boiling water for
   5 minutes, drained, and finely chopped
2 tablespoons butter
1 medium-sized onion, finely chopped
2 medium-sized potatoes, peeled and cut into ½-inch
   or smaller cubes
½ cup chopped celery leaves from the center of the
   bunch
6 cups beef broth
1 large ripe tomato, peeled, seeded, and finely chopped
¾ cup long-grain rice
Salt and freshly ground black pepper to taste
1 tablespoon chopped fresh chives

    1. In a large pot, over medium heat, cook the salt pork
with the butter for 4 mintues, or until the salt pork is golden.
Add the onion and cook for 3 minutes, or until the onion is
soft. Do not brown. Add the potatoes and celery leaves and
cook, stirring, for 2 minutes.
    2. Pour in the broth. Add the tomato and bring to a boil.
Lower the heat, add the rice, and simmer, covered, for 15 minutes, or until the potatoes and rice are tender. Taste for seasoning, adding salt and pepper, if needed. The broth may have
supplied enough seasoning. Serve sprinkled with the chives.

Caribbean Pumpkin and Rice Soup

SERVES 6 TO 8

3 tablespoons butter
1 medium-sized onion, chopped
1 garlic clove, minced
½ teaspoon salt
½ teaspoon each ground coriander and allspice
1 bay leaf
½ cup long-grain rice
4 cups chicken broth (or more, see below)
2 cups fresh pumpkin cut into ½-inch cubes
Pinch of hot red pepper flakes, crumbled
2 cups cooked chicken cut into ½-inch cubes
2 tablespoons chopped fresh coriander leaves, or 1
    tablespoon chopped fresh parsley leaves mixed
    with 1 tablespoon chopped fresh chives

1. In a large pot, over medium heat, melt the butter. Add the onion and garlic and cook for 3 minutes, or until they are soft. Do not brown. Add the salt, ground coriander and allspice, and bay leaf. Add the rice and cook, stirring, for 1 minute. Pour in the 4 cups of broth and bring to a boil. Stir with a wooden fork, lower the heat, cover, and simmer for 10 minutes. Add the pumpkin and hot red pepper flakes and simmer for 10 minutes, or until the rice and pumpkin are tender but still slightly firm. Remove and discard the bay leaf. Taste for seasoning, adding salt and pepper, if needed.

2. Stir in the chicken and cook until it is just heated through. If the soup seems too thick for your taste, add more hot broth. Sprinkle each serving with the fresh coriander or the parsley-chive mixture.

Rice with Yogurt Soup

SERVES 6 TO 8

3 tablespoons butter
1 medium-sized onion, finely chopped
¾ cup long-grain rice
8 cups chicken broth
1½ cups plain yogurt
1 egg
2 tablespoons chopped fresh mint leaves, or 2
    teaspoons dried mint
Salt and freshly ground black pepper

1. In a pot large enough to hold all the ingredients, over medium heat, melt the butter and cook the onion until it is soft and slightly golden. Stir in the rice and chicken broth. Bring to a boil, cover, lower the heat, and simmer for 15 minutes, or until the rice is almost tender.

2. In a bowl, beat the yogurt with the egg until smooth. Stir 1 cup of the broth into the yogurt-egg mixture. Stir the mixture and the mint into the pot with the rice. Heat, stirring (but do not boil), for 3 minutes. Taste and add salt and pepper, if needed. The broth may have supplied enough seasoning.

Note: This can also be served cold, but, if allowed to stand, the rice will absorb much of the liquid. If the soup seems too thick, stir in additional broth.

4
RICE
with FISH and SHELLFISH

All over Asia, the birthplace of rice, no matter what variety of seafood is served, or how it is prepared, it is always presented with rice. Often rice is an integral part of the dish or used as a border or a garnish—but it's always there.

We asked about this several times. Some, who knew America, compared it with our habit of serving potatoes with meat. Others merely smiled and said, "Rice first; everything else second. For Asians, rice always leads the way and sets our tables."

But perhaps we found the basic reason in the Typhoon Shelter in Hong Kong, the floating city of the Tam Ka people. One night we dined on one of the boats with a family of eight, friends of a friend of ours assigned to Hong Kong. It was an experience we'll remember for a long time.

One fish, a big red one that looked like our red snapper, called a *garoupa,* fed eleven hungry people. The fish was cooked in stock in a wok over a brazier on deck. We all had small portions of the fish in its stock, which was sparked with ginger, ladled over large servings of slightly gummy but very white and delicious rice. We didn't ask, but we were certain that the rice had been cooked in seawater, dipped from that dark, over-populated harbor.

Rice not only made that fish go a long way, but it magnified and extended its flavor. That, we believe, is the real magic of rice.

Fish Stock

MAKES ABOUT 2 QUARTS

There are several ways to obtain fish stock. The simplest way is to use Knorr fish bouillon cubes which are very good. The second simple way is to use equal parts of bottled clam juice, dry white wine, and water. The third is this classic way.

> *2 pounds fish heads, tails, and bones (Or, buy less*
> *expensive fish, using the whole fish, cut up.),*
> *washed*
> *2 quarts water*
> *2 cups dry white wine*
> *1 large onion, cut in half and each half nailed with a*
> *whole clove*
> *2 sprigs fresh parsley*
> *2 carrots, scraped and cut up*
> *Leaves from 2 celery stalks*
> *1 bay leaf*
> *1 teaspoon dried thyme*
> *10 whole black peppercorns, cracked*
> *2 teaspoons salt*

Combine all the ingredients in a large pot. Bring to a boil, lower the heat, and simmer, uncovered, for 45 minutes, skimming the scum off the top as it appears. Strain the stock through a fine sieve or cheesecloth, discarding all the solids. Store in glass jars in the freezer.

Lisbon Cod and Rice

SERVES 6

We've had this dish several ways in Portugal and Spain, with tomatoes and potatoes, but also just creamed. We found that the rice version always came off best. Cooked properly, salt cod is surprisingly delicious.

The Portuguese serve a green wine, *vinho verde,* with this. We like an Italian *pinot grigio.*

> 2 pounds dried salt cod (soaked for 24 hours in cold
>   water, the water changed 3 times)
> 1 bay leaf
> ½ teaspoon dried thyme
> 2 sprigs fresh parsley
> 2½ cups water
> 3 tablespoons butter
> 1 cup long-grain rice
> 3 tablespoons olive oil
> 3 large onions, chopped
> 2 garlic cloves, minced
> ½ teaspoon freshly ground black pepper
> 8 pimiento-stuffed olives, sliced
> 3 tablespoons chopped broadleaf (Italian) parsley
>   leaves

1. Drain the cod and put it in a deep saucepan with the bay leaf, thyme, parsley sprigs, and 2½ cups of water. Turn the heat to high and bring the water to a boil. Cover, lower the heat, and simmer for 20 minutes, or until the fish flakes with a fork. Remove the fish. Strain and reserve the liquid. Remove and discard the skin and bones from the fish and cut it into small bite-sized pieces. Reserve.

2. Melt 2 tablespoons of the butter in the saucepan. Stir in the rice and cook, stirring, for 2 minutes. Pour in the reserved fish cooking liquid. Bring to a boil, cover, lower the heat, and simmer for 20 minutes, or until the rice is tender and the liquid has been absorbed. If the liquid is absorbed before the rice is tender, add small amounts of hot water and continue cooking.

3. In a large heavy-bottomed pot, over medium heat, heat the remaining butter and olive oil and cook the onions and garlic for 5 minutes, or until they are soft, seasoning with the pepper. Do not brown. Carefully stir in the olives, fish, and rice, and simmer for 5 minutes, or until heated through. Serve garnished with the parsley.

Scalloped Fish and Rice

SERVES 4

A little leftover fish plus rice, served in scallop shells or small ramekins, topped with a cream sauce and sprinkled with cheese, produces an elegant offering. Leftover rice can also be used. We often use leftover haddock or cod, but any white-fleshed fish will do.

4 tablespoons butter
2 cups seasoned cooked rice
1 cup grated Gruyère cheese
2 cups flaked cooked fish
2 tablespoons all-purpose flour
1½ cups warm milk
¼ cup clam juice
2 tablespoons fresh lemon juice
1 egg, beaten
Salt and freshly ground black pepper to taste

1. In a saucepan, over medium heat, melt 2 tablespoons of the butter. Use a wooden fork to stir in the rice and 4 table-spoons of the cheese, blending well. Remove from the heat. Preheat the oven to 350 degrees.

2. Lightly butter 4 scallop shells or small ramekins. Divide the rice and fish among the shells, arranging a smooth layer of rice and topping it with one of fish. Transfer the scallop shells to a baking sheet.

3. In a saucepan (you can use the one in which you heated the rice), over medium heat, melt the remaining butter. Add the flour and cook, stirring, into a smooth paste. Lower the heat and gradually add the milk; then add the clam juice and lemon juice, stirring into a smooth sauce. Remove from the heat and quickly blend in the egg. Taste and season with salt and pepper.

4. Spoon the sauce over the fish and rice, sprinkle with the remaining cheese, and bake until golden and bubbling.

Fish and Rice Casserole

SERVES 6

2 pounds ½-inch-thick firm fish fillets, from any white
    fish (cod, haddock, scrod, etc.), cut into 6 serving
    pieces
Salt and freshly ground black pepper
Juice of ½ lemon
1 cup long-grain rice, simmered in 2½ cups of water
    until quite al dente (it will cook more later),
    drained
2 tablespoons butter
1 tablespoon olive oil
2 medium-sized onions, finely chopped
1 garlic clove, minced
4 medium-sized ripe tomatoes, peeled, seeded, and
    chopped
½ cup dry white wine
3 tablespoons chopped broadleaf (Italian) parsley
    leaves

1. Arrange the fillets in a buttered casserole or baking dish
with a cover, leaving some space between them. Sprinkle them
with salt, pepper, and lemon juice. Spoon the rice between the
fillets. Preheat the oven to 350 degrees.
2. In a frying pan, over medium heat, heat the butter and
oil. Add the onions and garlic and cook for 5 minutes, or until
they are soft. Do not brown. Add the tomatoes and wine and
cook briskly for 7 minutes. Spoon the tomato mixture over the
fillets and rice.
3. Bake, covered, for 30 minutes, or until the rice is tender
and the fish flakes (but not too easily, or it will probably be
overcooked) with a fork. Sprinkle with parsley before serving.

Bluefish Fillets
with Avocado and Saffron Rice

SERVES 4

2 tablespoons butter
1 cup long-grain rice
2½ cups chicken broth
¼ teaspoon powdered saffron (or ¼ teaspoon
    turmeric), mixed with 2 tablespoons of broth or
    water
1 large ripe but firm avocado, peeled and cubed
1 tablespoon rinsed and drained capers
2 whole scallions, trimmed and thinly sliced
1 medium-sized ripe tomato, peeled, seeded, and diced
2 tablespoons fresh lemon juice
2 tablespoons olive oil
A light dash of Tabasco sauce
Salt and freshly ground black pepper
4 6- to 8-ounce bluefish fillets with skin on
Soft butter

1. In a saucepan, over medium heat, melt the 2 table-spoons of butter. Stir in the rice and cook, stirring, for 2 minutes. Add the broth and bring to a boil. Stir with a wooden fork, cover, lower the heat, and simmer for 20 minutes, or until the liquid has been absorbed and the rice is tender. Stir in the saffron and cover again. Keep warm.

2. Combine and blend well, but carefully, the avocado, capers, scallions, tomato, lemon juice, olive oil, Tabasco sauce, and salt.

3. Preheat the broiler to hot. Arrange the bluefish on a large buttered baking sheet. Sprinkle the fillets with salt and pepper and coat them lightly with soft butter. Broil 3 to 4 inches from the heat for 5 minutes, or until the fish is golden and flakes easily with a fork (but not too easily, or it will probably be overdone).

4. Arrange the bluefish fillets on a large hot serving dish. Spoon the avocado mixture over them and surround with the saffron rice.

Pesce e Riso in Conchiglie

An Italian Rice and Seafood Specialty

SERVES 4

8 tablespoons (1 stick) butter
2 shallots, or 1 small white onion, minced
1 cup diced uncooked lobster, shrimp, crab meat, or
    scallops
3 tablespoons all-purpose flour
1½ cups milk, warmed
2 tablespoons dry vermouth
Salt to taste
⅛ teaspoon cayenne pepper
1 cup flaked, cooked white fish (sole, cod, halibut, etc.)
1½ cups cooked long-grain rice
2 tablespoons fine fresh bread crumbs
4 tablespoons grated Asiago or Parmesan cheese

1. In a frying pan, over medium heat, melt 3 tablespoons of the butter. Add the shallots and cook until they are soft. Do not brown. Stir in the shellfish and cook for 3 to 4 minutes. (If you are using lobster, shrimp, or crab, cook until they just start to turn pink; if you are using scallops, cook until they begin to become firm.)

2. In a saucepan, melt 3 tablespoons of the butter. Add

the flour and cook, stirring, into a smooth paste. Gradually add the milk and cook, stirring into a smooth, thickened sauce. Stir in the vermouth, salt, and cayenne. Mix the sauce with the shellfish and the flaked fish. Preheat the oven to 400 degrees.

3. Butter 4 scallop shells or small ramekins. Divide the rice among them. Spoon the sauced seafood over the rice. Sprinkle with the bread crumbs, then the cheese, and dot with remaining butter.

4. Bake for 15 minutes, or until the top is golden and the sauce bubbling.

Mussels Greek Style

SERVES 6

36 large fresh mussels with tightly closed, unbroken
  shells
½ cup olive oil
2 medium-sized onions, finely chopped
½ cup pignoli
¾ cup long-grain rice
¼ cup currants
½ teaspoon ground allspice
⅓ teaspoon ground cinnamon
1 teaspoon salt
¼ teaspoon freshly ground black pepper
1¼ cups chicken broth
½ cup dry white wine
Water
1 bay leaf
Lemon wedges

1. Scrub the mussels with a wire brush and remove the beards. Rinse in several changes of cool water, or under cool running water.

2. In a saucepan, heat ¼ cup of the olive oil. Add the onions and cook until soft and golden, for about 6 minutes. Add the *pignoli* and cook for 2 minutes, or until they are golden and crisp. Stir in the rice, currants, allspice, cinnamon, salt, pepper, and broth. Bring to a boil, stir with a wooden fork, cover, lower the heat, and simmer for 20 minutes, or until the liquid has been absorbed.

3. Open the mussels with a sharp knife, leaving the 2 parts of the shell attached at the joint. Stuff each mussel with 1 tablespoon of the rice filling. Close the shells and tie with kitchen string.

4. Arrange the stuffed mussels in a large heavy saucepan, in two layers. Pour on the wine, remaining olive oil, and just enough water to cover. Add the bay leaf. Set a heavy plate on top to prevent the mussels from moving around. Bring to a boil, cover, lower the heat, and simmer for 20 minutes. Remove from the heat and cool in the pan.

5. Remove the mussels with a slotted spoon. Remove the string and serve the mussels at room temperature, garnished with lemon wedges.

Note: The mussels can be cooked in advance, chilled, and then brought to room temperature before serving.

Paella

SERVES 6 TO 8

Paella could be the national dish of Spain, with different varieties being offered in various parts of the country. Sometimes it's mainly seafood; some prefer it with poultry, others with sausage; often with a mixture. But the "Queen of the Paellas" is *Paella Valenciana,* which contains everything. Rice remains the principle and most important ingredient; yellow rice, made so by saffron. Saffron (dried stamens of the crocus) is expensive and, we believe, contributes little to the flavor of the dish. Thus, as it is mainly cosmetic, turmeric can be substituted. But do it your own way as this is simply an economic tip.

We learned how to make the dish at Madrid's Botin Restaurant, working with their chef for several days, and, even bringing back to the United States a couple of Botin's special metal paella pans, the *paelleras.* These pans aren't necessary to produce the dish, but, as you cook and serve in them, they're handy, and, we think, dramatic.

> 3 chorizos (*Spanish sausages*), or ½ pound Italian
>   *sweet sausage*
> ½ cup olive oil, approximately
> 1 2- to 2½-pound chicken, cut into at least 8 pieces
>   (Do not use wings or back.)
> Salt and freshly ground black pepper to taste
> 6 to 8 small serving pieces fresh haddock
> 1 cup diced lean ham
> 1 large onion, finely minced
> 1 garlic clove, minced
> 3 cups long-grain rice
> ½ teaspoon powdered saffron
> 1 large ripe tomato, peeled, seeded, and chopped, or 1
>   cup canned tomatoes, drained and chopped

7 to 8 cups chicken broth
½ cup shelled peas, slightly undercooked in salted
boiling water, or use the same amount of frozen
peas, defrosted
12 medium-sized shrimp, shelled and deveined
12 mussels or clams, scrubbed and beards removed
from the mussels
1 large pimiento, cut into 8 or more strips
1 lemon, cut into 8 wedges

1. Prick the skins of the sausages in several places and simmer them in water for 10 minutes. Drain and brown in 2 tablespoons of the olive oil. Drain on paper towels and cut into ¼-inch-thick slices. Reserve.

2. In a large paella pan, a large deep frying pan, or a large flameproof casserole, over medium-high heat, heat ¼ cup of the olive oil and evenly brown the chicken pieces, seasoning them with salt and pepper. Remove and reserve. Add the haddock and season lightly with salt and pepper. Cook for 45 seconds on each side, adding more oil, if needed. Remove and reserve. Add the ham and more oil, if needed, to the pan and cook for 2 minutes. Remove with a slotted spoon and reserve.

3. Add the onion and garlic to the pan and cook for 5 minutes, or until they are soft. Do not brown. Add the rice and cook, stirring, for 2 minutes. Stir in the saffron, tomato, and 7 cups of the broth. Simmer for 10 minutes. Preheat the oven to 350 degrees.

4. Stir in the peas. Arrange the sausage slices and chicken on the rice, partially burying them. Bring to a boil on top of the stove, cover with foil, and bake for 20 minutes. Add the haddock, shrimp, mussels or clams, partially burying them, and bake, uncovered, for 15 minutes, or until the meats, rice, and shellfish are cooked. Halfway through the cooking time, taste for seasoning, adding more salt and pepper, if needed. If the liquid is absorbed before the rice is tender, add small amounts of hot broth.

5. Garnish with the pimiento strips and lemon wedges just before serving.

Curried Lobster
in a Singhalese Rice Ring

SERVES 6

Singhalese Rice Ring

6 tablespoons butter
2 medium-sized onions, finely chopped
2 cups short- or medium-grain rice
3 whole cloves
4½ cups chicken broth
½ cup unsalted cashews, toasted and broken into
    small pieces
½ cup golden raisins, plumped in 1 tablespoon butter
    over medium heat and then halved
3 tablespoons finely chopped fresh coriander leaves, or
    1½ tablespoons chopped fresh parsley leaves and
    1½ tablespoons chopped fresh chives
Salt and freshly ground black pepper to taste

The Curried Lobster

4 tablespoons butter
2 medium-sized onions, finely chopped
1½ tablespoons curry powder, or to taste
3 tablespoons all-purpose flour
1 cup chicken broth
½ cup clam juice
½ cup dry sherry
2 tablespoons tomato purée
½ cup heavy cream
⅛ teaspoon cayenne pepper, or to taste
Salt to taste
4 cups diced cooked lobster meat

1. To make the Rice Ring, melt 3 tablespoons of the butter, over medium heat in a saucepan. Add the onions and cook for 5 minutes, or until they are soft. Do not brown. Add the rice and stir until it is well coated. Cook for 2 minutes. Add the cloves and broth and bring to a boil. Cover, lower the heat, and simmer for 20 minutes, or until the rice is just *al dente* and the liquid has been absorbed. Discard the cloves.

2. Stir in the cashews, raisins, coriander, salt and pepper, and the remaining butter (in small pieces). Preheat the oven to 350 degrees.

3. Press into a buttered 6- or 8-cup ring mold (the rice should fill the mold), cover with foil, and bake for 10 minutes. Unmold onto a hot serving dish and spoon the lobster and sauce into the ring. If the ring cannot accommodate all of the lobster, serve the remainder in a bowl.

4. To make the Curried Lobster, melt the butter in a saucepan over medium heat. Add the onions and cook for 5 minutes, or until they are soft. Do not brown. Stir in the curry powder and flour, stirring until well blended. Gradually stir in the chicken broth, clam juice, sherry, and tomato purée and cook, stirring into a smooth sauce. Stir in the cream and cayenne. Taste and season with salt. Add the lobster meat and heat through. Do not overcook as the lobster will toughen.

Risotto di Frutti di Mare

SERVES 4

This seafood-rice offering that we found on the Italian "Riviera"
could be our favorite.

> *12 clams in their shells, well scrubbed*
> *12 mussels in their shells, well scrubbed and*
> *   debearded*
> *4 tablespoons butter*
> *2 tablespoons olive oil*
> *1 medium-sized onion, finely chopped*
> *1 garlic clove, minced*
> *1 celery stalk, scraped and finely chopped*
> *12 medium-sized shrimp, shelled and deveined*
> *1½ cups long-grain rice*
> *1½ cups clam juice or fish stock (page 51)*
> *1½ cups water or fish stock (page 51)*
> *¼ teaspoon powdered saffron*
> *½ cup dry white wine*
> *3 tablespoons chopped broadleaf (Italian) parsley*
> *   leaves*
> *Salt and freshly ground black pepper to taste*

1. Put the clams and mussels in a large pot with 2 cups of
water and steam over medium heat until the shells open. As
they open, remove the clams and mussels from the shells and
pour the liquid from the shells into a bowl. Discard any mussels and clams that do not open. Reserve the shellfish.

2. In a deep saucepan, over medium heat, heat 2 tablespoons of the butter with the olive oil. Add the onion, garlic,
and celery and cook for 5 minutes, or until they are soft. Do
not brown. Stir in the clams, mussels, and shrimp and cook for
4 minutes, or until the shrimp are pink and the clams and

mussels become firm. Do not overcook or they'll toughen. Remove the clams, mussels, and shrimp with a slotted spoon. Reserve and keep them warm.

3. Stir the rice into the saucepan. Pour in the clam juice and water and the liquid saved from the shells. Dissolve the saffron in the wine and stir the mixture into the rice with a wooden fork, blending it well. Bring to a boil, lower the heat, stir with a wooden fork, cover, and simmer for 20 minutes, or until the rice is *al dente* and most of the liquid has been absorbed. The *risotto* should be slightly moist but not soupy. If it seems dry, add a small amount of hot liquid.

4. Stir in the shellfish, remaining butter (in small pieces), and parsley with a metal fork, fluffing up the rice. Taste for seasoning and add salt and pepper, if necessary. Cover the pot and heat for 1 minute.

Crab Meat Cocer

SERVES 4 TO 6

1 pound crab meat, fresh or canned
1 bunch (about 1½ pounds) broccoli
7 tablespoons butter
4 tablespoons all-purpose flour
3 cups light cream or half-and-half, heated
Salt to taste
⅛ teaspoon cayenne pepper
⅓ cup thinly sliced scallions (white part only)
1 canned pimiento, coarsely chopped
3 cups al dente-cooked long-grain rice
3 tablespoons fresh lemon juice
¼ cup toasted slivered almonds

1. Pick over the crab meat to remove any bits of cartilage or shell.

2. Separate the flowerets from the stems of the broccoli. Scrape the stems and cook them in salted boiling water until crisp-tender. Remove from the water with a slotted spoon. Cook the flowerets in the same water until crisp-tender; then drain. Reserve and keep warm. Coarsely chop the broccoli stems and reserve separately.

3. In a saucepan, over medium heat, melt 4 tablespoons of the butter. Stir in the flour and cook, stirring, into a smooth paste. Gradually add the cream and cook, stirring into a smooth sauce. Season with salt and cayenne. Stir in the crab meat, scallions, and pimiento. Preheat the oven to 375 degrees.

4. In a shallow buttered baking dish, spread a smooth layer of the rice. Arrange a layer of the chopped broccoli stems over the rice. Spoon the crab meat mixture over the broccoli. Bake for 20 minutes, or until heated through and the sauce is bubbling.

5. Heat the lemon juice with the remaining butter and pour the mixture over the broccoli flowerets.

6. Arrange the flowerets around the rim of the dish with the crab meat and rice and sprinkle the almonds over the top.

Tuna with Rice

SERVES 4

Let's face it, canned tuna is an All-American favorite, and with good reason: flavor, ease of handling, and versatility. And teamed with rice it's a winner. We like the "solid white, albacore"; it's finer textured, less oily, and more delicate than regular tuna.

> 6 tablespoons butter
> 2 medium-sized white onions, chopped
> 1 cup long-grain rice
> 2½ cups chicken broth
> 1 10-ounce package frozen tiny peas
> 8 medium-sized fresh mushrooms, thinly sliced
> Salt and freshly ground black pepper to taste
> 1 7-ounce can solid white tuna (albacore), drained
>   and flaked

1. In a large deep frying pan, over medium heat, melt 3 tablespoons of the butter and cook the onions for 5 minutes, or until they are soft. Do not brown. Add the rice and cook, stirring, for 1 minute. Pour in 1 cup of the broth, bring to a boil, lower the heat, cover, and simmer for 10 minutes. Stir in the peas and the remaining broth. Bring to a boil, lower the heat, cover, and simmer for 10 minutes, or until the peas and rice are tender and the broth has been absorbed.

2. In another small frying pan, over medium-high heat, melt the remaining butter and cook the mushrooms for 3 minutes, or until any liquid has cooked off and they are slightly brown. Use a metal fork to combine the mushrooms and the butter they cooked in with the rice. Taste and season with salt and pepper.

3. Blend in the tuna and heat through, fluffing the rice mixture with a metal fork. Spoon into a hot serving dish.

Mussels Marinara

SERVES 4

This one we discovered in Taranto, in the south, on the heel of the boot that is Italy.

> 4 tablespoons olive oil
> 2 garlic cloves, flattened with the broad blade of a
>   knife and peeled
> ½ cup dry red wine
> 36 fresh mussels, well scrubbed and debearded
> 1 1-pound can imported Italian plum tomatoes (Finely
>   chop the tomatoes and save the liquid.)
> ½ to 1 cup clam juice
> 5 tablespoons butter
> 1 medium-sized onion, finely chopped
> 1 garlic clove, minced
> 1 cup long-grain rice
> Salt and freshly ground black pepper to taste
> 3 tablespoons chopped broadleaf (Italian) parsley
>   leaves

1. In a large pot, heat 2 tablespoons of the olive oil. Add the flattened garlic cloves and cook until they are golden. Discard the garlic. Remove the pot from the heat and quickly (to avoid spattering) pour in the wine. Add the mussels, cover tightly, and cook over high heat, shaking the pot occasionally, for 5 minutes, or until they open. Discard any mussels that do not open.

2. Drain the mussels in a strainer over a bowl to reserve the liquid. Set aside 4 mussels in their shells. Remove the remaining mussels from their shells, adding any liquid in the shells to the liquid in the bowl. Strain all the liquid through cheesecloth. Pour the strained liquid into a 4-cup measuring cup. Add the liquid from the tomatoes and enough clam juice to bring the liquid up to the 2½-cup mark.

3. In a large saucepan, over medium heat, heat 2 tablespoons of the butter with the remaining oil. Add the onion and minced garlic and cook for 5 minutes, or until they are soft. Do not brown. Stir in the rice and cook, stirring, for 2 minutes.

4. Heat the clam juice-tomato liquid to a boil. Pour 1 cup of it onto the rice. Stir with a wooden fork, cover, lower the heat, and cook for 10 minutes, or until the liquid has been absorbed. Add the remaining hot liquid with the tomatoes and cook for 15 minutes, or until the rice is almost tender, but still quite *al dente,* allowing the rice to absorb the liquid.

5. Stir in the mussels (including the four in the shells) and cook for 5 minutes, or until the mussels are just firm. Do not overcook or they will toughen. Taste for seasoning and add salt and pepper, if necessary. Stir in the parsley and the remaining butter (in small pieces) with a metal fork, fluffing the rice. Transfer to a hot serving dish, setting the 4 mussels in their shells on top. Place 1 on each individual serving.

Creole Rice and Shrimp

SERVES 6

Rice

2 tablespoons butter
1 medium-sized onion, finely chopped
2 cups long-grain brown rice
1 small sweet green pepper, cored, seeded, and
      coarsely chopped
2 celery stalks, scraped and coarsely chopped
4½ cups chicken broth
2 whole cloves
4 tablespoons soft butter
1 cup grated Asiago or Parmesan cheese
Salt to taste

Shrimp

8 tablespoons (1 stick) butter
2 tablespoons olive oil
2 pounds medium-sized shrimp, shelled and deveined
1 large garlic clove, minced
¼ teaspoon cayenne pepper, or to taste
Salt to taste
3 tablespoons chopped broadleaf (Italian) parsley
      leaves

1. To prepare the rice, melt the 2 tablespoons of butter in a saucepan, over medium heat. Add the onion and cook for 3 minutes, or until the onion is soft. Do not brown. Stir in the rice and cook, stirring, for 2 minutes. Add the pepper, celery, chicken broth, and cloves and bring to a boil. Lower the heat, stir with a wooden fork, cover, and simmer for 30 minutes, or until the rice is tender and the liquid has been absorbed. Discard the cloves. Just before serving, stir in the soft butter and

cheese, fluffing up the rice with a metal fork. Taste for seasoning and add salt, if needed.

2. To prepare the shrimp, heat the butter and oil in a large
frying pan over medium-high heat. Add the shrimp and garlic
and sprinkle with the cayenne and salt. Cook, turning, just
until the shrimp are pink and firm. This will take about 3 minutes. Do not overcook or the shrimp will toughen.

3. Spoon the rice onto a hot serving dish. Arrange the
shrimp over the rice and pour the sauce in the frying pan over
it. Sprinkle with the parsley.

Rice Savannah

SERVES 4

*3 medium-sized ripe tomatoes, peeled, seeded, and
      chopped, or 1 1-pound can imported Italian plum
      tomatoes, drained and chopped*
6 tablespoons butter
1 cup long-grain rice
2½ to 3 cups chicken broth
1 cup grated Asiago or Parmesan cheese
*1 pound medium-sized shrimp, shelled, deveined, and
      cut in half lengthwise*
2 tablespoons brandy
*1 cup shelled fresh peas, cooked al dente, or frozen
      peas, defrosted*
Salt and freshly ground black pepper to taste

1. In a saucepan, over medium heat, cook the tomatoes
for 10 minutes, or until much of their liquid has evaporated.
Set aside.

2. In another saucepan, over medium heat, melt 3 tablespoons of the butter, stir in the rice, and cook, stirring, for 2 minutes, or until well coated. Pour in 2½ cups of the broth, bring to a boil, stir with a wooden fork, lower the heat, cover, and simmer for 15 minutes, or until the rice is almost tender and most of the liquid has been absorbed. If necessary, add more broth. The rice should be slightly moist, but not soupy. Taste for seasoning, adding salt and pepper, if needed.

3. Stir ¼ cup of the cheese into the rice with a wooden fork and cook for another 3 minutes, or until the rice is tender. Remove from the heat and keep warm.

4. While the rice is cooking, melt the remaining butter in a large frying pan over medium-high heat. Add the shrimp and cook for 1 minute, stirring. Add the brandy and cook off half of it. Stir in the tomatoes and peas and simmer for 2 minutes, or until the shrimp just turn pink. Stir in the salt and pepper.

5. Transfer the rice to a hot serving dish. Spoon the shrimp-peas-tomato sauce over the top and serve with the remaining cheese at the table.

Tuna Rice Quiche

SERVES 6

3 cups cooked short- or medium-grain rice, cooled
1 egg, beaten
⅔ cup grated Gruyère or Swiss cheese
1 medium-sized tomato, peeled, seeded, and chopped
1 7-ounce can solid white tuna (albacore), drained,
    and flaked
2 tablespoons butter
1 medium-sized onion, finely chopped
2 tablespoons all-purpose flour
1½ cups light cream or half-and-half, warmed
3 eggs, beaten
1 teaspoon salt
¼ teaspoon ground mace
⅛ teaspoon cayenne pepper
¼ teaspoon paprika
¼ cup grated Asiago or Parmesan cheese

1. In a bowl, combine and blend well the rice, the single beaten egg, and the Gruyère cheese. Press evenly onto the bottom and side of a buttered 10-inch pie plate.

2. Distribute the tomato over the "crust" and the tuna over the tomato.

3. In a saucepan, over medium heat, melt the butter. Add the onion and cook until it is soft. Do not brown. Stir in the flour and blend well. Gradually add 1 cup of the cream and cook, stirring into a thickened sauce. Remove from the heat. Preheat the oven to 350 degrees.

4. In a bowl, combine and blend well the remaining cream, the 3 beaten eggs, salt, mace, cayenne, and paprika. Stir into the sauce. Carefully pour over the tuna. Sprinkle on the Asiago cheese.

5. Bake for 30 minutes, or until set and a knife blade inserted just off center emerges clean. Do not overbake.

Sweet and Sour Shrimp
in a Spinach-Rice Ring

SERVES 4 TO 6

Rice Ring

10 tablespoons butter
1 medium-sized onion, minced
2 cups short- or medium-grain rice
4½ cups chicken broth
1 cup finely chopped spinach
6 medium-sized fresh mushrooms, finely chopped

Sweet and Sour Shrimp

¼ cup white vinegar
½ cup chicken broth
¼ cup dark brown sugar
2 teaspoons soy sauce
1½ pounds medium-sized shrimp, shelled and
    deveined
1 tablespoon peanut oil or vegetable oil
2 medium-sized carrots, scraped and thinly sliced
1 garlic clove, minced
3 whole scallions, trimmed and cut into ½-inch
    lengths
1 sweet green pepper, seeds and ribs removed, cut into
    narrow strips
1 tablespoon cornstarch, dissolved in 2 tablespoons
    cold water

1. To make the Rice Ring, melt 2 tablespoons of the butter
in a saucepan over medium heat. Add the onion and cook for 3
minutes, or until it is soft. Do not brown. Add 2 more tablespoons of butter to the pan. When it is melted, add the rice and

cook, stirring, for 2 minutes. Pour in the broth and bring to a boil. Lower the heat, cover, and simmer for 25 minutes, or until the rice is tender and the broth has been absorbed. Stir in the spinach.

2. In a frying pan, melt 2 tablespoons of the butter and cook the mushrooms over medium-high heat, cooking off all of the liquid that the mushrooms produce. Add to the rice with the remaining butter (in small pieces), and blend well with a fork. Press into a 6- or 8-cup ring mold (the rice should fill it), cover, and keep warm in a 200-degree oven until ready to unmold.

3. To prepare the Sweet and Sour Shrimp, combine and blend well the vinegar, broth, sugar, and soy sauce. Set aside.

4. Bring a large saucepan of water to a boil. Drop in the shrimp and the moment they start to turn pink (about 30 seconds after you have added them to the water) remove from the heat and drain. Set aside and keep warm.

5. Heat the oil in a wok or a large frying pan. Add the carrots, garlic, scallions, and green pepper and stir-fry over medium-high heat for 2 or 3 minutes, or until crisp-tender.

6. Pour in the vinegar-broth-sugar mixture and simmer for 1 minute, stirring to dissolve the sugar.

7. Add the cornstarch and water and stir for 1 or 2 minutes, or until the sauce starts to thicken. Add the shrimp and heat through. The shrimp should be pink but tender and the sauce thick. Taste for seasoning, adding salt, if necessary.

8. Unmold the rice ring onto a serving dish. Spoon the shrimp into the center of the ring. If the ring won't accommodate all of the shrimp, serve the remainder in a bowl.

Scallops à la Kerala

SERVES 4

We discovered this, or an approximation of it, in Kerala on
India's west coast. This is a South Sea-like area where we were
introduced to several interesting dishes. This was prepared
with very small, very sweet shrimp, but we have substituted
scallops to offer variety, and we have also added what we hope
are palate-pleasing touches of our own.

Rice

3 tablespoons butter
2 medium-sized onions, finely chopped
1 cup long-grain rice
5 whole black peppercorns, cracked
1 ½-inch piece cinnamon stick
1 small bay leaf
¼ teaspoon ground cardamom
2½ cups water

Scallops

7 tablespoons butter
2 garlic cloves, minced
1 tablespoon curry powder, or to taste
1 pound scallops (If you are using bay scallops, leave
     them whole; if you are using sea scallops, cut
     them in half.)
Salt and freshly ground black pepper to taste
3 tablespoons all-purpose flour
2 cups fish stock (page 51)

1. To prepare the rice, melt the butter in a deep saucepan over medium heat and cook the onions for 5 minutes, or until they are soft and golden. Do not brown. Add the rice and cook, stirring, for 2 minutes. Stir in the peppercorns, cinnamon, bay leaf, cardamom, and water. Raise the heat and bring the liquid to a boil. Cover, lower the heat, and simmer for 20 minutes, or until the rice is tender and the liquid has been absorbed. Remove and discard the peppercorns, cinnamon stick, and bay leaf. Keep the rice warm while preparing the scallops.

2. To prepare the scallops, melt 3 tablespoons of the butter in a saucepan over medium heat and sauté the garlic until it is soft. Do not brown. Stir in the curry powder and cook for 1 minute, stirring. Add the scallops, seasoning with salt and pepper, and cook for 5 minutes, turning. They should be just firm. Do not overcook or they will toughen. Remove the scallops and keep them warm.

3. Stir the remaining 4 tablespoons of butter into the saucepan. When it has melted, stir in the flour, blending and stirring into a smooth paste. Lower the heat and gradually add the fish stock, stirring into a smooth sauce. Return the scallops to the pan; cook for 1 minute to heat through. Taste for seasoning, adding salt and pepper, if needed. Spoon the scallops with their sauce over the rice.

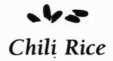

Chili Rice

SERVES 4 TO 6

Although chili peppers were developed by the Aztecs in Mexico, the Spaniards brought them to Europe, making them their own. The peppers eventually landed in Asia where they are very popular. We discovered this dish in Bangkok. If fresh chilies aren't available, most supermarkets have them canned. They'll do as a substitute.

> 3 tablespoons peanut oil
> 2 medium-sized onions, chopped
> 2 fresh (or canned) green chilies, seeded and thinly
>   sliced
> 1 large pork chop, both fat and lean, finely chopped
> ½ pound fresh shrimp, shelled, deveined, and coarsely
>   chopped
> 4 cups cooked long-grain rice
> 2 eggs, beaten
> Salt and freshly ground black pepper to taste
> 6 whole scallions, trimmed and chopped

1. In a large frying pan, over medium heat, heat the oil and cook the onions and chilies for 5 minutes, or until they are soft. Do not brown. Stir in the pork and cook for 10 minutes. Add the shrimp and cook just until the shrimp start to turn pink, about 3 minutes.

2. Add the rice and eggs, and use a wooden fork to blend them well with the other ingredients. Season with salt and pepper. When the eggs have set, quickly stir in the chopped scallions and serve.

Shrimp Jambalaya

SERVES 6 TO 8

The Creoles of Louisiana (descended from French settlers, their cooking a mixture of French *haute cuisine* and provincial, also African and Indian) probably are as versatile with rice as the Orientals and eat almost as much. Here's one of their classics.

3 tablespoons bacon fat
2 medium-sized onions, finely chopped
1 garlic clove, minced
1 celery stalk, scraped and finely chopped
1 small sweet green pepper, cored, seeded, and finely chopped
1½ cups long-grain rice
3 cups chicken broth
3 medium-sized ripe tomatoes, peeled, seeded, and chopped
¼ teaspoon dried thyme
¼ teaspoon hot red pepper flakes, crushed
Salt to taste
1 cup cubed cooked ham
3 scallions, trimmed and thinly sliced
1½ pounds medium-sized shrimp, shelled and deveined

1. In a large pot, over medium heat, heat the bacon fat. Add the onions, garlic, celery, and green pepper and cook, stirring, for 2 minutes. Stir in the rice, mixing well. Add the broth, tomatoes, thyme, hot red pepper flakes, and salt. Bring to a boil, stir with a wooden fork, cover, lower the heat, and simmer for 30 minutes, or until the rice is almost tender but still *al dente*.
2. Stir in the ham and scallions and cook for 5 minutes.

Stir in the shrimp and cook for 5 minutes, or until they just turn pink (do not overcook the shrimp or they will toughen). Taste for seasoning, adding salt and pepper, if needed, and serve.

Scallops en Brochette on Curried Rice

SERVES 6

We learned to respect scallops in Spain, in Santiago de Compostela, home of the magnificent Cathedral of St. James, and, at one time, a holy place, second only to Rome in all of Christendom. Pilgrims came from all over Europe to visit the shrine of St. James of Compostela. They ate scallops as a "penance," and wore their shells on their hats on the trip home.

A favorite dish of ours, Coquilles St. Jacques, is also named after St. James. Santiago is one of our favorite places, a historic, yet sparkling city that hasn't been overwhelmed by the present, it offers the best seafood, in our view, in Europe. In the province of Galicia, in the mountains of the northwest, with the Bay of Biscay to the north, Portugal to the south, and the Atlantic Ocean breasting the west, Santiago introduced us to this dish—and many others. The chef at the beautiful Hostal de los Reyes Católicos, beside the cathedral, was delighted to give us his recipes for the dishes we applauded. In France we would have needed a gun to get them.

The Scallops

30 sea scallops, about 1 inch in diameter (If they are larger, use fewer and halve them.)
1 medium-sized onion, chopped
½ cup chopped broadleaf (Italian) parsley leaves

1 teaspoon ground cumin
½ teaspoon ground coriander
4 whole cloves
⅓ cup olive oil
⅓ cup fresh lemon juice
⅓ cup dry sherry
1 teaspoon salt
½ teaspoon freshly ground black pepper

The Curried Rice

3 tablespoons butter
1 medium-sized onion, finely chopped
1 garlic clove, minced
1½ cups long-grain rice
3½ cups chicken broth
2 teaspoons curry powder, or to taste
2 canned chili peppers, drained and cut into short
    strips
3 tablespoons golden raisins

Vegetables for the Brochettes
and Assembling Them

2 large firm sweet green peppers, halved, seeded,
    deribbed, and parboiled for 5 minutes
12 very small white onions, root ends scored,
    parboiled for 7 minutes
12 fresh mushroom caps, sautéed in 2 tablespoons
    butter for 2 minutes
Salt and freshly ground black pepper to taste

1. To prepare the scallops, combine and blend well the onion, parsley, cumin, coriander, cloves, olive oil, lemon juice, sherry, salt, and pepper in a large stainless steel or Pyrex bowl. Add the scallops and stir to coat them evenly. Cover tightly and marinate in the refrigerator for at least 6 hours, stirring 2 or 3 times. Bring to room temperature before assembling the brochettes.

2. To prepare the rice, melt the butter in a deep saucepan over medium heat. Add the onion and garlic and cook for 5 minutes, or until they are soft. Do not brown. Stir in the rice and cook for 2 minutes, stirring. Pour in the broth and bring to a boil. Cover, lower the heat, and simmer for 20 minutes, or until the rice is slightly *al dente,* almost tender. With a metal fork, stir in the curry powder, chilies, and raisins, fluffing up the rice as you stir. Cover and allow to sit for 10 minutes.

3. To prepare the brochettes, thoroughly drain the peppers and onions. Cut the peppers into bite-sized squares. Drain the scallops, reserving the marinade. Starting with a scallop and ending with one, arrange the scallops, green peppers, onions, and mushrooms on 6 skewers, dividing them equally. Brush with the marinade and sprinkle with salt and pepper.

4. Cook in a preheated broiler (with a drip pan) 3 or 4 inches from the heat for about 1 minute; then turn and brush with the marinade every minute for 5 minutes, or until the scallops are golden and somewhat firm. Do not overcook or they will toughen.

5. Serve each skewer on a bed of rice, spooning any drippings collected in the drip pan over the rice.

5

RICE

with POULTRY and GAME

Often recipes have stories. This one takes us into the jungles of Central India where we were studying the habitat of the tiger, as research for a novel. Our camp cook, a wisp of a man with a thick gray moustache and few words of English, was from Goa, a Portuguese possession in India. Every time he prepared a meal he gave us an inferiority complex. His stove was a few stones on which he rested his pots; his fire, wood reduced to glowing ashes. On this he prepared everything from bread to a sort of pot roast called "boily-brown."

In camp were a pair of brown-and-white goats, cute as kittens, brought along in case our rations ran short. This was probably a psychological gambit, for whenever we needed fresh meat, our hunter, or *shikari,* Rao Naidu, would say, "Shall we have some nice fresh kid in a curry tonight, or do you want to shoot for the pot?"

So, of course, we shot for the pot—doves or more often peacock, for the jungles were full of exotic birds. On page 86 is an approximation of one of the dishes we had. We've substituted chicken for the peacock, but we encourage you to try for peacock. The cook made his own curry powder, so we offer that recipe as well.

Nested Rice and Chicken

SERVES 6

4 tablespoons (½ stick) butter
1 tablespoon olive oil
6 chicken thighs
6 chicken drumsticks
Salt and freshly ground black pepper to taste
⅓ pound pork sausage meat (about ½ cup)
2 medium-sized onions, chopped
1 celery stalk, scraped and chopped
1 cup long-grain rice
1 10-ounce package frozen corn kernels, defrosted, or
*   an equal amount of fresh corn kernels*
2½ cups chicken broth
1 large pimiento, cut into strips

1. Preheat the oven to 350 degrees.

2. Over medium heat, in a large flameproof casserole, heat the butter and oil and evenly brown the chicken pieces, sprinkling them with salt and pepper.

3. Remove the chicken and pour off any excess fat. Over medium heat, in the same casserole, cook the sausage for 5 minutes, breaking it up with a wooden fork. Add the onions and celery and cook, stirring, for 5 minutes. Do not brown. Stir in the rice and corn. Pour in the chicken broth and bring to a boil.

4. Remove from the heat and place the chicken on top, pushing it down slightly into the rice. Cover and bake for 25 minutes, or until the liquid has been absorbed and the chicken and rice are tender. Garnish with the pimiento strips.

Curried Chicken with Rice

SERVES 4

Curry Powder

2 teaspoons ground cumin
½ teaspoon ground ginger
2 teaspoons ground coriander
1 teaspoon ground turmeric
⅛ teaspoon cayenne pepper
¼ teaspoon freshly ground black pepper
1 teaspoon ground cardamom

Chicken-Rice Curry

3 tablespoons butter
2 tablespoons olive oil
2 pounds boned chicken breast, cut into 1-inch cubes
Salt and freshly ground black pepper
3 medium-sized white onions, chopped
2 garlic cloves, minced
1 medium-sized apple, peeled, cored, and chopped
2 tablespoons all-purpose flour
All of the above curry powder
2 cups chicken broth
½ cup dry white wine
2 medium-sized ripe tomatoes, peeled, seeded, and
     chopped
1 cup long-grain rice

    1. Blend all of the ingredients for the curry powder to-
gether. Makes approximately 2⅓ tablespoons.
    2. Preheat the oven to 350 degrees.
    3. In a flameproof casserole, over medium heat, heat the
butter with the oil. Add the chicken and season lightly with salt

and pepper. Brown the chicken evenly. Stir in the onions and garlic and cook for 5 minutes, or until they are soft. Stir in the apple and blend in the flour and curry powder.

4. Gradually stir in the broth and then the wine and tomatoes. Bring to a boil; then, with a wooden fork, stir in the rice. Cover and bake for 35 minutes, or until the chicken and rice are tender and the liquid has been absorbed. Taste for seasoning, adding salt and pepper, if needed. The broth may have supplied enough.

Roman Chicken and Rice

SERVES 6 TO 8

1 cup all-purpose flour
2 teaspoons salt
1 teaspoon freshly ground black pepper
½ teaspoon dried oregano
*2 3-pound chickens, cut into serving pieces (Do not
    use the backs or wing tips; save them for making
    stock.)*
8 tablespoons (1 stick) butter
2 tablespoons olive oil
3 tablespoons all-purpose flour
2½ cups chicken broth
½ cup heavy cream
Juice of ½ lemon
Salt and freshly ground black pepper to taste
1 medium-sized white onion, minced
*3 tablespoons chopped broadleaf (Italian) parsley
    leaves*
⅛ teaspoon dried thyme
2 cups long-grain rice, cooked al dente

1. Combine the 1 cup flour, salt, pepper, and oregano. Dredge the chicken pieces in the seasoned flour.

2. In a deep frying pan, over medium heat, heat 4 tablespoons of the butter and the oil. Add the chicken, cooking as many pieces as you can at a time until they are evenly browned. Remove and reserve.

3. Pour off any fat remaining in the pan. Melt the remaining butter in the frying pan. Slowly blend in the 3 tablespoons of flour, stirring into a smooth paste. Gradually pour in the chicken broth, stirring into a smooth, thin sauce. Stir in the cream and lemon juice and season with salt and pepper. Stir in the onion, parsley, and thyme, and simmer, for 1 minute, stirring. Preheat the oven to 375 degrees.

4. In a large casserole, arrange the rice in a smooth layer, but do not pack it. Spoon one third of the sauce over the rice. Arrange the chicken pieces on top, overlapping, if necessary. Spoon on the remaining sauce. Cover the casserole and bake for 30 minutes, or until the chicken is tender and the sauce has thickened. Taste for seasoning, adding salt and pepper, if needed.

Frango com Arroz

Portuguese Chicken and Rice

SERVES 4

8 slices bacon, chopped
8 medium-sized chicken thighs
Salt and freshly ground black pepper to taste
3 medium-sized onions, chopped
1 medium-sized sweet red pepper, cored, seeded, and
chopped
1 cup long-grain rice
½ cup port wine
2½ cups chicken broth
Pimiento-stuffed olives
Peeled and seeded orange slices

1. In a large deep, heavy saucepan, over medium heat, cook the bacon until it is almost crisp. With a slotted spoon, remove and reserve the bacon.

2. Add the chicken to the saucepan, season with salt and pepper, and brown it evenly. Remove and reserve the chicken.

3. Stir the onions and pepper into the fat remaining in the pan. Cook for 5 minutes. Add the rice, port wine, and chicken broth. Return the bacon and the chicken to the pan. Blend well. Bring to a boil, lower the heat, cover, and simmer for 20 minutes, or until the chicken and rice are tender. Taste for seasoning, adding salt and pepper, if needed.

4. Serve the chicken on the rice. Garnish with the olives and the orange slices.

Casablanca Chicken and Rice

SERVES 4

One of rice's great assets is its ability to complete a quick and easy meal. We had a dish much like this in North Africa, except that the meat was pigeon.

Serve this spicy dish with individual bowls of plain yogurt and a simple tomato or avocado salad or with slices of fresh pineapple.

> 3 tablespoons butter
> 1 tablespoon olive oil
> 4 large chicken thighs
> Salt to taste
> 2 medium-sized onions, chopped
> 2 large garlic cloves, minced
> 1 cup long-grain rice
> ½ teaspoon ground cumin
> ½ teaspoon ground coriander
> 1 tablespoon chopped fresh ginger
> ⅛ teaspoon hot red pepper flakes
> 1 8-ounce can stewed tomatoes, mashed with a fork
> ½ cup peanut butter, blended with 1½ cups cold
>   chicken broth into a smooth mixture
> 4 hard-cooked eggs

1. In a heavy-bottomed casserole, over medium heat, heat the butter and oil, and evenly brown the chicken, seasoning with salt. Remove the thighs, and stir in the onions and garlic. Cook for 5 minutes, or until they are soft. Do not brown. Return the thighs to the pot and spoon the rice between them.

2. Blend the cumin, coriander, ginger, and hot red pepper flakes with the tomatoes and the peanut butter-broth mixture and spoon over the chicken and rice. Bring to a boil, cover, lower the heat, and simmer for 30 minutes, or until the thighs and rice are just tender.

3. Add the eggs to the pot, spooning the rice over them, cover, and cook for 5 minutes, or until the eggs are heated through.

Lemon Rice with Curried Chicken

SERVES 6

Lemon Rice

2 tablespoons butter
1 tablespoon olive oil
1 medium-sized onion, finely chopped
2 cups long-grain rice
4½ cups water
1 teaspoon salt
3 tablespoons fresh lemon juice
½ cup toasted blanched and slivered almonds

Curried Chicken

¾ cup all-purpose flour
1 teaspoon sweet Hungarian paprika
2 tablespoons curry powder, or to taste
1 teaspoon salt
3 whole chicken breasts, skinned, boned, and halved, and each half cut into halves, crosswise
6 chicken thighs, skinned and boned
5 tablespoons butter
1 cup heavy cream
1 cup dry sherry
1¾ cups chicken broth
1 teaspoon Worcestershire sauce
Salt and freshly ground black pepper

1. To prepare the Lemon Rice, melt the butter with the oil in a heavy saucepan over medium-high heat. Add the onion and cook for 3 minutes, or until it is soft and slightly golden. Do not brown. Add the rice and cook, stirring, for 2 minutes, or until it is well coated with the butter and oil.

2. Add the water, salt, and lemon juice and bring to a boil. Lower the heat, cover, and simmer for 25 minutes, or until the rice is tender and the liquid has been absorbed.

3. To prepare the Curried Chicken, combine the flour, paprika, curry powder, and salt in a clean paper or plastic bag. Add the chicken pieces and shake to coat them evenly.

4. In a large frying pan, heat the butter over medium-high heat and evenly brown the chicken. Add more butter, if needed.

5. In a large measuring cup combine and blend the cream, sherry, broth, and Worcestershire sauce and pour the mixture over the chicken. Bring to a boil, lower the heat, cover, and simmer, stirring occasionally, for 30 minutes, or until the chicken is tender and the sauce has thickened. If the chicken seems to be getting tender before the sauce thickens, remove the cover from the pan. Taste for seasoning, adding salt and pepper, if needed.

6. Serve with a border of the Lemon Rice, sprinkled with almonds.

Rice and Chicken Oregano

SERVES 4

4 tablespoons olive oil
4 chicken thighs
4 chicken drumsticks
Salt and freshly ground black pepper to taste
2 teaspoons dried oregano
2 medium-sized onions, chopped
¼ cup dry vermouth
1 cup long-grain rice
2½ cups chicken broth

1. In a flameproof casserole, over medium heat, heat the oil. Sprinkle the chicken with salt, pepper, and oregano and brown it evenly. Remove the chicken. Preheat the oven to 350 degrees.

2. Add more oil to the casserole, if necessary, and stir in the onions. Cook for 3 minutes.

3. Pour in the vermouth and cook, stirring well, scraping up the browned-on bits in the bottom of the pot.

4. Add the rice and stir to blend well.

5. Return the chicken to the pan and pour on the broth. Bring to a boil on top of the stove. Cover the casserole and bake for 40 minutes, or until the chicken and rice are tender and most of the liquid has been absorbed. It should be somewhat moist. Taste for seasoning, adding salt and pepper, if needed.

India's Rice

We can't claim to *know* India. No one but an Indian knows that subcontinent, and even many of them are uncertain. But after six visits, the length of stay increasing with each visit, we feel that we have learned much about the areas we traveled— the villages, cities, and jungles. In fact, we have presumptuously written three books about India. We are absolutely convinced, however, of a single fact: Indians love rice and cook it in many interesting and exotic ways unknown to the Western world.

Two words jump out of India's remarkable rice repertoire: *pulao* and *biryani*. In *pulaos,* which are probably the most popular, the rice is first sautéed in *ghee* (butter from buffalo cream) and then steamed and spiced, with a variety of ingredients added, varying in the different areas, ranging from the sumptuous to the simple.

Biryanis are fancier, offered to please and impress guests on special occasions. Often main courses, they are layered dishes (casseroles, if you will) alternating rice with various meats and vegetables, which are then baked. Before serving, the dishes are garnished with fried onion rings, eggs, nuts, raisins, or anything an imaginative hostess can dream up. We once had a *biryani* served with the gold-tinted coconut called *sajavat*.

Chicken Biryani

SERVES 4

1 cup plain yogurt
1 medium-sized onion, grated
2 garlic cloves, minced
2 teaspoons grated fresh ginger

⅛ teaspoon ground cloves
½ teaspoon ground cardamom
⅛ teaspoon ground mace
¼ teaspoon ground cinnamon
2 tablespoons chopped parsley leaves
2 large chicken thighs, boned and cut into 2-inch
    pieces
1 large whole chicken breast, boned and cut into 2-
    inch pieces
Salt to taste
2 cups chicken broth
1 cup long-grain rice
½ teaspoon of powdered saffron, blended with ½ cup
    warm water
4 tablespoons butter

1. In a large bowl, combine and blend well the yogurt, onion, garlic, ginger, cloves, cardamom, mace, cinnamon, and parsley. Add the chicken and blend well to thoroughly coat the pieces. Cover and marinate in the refrigerator for 3 to 4 hours, turning 2 or 3 times. Remove from the refrigerator 1 hour before cooking.

2. Transfer the chicken mixture to a saucepan. Bring to a boil, cover, lower the heat, and simmer for 20 minutes, or until the chicken is very nearly tender. Taste for seasoning, adding salt, if needed.

3. While the chicken is cooking, bring the broth to a boil in another saucepan. Stir in the rice, cover, lower the heat, and simmer for 15 minutes. The rice should be quite *al dente*. Taste before seasoning, as the broth may have supplied enough.

4. Preheat the oven to 350 degrees. In a medium-sized casserole, arrange a layer of half of the chicken and a layer of half of the rice on the chicken, sprinkling each layer lightly with the saffron blend. Repeat. Dot the top layer of rice with the butter. Cover the casserole with aluminum foil and then with its cover. Bake for 25 minutes, or until the chicken and rice are tender.

Castilian Arroz con Pollo

Castilian Rice with Chicken

SERVES 6 TO 8

2 3-pound chickens, cut into serving pieces (Do not
    use the backs or wing tips; save them for making
    stock.)
All-purpose flour for dredging
¼ pound lean fatback, cut into ½-inch cubes,
    blanched in boiling water for 5 minutes and well
    drained
4 tablespoons (¼ cup) olive oil
Salt and freshly ground black pepper
4 shallots, finely chopped
2 garlic cloves, minced
2 cups long-grain rice
3 cups chicken broth
3 large ripe tomatoes, peeled, seeded, and chopped, or
    2 cups canned tomatoes, broken up
1 bay leaf
3 whole cloves
¼ teaspoon powdered saffron, dissolved in a little
    broth
½ cup Madeira
1 cup partially cooked fresh peas or defrosted frozen
    peas
½ cup coarsely chopped pimiento
3 tablespoons chopped broadleaf (Italian) parsley
    leaves

    1. Lightly dredge the chicken parts in the flour, shaking
off any excess. Preheat the oven to 375 degrees.
    2. In a large flameproof casserole, cook the fatback until it

is golden. Remove with a slotted spoon and reserve.

3. Add the oil to the casserole and heat over medium heat. Add the chicken, cooking as many pieces as you can at a time, until they are evenly browned. Season with salt and pepper. Remove from the pot as they brown and reserve.

4. Add the shallots and garlic to the pot and cook until soft, about 5 minutes. Do not brown. Stir in the rice and cook for 2 minutes, stirring to coat the rice well. Add a little more oil if the chicken has absorbed all the fat.

5. Pour in the broth and cook, stirring, scraping up the browned-on bits on the bottom of the pot.

6. Add the tomatoes, bay leaf, cloves, saffron, and Madeira. Return the chicken and fatback to the pot, mixing them in with the rice. Bring to a boil on top of the stove. Cover and bake for 25 minutes. Fluff the rice with a metal fork. Remove and discard the bay leaf and cloves. Taste for seasoning, adding salt and pepper, if needed.

7. Stir in the peas and pimiento and bake for 10 minutes longer, or until the rice and chicken are tender and most of the liquid has been absorbed. If the liquid is absorbed before the rice is tender, add a small amount of hot broth and continue to bake.

8. Sprinkle with the parsley and serve from the casserole.

Deviled Chicken with "Greek" Rice in Pepper Cups

SERVES 4

The French like to offer more or less plain chicken with fancy little side dishes of baked red peppers filled with rice that they call *Riz à la Grecque*, although the Greeks probably never saw the rice. But it's a nifty presentation.

"Greek" Rice

6 to 8 medium-sized sweet red peppers, tops cut off
    and seeds and white ribs carefully removed,
    leaving the pepper shells intact
3 tablespoons olive oil
4 large shallots, chopped
1 cup long-grain rice
4 medium-sized fresh mushrooms, coarsely chopped
½ cup diced Canadian bacon or ham
12 pitted dark plump "Greek" olives, coarsely chopped
2½ cups chicken broth
½ cup tomato purée, blended with ½ cup water

Deviled Broiled Chickens

2 chickens, weighing no more than 2½ pounds each
2 tablespoons olive oil
Lawry's seasoned salt
6 tablespoons fine fresh bread crumbs
1 teaspoon Coleman's dry mustard
⅛ teaspoon cayenne pepper
3 tablespoons butter
8 slices bacon, fried or broiled until crisp and drained
    on paper towels

1. To prepare the pepper cups, parboil the peppers in boiling water for 5 minutes. Remove from the water and invert the peppers to drain thoroughly. Preheat the oven to 375 degrees.

2. In a flameproof casserole, over medium heat, heat the olive oil and cook the shallots for 3 minutes, or until they are soft. Do not brown. Stir in the rice and cook for 2 minutes, stirring to coat the rice well. Stir in the mushrooms, Canadian bacon, olives, and broth. Bring to a boil, cover, and bake for 25 minutes, or until the rice is tender and the liquid has been absorbed.

3. Spoon the rice stuffing loosely into the peppers. Arrange them in a baking dish with a cover, or a casserole, just large enough to hold them snugly without crowding them. Pour the tomato purée-water mixture around the peppers, cover, and bake for 30 minutes, or until the peppers are tender, basting 2 or 3 times (see Note).

4. Meanwhile, split the chickens into halves, cutting down the backbones. Remove the backbones and save them for soup. Breast side up, striking firmly, flatten the halves with the flat side of a cleaver.

5. Rub the outside of the chicken halves with the olive oil and seasoned salt. Place on a lightly oiled baking sheet or in shallow broiler-proof baking dish. Bake in a preheated 450-degree oven for 20 minutes, or until just tender.

6. Combine the bread crumbs, dry mustard, and cayenne pepper together in a small bowl. Sprinkle the mixture evenly over the chickens and dot with flecks of butter.

7. Place under a preheated broiler (5 inches from the heat) for 10 minutes, or until the chickens are golden.

8. Serve with 2 strips of bacon over each chicken half, accompanied by 2 rice-stuffed peppers.

Note: If you are not fortunate enough to have two ovens, you can prepare the peppers and bake them before you bake the chickens. The peppers can then be reheated in the oven while the chickens are in the broiler.

Chicken and Sausage Risotto

SERVES 4

The Italians have almost as many interesting combinations of various foods with rice as they have with pasta. Here's one that we like which comes from the Veneto region.

> *4 Italian sweet sausages, in their casings*
> *6 tablespoons butter*
> *2 tablespoons olive oil*
> *1 medium-sized onion, finely chopped*
> *1 celery stalk, scraped and finely chopped*
> *1 medium-sized carrot, scraped and finely chopped*
> *4 large chicken thighs, boned and the flesh cut into ½-inch-wide strips*
> *Salt and freshly ground black pepper to taste*
> *½ cup dry white wine*
> *1 cup long-grain rice*
> *2½ cups chicken broth*
> *½ cup grated Asiago or Parmesan cheese*

1. Prick the sausages with the point of a knife and poach them in boiling water for 10 minutes. Drain, quarter, and set aside.

2. In a large deep frying pan, over medium heat, heat half of the butter with the oil and cook the onion, celery, and carrot for 5 minutes, or until the onion is soft. Do not brown. Add the chicken strips and sausage and brown evenly, seasoning with salt and pepper. Pour in the wine, cover, and simmer for 20 minutes.

3. Stir in the rice, mixing it in well with a wooden fork. Stir in the broth. Bring to a boil, lower the heat, cover, and simmer for 20 minutes, or until the rice and chicken are tender and the liquid has been mostly absorbed. If the rice is not

cooked when the liquid is absorbed, add a small amount of hot broth and continue cooking. The *risotto* should be slightly moist. Taste for seasoning, adding salt and pepper, if needed.

4. Stir in the remaining butter (in small pieces) with a metal fork, fluffing the rice. Serve on a hot serving dish and pass the cheese at the table.

Pollo con Arroz Verde

Spanish Chicken with Green Rice in a Mushroom-Sherry Sauce

SERVES 4

1 3-pound chicken, trussed
5 cups chicken broth
8 tablespoons (1 stick) butter
1 medium-sized onion, chopped
1 cup long-grain rice
½ cup chopped broadleaf (Italian) parsley leaves
4 tablespoons all-purpose flour
¼ cup dry sherry
6 medium-sized fresh mushrooms, sliced and cooked
    in 3 tablespoons butter until brown but still firm
½ cup grated Asiago or Parmesan cheese

1. Put the chicken in a large deep pot. Pour in the broth and bring to a boil over high heat. Lower the heat, cover, and simmer the chicken until it is tender, about 45 minutes. Remove the chicken from the liquid and strain the broth. Reserve *all* of the broth, setting aside 3 cups for the sauce.

2. In a deep saucepan, over medium heat, melt 2 tablespoons of the butter. Add the onion and cook until it is soft, about 3 minutes. Do not brown. Stir in the rice and cook for 2 minutes, coating it well with the butter. Pour the broth that remained after the 3 cups were reserved for the sauce into a 2-cup measuring cup. If it does not fill the cup, add enough water to make 2 cups of liquid. Add to the rice in the saucepan. Bring to a boil, lower the heat, stir with a wooden fork, cover, and simmer for 15 minutes, or until the liquid has been absorbed and the rice is barely tender, still quite *al dente*. Stir in 2 tablespoons of the butter and the parsley.

3. Remove the chicken meat from the bones, discarding the skin and bones. Preheat the oven to 375 degrees.

4. In a saucepan, over medium heat, melt the remaining 4 tablespoons of butter. Add the flour and cook, stirring into a smooth paste. Gradually stir in the reserved 3 cups of chicken broth and cook, stirring into a smooth, slightly thickened sauce. Stir in the sherry and mushrooms.

5. Arrange the rice in a smooth layer in a buttered baking dish. Place the chicken meat on the rice and spoon the mushroom-sherry sauce over the chicken. Sprinkle the cheese on the sauce. Bake for 30 minutes, or until the top is golden and the sauce bubbling.

Shanghai Stewed Chicken

SERVES 4

4 large chicken drumsticks
4 large chicken thighs
½ cup rice wine or light dry sherry
½ cup chicken broth
⅓ cup soy sauce
⅛ teaspoon hot red pepper flakes
¼ teaspoon ground ginger
¼ teaspoon ground coriander
4 garlic cloves, flattened with the broad side of a knife
    blade and peeled
2 teaspoons cornstarch, dissolved in 3 tablespoons cold
    water or chicken broth
4 cups hot cooked long-grain rice

1. In a large deep frying pan arrange the chicken parts in one layer. Combine the rice wine, broth, soy sauce, hot red pepper flakes, ginger, and coriander in a cup. Pour the mixture over the chicken. Drop in the garlic. Bring the liquid to a boil, lower the heat, cover, and simmer for 30 minutes, or until the chicken is tender.

2. Transfer the chicken to a hot dish and keep it warm. Stir the cornstarch into the liquid in the pan and cook until slightly thickened. Serve the chicken on a bed of hot rice with the sauce spooned over the chicken.

Rice, Chicken, and Spinach Casserole

SERVES 4

3 cups al dente-cooked long-grain rice
1 pound fresh spinach, cooked just until wilted, or 2
    10-ounce packages frozen leaf spinach, defrosted,
    well-drained
3 cups cooked chicken, cut into large bite-sized pieces
3 tablespoons butter
3 tablespoons all-purpose flour
2 cups chicken broth
¼ cup Madeira
⅛ teaspoon ground nutmeg
Salt and freshly ground black pepper to taste

1. Preheat the oven to 350 degrees.

2. In a baking dish or casserole, arrange the rice in a smooth layer (do not pack it down). Top with a smooth layer of the spinach, and then with the chicken.

3. In a saucepan, over medium heat, melt the butter. Stir in the flour and cook, stirring, into a smooth paste. Gradually add the broth and cook, stirring into a smooth, medium-thick sauce. Stir in the Madeira, nutmeg, salt, and pepper.

4. Spoon the sauce over the chicken and bake, uncovered, until bubbly and slightly golden, about 25 minutes.

Rice Tetrazzini

SERVES 4

3 tablespoons butter
3 tablespoons all-purpose flour
2½ cups half-and-half
Salt and freshly ground black pepper to taste
½ teaspoon ground nutmeg
1 egg yolk, beaten
1½ cups al dente-cooked long-grain rice
1 cup grated Asiago or Parmesan cheese
2 cups cubed cooked turkey or chicken (the breast is
     classic)
8 small fresh mushrooms, quartered and cooked in 2
     tablespoons butter for 2 minutes
1 10-ounce package frozen chopped spinach, defrosted
     and drained

1. In a saucepan, over medium heat, melt the butter. Stir in the flour, stirring into a smooth paste. Gradually add the half-and-half, stirring into a smooth, thickened sauce. Season with salt, pepper, and nutmeg. Remove from the heat and stir in the egg yolk. Reserve. Preheat the oven to 400 degrees.

2. In a large bowl, combine and blend well the rice and half of the cheese. Thoroughly, but carefully, stir in the turkey pieces, mushrooms, and spinach.

3. Arrange the rice-turkey mixture in a buttered casserole. Pour the sauce over it and sprinkle with the remaining cheese. Bake, uncovered, for about 15 minutes, or until bubbling and golden.

Rice Croquettes
with Pojarski Côtelettes

SERVES 6 TO 8

We like these recipes so much that we're coupling them as a dinner suggestion.

Croquettes used to be quite difficult to master until we discovered this method after a dozen attempts. It's not easy to keep the croquette patties "together" (intact). Just "rice" cannot be listed in the ingredients. A "clinging" rice, short or medium grain, is a must, preferably California short-grain rice. Also, with many of us today preferring lighter foods, keeping away from the deep-fried method as croquettes are usually cooked, we worked on a different approach. Much ado about croquettes? Perhaps. But they are delicious, different, and rarely served (a welcome change from potatoes or pasta), so perhaps this recipe will be a find for some, a discovery for others. It was for us.

This recipe makes approximately 20 "cutlets." (Cook whatever number you need, and freeze the remainder [uncooked]. They freeze exceptionally well.)

We like to serve this combination with puréed carrots.

Rice Croquettes

1 cup short-grain rice
2 cups water
1 teaspoon salt
3 tablespoons heavy cream
1 large egg, beaten
2 tablespoons minced parsley leaves
4 tablespoons melted butter
Salt and freshly ground black pepper to taste
½ cup grated Asiago or Parmesan cheese

*Approximately 2 cups fine dry bread crumbs for
    dredging*
4 tablespoons butter
3 tablespoons olive oil

Pojarski Côtelettes

6 slices white bread, crusts removed
2 cups chicken broth
8 tablespoons (1 stick) butter, melted
*4 pounds skinned and boned chicken breasts, finely
    ground*
½ pound lean pork, finely ground
4 large eggs, beaten
1 teaspoon salt
½ teaspoon freshly ground black pepper
4 tablespoons dried dill
All-purpose flour for dredging
*Butter and olive oil (amount depends on the number of
    cutlets to be cooked)*
1 pint sour cream

1. To prepare the Rice Croquettes, combine the rice, water, and salt in a saucepan. Bring to a boil, cover, lower the heat, and simmer for 25 minutes, or until the liquid has been absorbed and the rice is very soft. Remove from the heat and cool. In a large bowl, combine and blend well with a metal fork the rice, cream, egg, parsley, melted butter, salt, pepper, and cheese. Refrigerate for 2 hours.

2. Remove from the refrigerator, and, using the "mud-pie" method, scoop up a handful of rice, sprinkle bread crumbs liberally on one side and then the other. Then re-mold the croquette with both hands, shaping it until the bread crumbs adhere to the outside. Place the croquettes on a large plate and refrigerate until ready to cook.

3. In a large frying pan, over medium heat, heat the 4 tablespoons of butter with the olive oil. Place the croquettes in

the pan, not touching, and brown them evenly, carefully turning them with a spatula. As they become golden brown, they
will be well-formed and intact. The croquettes can be browned
while the côtelettes are in the oven in their last cooking stage.
Serve immediately with the Pojarski Côtelettes.

4. To prepare the Pojarski Côtelettes, break up the bread
and put it in a very large bowl. Stir in the chicken broth and
melted butter. Using a large fork, stir in the chicken, pork,
eggs, salt, pepper, and 2 tablespoons of the dried dill. With the
fork, blend well. Cook a small patty to test the seasoning; then
add more salt and pepper, if needed. Form plump, oblong patties (not flattened like hamburgers), about 2 inches by 3
inches. Lightly dredge in the flour. Preheat the oven to 300
degrees.

5. In a large frying pan, over medium heat, heat 3 tablespoons of butter and 1 of olive oil. Cook 6 cutlets at a time,
browning them evenly on both sides. Arrange in a single layer
in a baking dish. Bake, uncovered, for 15 minutes.

6. Just before serving, heat the sour cream. Spoon it over
the cutlets and sprinkle them with the remaining dried dill.

Boned Chicken Breasts with Scallioned Rice

SERVES 4

1 tablespoon olive oil
8 tablespoons (1 stick) butter
2 large whole chicken breasts, split, skinned, and
    boned
Salt and freshly ground black pepper to taste
½ teaspoon ground cumin
¼ cup dry vermouth
1 cup long-grain rice
2 cups chicken broth
¼ cup dry white wine
6 whole scallions, trimmed and thinly sliced
2 celery stalks, scraped and thinly sliced
6 medium-sized fresh mushrooms, sliced

1. In a frying pan, over medium heat, heat the oil and half of the butter. Evenly brown the chicken breasts, sprinkling them with salt, pepper, and cumin. Remove the breasts. Stir in the vermouth, mixing it with the browned-on bits on the bottom of the pan. Return the breasts to the pan, cover, lower the heat, and simmer for 15 minutes, or until the chicken is nearly tender. Remove from the heat.

2. In a large deep saucepan, melt the remaining butter. Stir in the rice, coating it well. Stir in the chicken broth and white wine. Bring to a boil, stir with a wooden fork, cover, lower the heat, and simmer for 15 minutes.

3. Stir in the scallions, celery, and mushrooms and push the chicken breasts into the rice-vegetable mixture. Cover the pan and cook for 8 minutes, or until the chicken and rice are tender. If liquid cooks off before the chicken and rice are tender, add a small amount of hot broth and continue cooking. Fluff the rice with a metal fork before serving.

Cornish Game Hens Mole with Wild Pecan Rice

SERVES 4

Don't let this long list of ingredients deter you. This is not complicated, and it's rewarding. See the recipe for Pheasant with Wild Pecan Rice, page 120, for more about this rice.

4 Cornish game hens, about 1 pound each, trussed
1 large whole onion
1 celery stalk, scraped and quartered
1 carrot, scraped and quartered
2 teaspoons salt
3 to 4 cups chicken broth
½ cup toasted, coarsely chopped almonds
1 tablespoon toasted sesame seeds
½ teaspoon ground aniseed
1 tortilla, or 1 slice toasted stale bread
½ cup raisins
½ square bitter chocolate, grated
1 tablespoon chili powder, or to taste
½ teaspoon ground cinnamon
⅛ teaspoon ground cloves
2 tablespoons lard or olive oil
2 medium-sized onions, chopped
2 garlic cloves, minced
2 tablespoons all-purpose flour
½ cup tomato purée
1 7-ounce package Wild Pecan Rice

1. Put the game hens with the whole onion, celery, carrot, and 1 teaspoon of the salt in a large pot. Barely cover with water. Bring to a boil, cover, and simmer for 15 minutes. Remove the birds; they will cook more later.

2. In a blender container, combine 1 cup of the chicken broth, the almonds, sesame seeds, aniseed, tortilla, raisins, chocolate, chili powder, cinnamon, and cloves and blend into a smooth purée.

3. In a large heavy pot, over medium heat, melt the lard and cook the chopped onions and garlic for 4 minutes. Lower the heat, stir in the flour, and blend well with the onions and garlic. Stir in the purée from the blender, mixing well. Simmer, stirring, for 2 minutes.

4. Stir in the tomato purée, 1 cup of the chicken broth, and the remaining teaspoon of salt. Simmer, stirring occasionally, for 5 minutes, or until the sauce just begins to thicken.

5. Add the rice and the partially cooked game hens. Simmer, covered, for 25 minutes, or until the rice and birds are tender. If the sauce becomes too thick before the rice and birds are tender, add small amounts of hot broth to thin it.

Note: This dish is also served with plain boiled white rice, but we like this version where the rice is cooked with the birds, making the sauce doubly delicious.

Cornish Game Hens Nested in Wild and Long-Grain Rice

SERVES 4

For this we prefer squabs to Cornish hens, but those baby pigeons are hard to come by and very expensive. However, get them, if you can.

> 6 tablespoons butter
> 4 scallions, trimmed and chopped
> ¾ pound chicken livers, trimmed and quartered
> Salt and freshly ground black pepper to taste
> 2 tablespoons Madeira
> 4 Cornish game hens, about 1 pound (or less) each
> 1 pint sour cream
> 1½ cups wild rice and long-grain rice combination
>   (available in boxes in supermarkets), cooked
>   according to package directions

1. In a frying pan, over medium heat, melt 3 tablespoons of the butter and cook the scallions for 5 minutes, or until they are soft. Do not brown. Add the livers and cook for 3 minutes. (They should be brown on the outside and quite pink on the inside.) Season with salt and pepper. Stir in the Madeira and cook, stirring, for 2 minutes.

2. Preheat the oven to 350 degrees.

3. Stuff the birds with the livers. Then truss them and rub them with the remaining butter. Sprinkle with salt and pepper. Place in a flameproof roasting pan, just large enough to hold them. Bake, uncovered, for 30 minutes, basting well after 20 minutes. Coat the birds with half of the sour cream and bake

for another 30 minutes, or until fork-tender. Transfer to a hot dish and remove the trussing cord.

4. Stir the remaining sour cream and the rice into the pan the birds roasted in, blending the rice into the juices and brown particles in the pan. Heat through over medium heat. Serve the birds, each on a nest of the rice.

Indian Duck and Brown Rice

SERVES 4

India has also been called "Spiceland" and its cooking is firm testament to their wide and constant use.

> 3 tablespoons butter
> 1 tablespoon olive oil
> 1 5- to 6-pound duck, cut into serving pieces (discard the wing tips)
> Salt and freshly ground black pepper to taste
> 4 medium-sized onions, quartered
> 1 small fresh hot red pepper, quartered and seeds discarded, or ¼ teaspoon hot red pepper flakes
> ½ teaspoon ground ginger
> 1 teaspoon ground turmeric
> 1 teaspoon ground coriander
> ¼ teaspoon ground cloves
> ¼ teaspoon ground cinnamon
> 3 cups chicken broth
> 1 cup long-grain brown rice
> 1 cup small green peas (defrosted frozen peas may be used)

1. Preheat the oven to 350 degrees.

2. In a large flameproof casserole, over medium heat, heat the butter with the oil and evenly brown the duck pieces, seasoning them lightly with salt and pepper. Remove the duck.

3. Add the onions and red pepper to the casserole and cook for 5 minutes, or until the onion is golden. Do not brown.

4. Return the duck to the casserole and sprinkle it with the ginger, turmeric, coriander, cloves, and cinnamon. Pour in the chicken broth. Bring to a boil, cover, and bake for 45 minutes.

5. Stir in the rice and bake for 40 minutes. Stir in the peas and bake for 10 minutes, or until the duck and rice are tender. Serve the duck pieces over the rice and peas.

Arroz con Pato Cervesa Inglesa
Duck with Rice and Ale South American Style

SERVES 4

Juice of 4 limes
½ teaspoon ground coriander
1 teaspoon salt
⅛ teaspoon hot red pepper flakes, or to taste
1 5-pound duck, cut into serving pieces, trimmed of
  excess fat
3 tablespoons olive oil
2 12-ounce bottles dark ale
1½ cups long-grain rice
½ cup finely chopped broadleaf (Italian) parsley
  leaves, blended with ½ cup finely chopped chives

1. In a large bowl, blend the lime juice, coriander, salt, and hot red pepper flakes. Add the duck pieces and turn several times to evenly coat with the marinade. Cover and marinate at room temperature for 2 hours, turning several times.

2. In a deep heavy saucepan, over medium heat, heat the oil and evenly brown the duck. Drain the fat from the pan and pour in the ale. Bring to a boil, cover, lower the heat, and simmer for 40 minutes, or until the duck is fork-tender. Remove the duck and keep it warm in a 200-degree oven.

3. Stir the rice into the liquid in which the duck cooked. Bring to a boil, stir with a wooden fork, cover, lower the heat, and simmer for 20 minutes, or until the rice is tender and the liquid has been absorbed. If the liquid is absorbed before the rice is tender, add small amounts of hot water and continue cooking. Or, if the rice is tender and there is an excess of liquid, raise the heat and cook, uncovered, watching carefully so that the rice does not burn. With a metal fork, blend the parsley-chives mixture with the rice, tossing as you mix. Spread the rice on a hot serving dish and top with the duck.

Roast Goose
with Cranberry-Rice Stuffing

SERVES 4 TO 6

1 7-pound goose
Cranberry-Rice Stuffing (see following recipe)
3 tablespoons soft butter
1 teaspoon salt
½ teaspoon freshly ground black pepper
¼ teaspoon dried rosemary

1. Preheat the oven to 375 degrees.

2. Geese are quite fatty, so pierce the breast and thighs in several places with the sharp point of a knife so the fat will cook off. Lightly stuff the bird with the Cranberry-Rice Stuffing (the rice will expand as the bird cooks). Any extra stuffing can be put into a small baking dish, wrapped in foil, and baked with the bird. Place the bird on a rack in a deep roasting pan. This will prevent the goose from cooking in its fat.

3. Blend the butter, salt, pepper, and rosemary into a paste. Rub the bird with this paste.

4. Roast, uncovered, 19 minutes to the pound (about 2 to 2½ hours), or until fork-tender. Do not overcook as the bird will dry out. Baste occasionally with 2 or 3 tablespoonfuls of boiling water and siphon the fat from the pan. We use a bulb baster and find it efficient.

Cranberry-Rice Stuffing

MAKES APPROXIMATELY 5 CUPS

4 tablespoons (½ stick) butter
1½ cups whole cranberries, washed, picked over, and
    coarsely chopped
4 cups al dente-cooked wild rice
2 tablespoons superfine sugar, dissolved in 2
    tablespoons warm water and 2 tablespoons
    brandy
4 scallions (white part only), minced
1 teaspoon salt
½ teaspoon freshly ground black pepper
¼ teaspoon ground nutmeg

In a deep saucepan, over medium heat, melt the butter.
Stir in the remaining ingredients. Lower the heat and simmer,
stirring with a metal fork, for 10 minutes.

Partridge Tandoori
with Wild Pecan Rice

SERVES 6

They can say all they want to about the Italian and Indian rices, but we think American Wild Pecan Rice (more about this rice in the recipe for Pheasant and Wild Pecan Rice, page 120) is superior to them all. It is especially good with this classic from India which we've adapted. Actually, to be authentic, the birds should be cooked in a *tandoor,* a four-foot, cylindrical clay oven buried in the ground. Wood, sometimes charcoal, is the fuel. When the fire is banked and the coals glowing, the heat in the oven becomes intense. These partridges would be tastier cooked *tandoor* fashion, as we've had them in New Delhi, but we've borrowed the sauce and some of the method, which produces good results.

> 3 *chukar partridges (sold at game farms and specialty markets), split and skinned*
> 3 *cups plain yogurt*
> ½ *cup fresh lime juice*
> ¼ *cup olive oil*
> 4 *garlic cloves, crushed*
> 1½ *tablespoons curry powder (page 86)*
> ¼ *teaspoon ground ginger*
> ½ *teaspoon ground cumin*
> ¼ *teaspoon ground coriander*
> 1 *7-ounce package Wild Pecan Rice*
> 1 *teaspoon salt*
> 2 *cups water*

1. Cut two small slits in each leg and each breast of the partridges. Place in a shallow glass dish or casserole, large enough to hold the halves spread flat.

2. In a bowl, combine and blend well the yogurt, lime juice, olive oil, garlic, curry powder, ginger, cumin, and coriander. Spoon the mixture over the partridges, turning to coat evenly. Cover and marinate in the refrigerator for 4 hours. Remove from the refrigerator 1 hour before cooking. Discard the garlic. Reserve the marinade. Preheat the broiler.

3. Put the partridges on a rack in the broiler, over a drip pan, 4 inches from the heat. Broil for 20 minutes on each side, turning frequently to prevent burning, or until tender, basting with marinade.

4. While the birds are cooking, combine the rice, salt, and water in a saucepan. Bring to a boil over medium heat. Stir with a wooden fork, cover, lower the heat, and simmer for 20 minutes, or until the water has been absorbed and the rice is tender.

5. Spoon the marinade that has collected in the drip pan, after basting the birds, into the rice, tossing with a metal fork. Serve each partridge half on its own bed of spicy rice.

Pheasant with Wild Pecan Rice

SERVES 6

We don't claim to have discovered Wild Pecan Rice (but ask yourself if you've ever used it before, or even heard of it), but we certainly feel as if we have. As we mentioned earlier, Wild Pecan Rice is neither wild nor flavored with pecans, but is a very flavorful unique American long-grain rice with a nutty aroma. It is grown only in the Acadian country of South Louisiana. We've found it in several of the larger supermarket chains, but it can also be ordered directly from Conrad Rice Mill, P. O. Box 296, New Iberia, Louisiana 70560. It comes sealed in foil in 7-ounce brown boxes.

> 1 7-ounce package Wild Pecan Rice
> 3 teaspoons salt
> 10 tablespoons butter
> 1½ cups water
> ¾ cup all-purpose flour
> 1 teaspoon dried thyme
> 2 3-pound pheasants, cut into serving pieces
> 2 tablespoons olive oil
> 4 tablespoons all-purpose flour
> 1½ cups chicken broth
> 1 cup light cream or half-and-half
> ½ cup Madeira
> Juice of ½ lemon
> Salt and freshly ground black pepper to taste
> 2 leeks, all of the white and some of the green part,
>   well washed and finely chopped
> 2 tablespoons chopped broadleaf (Italian) parsley
>   leaves

1. In a saucepan, stir in the rice, 1 teaspoon of the salt, and 1 tablespoon of the butter. Add the water, bring to a boil, stir with a wooden fork, cover, lower the heat, and simmer for 10 minutes. If the water hasn't been absorbed, drain and reserve the rice. Preheat the oven to 375 degrees.

2. Blend the ¾ cup of flour, remaining 2 teaspoons of salt, and thyme. Dredge the pheasants in the seasoned flour.

3. In a frying pan, over medium heat, heat 4 tablespoons of the butter with the olive oil, and evenly brown the pheasant pieces. Remove and reserve them.

4. Discard whatever fat remains in the pan. Over medium heat, melt the remaining 5 tablespoons of butter in the pan. Add the 4 tablespoons of flour and cook, stirring into a smooth paste.

5. Lower the heat and gradually stir in the chicken broth, stirring into a smooth sauce. Stir in the cream, Madeira, and lemon juice. Simmer for 2 minutes. Taste and season with salt and pepper, if necessary. Stir in the leeks and parsley and simmer for 1 minute.

6. In a casserole, spread the rice in a smooth layer. Pour half of the sauce over the rice. Arrange the pheasants on top and cover with the remaining sauce. Cover and bake for 25 minutes, or until the rice and pheasants are tender. If the sauce becomes too thick before the pheasants and rice are tender, add small amounts of hot broth or water.

Note: Admittedly, this is an elegant dish for special occasions, but if you aren't a hunter or don't have generous hunter friends for the game dishes in this chapter, don't despair. Many specialty markets sell game of all kinds.

Isle of Pines Quail Picante

SERVES 4

We had this dish on the Isle of Pines, which is just off the coast of Cuba, where we were quail shooting just a few weeks before Castro overran the area and put Cuba off limits for Americans.

> 6 tablespoons butter
> 2 tablespoons olive oil
> 1 large onion, chopped
> 4 bobwhite quails, or 8 coturnix quails
> Salt to taste
> 6 medium-sized ripe tomatoes, peeled, seeded, and
>   chopped, or 3 cups drained canned tomatoes,
>   chopped
> ½ cup dry red wine
> ½ teaspoon cayenne pepper
> 1 bay leaf
> ¼ teaspoon dried thyme
> ½ cup pitted black olives, halved (Use the plump dark
>   purple Greek olives, if possible.)
> 3 cups hot cooked long-grain rice
> ½ cup pimiento-stuffed olives
> 3 scallions (white part only)
> 3 hard-cooked eggs
> ½ cup raisins
> ½ cup toasted blanched almonds
> 3 tablespoons chopped parsley leaves

1. In a deep heavy frying pan, over medium heat, heat 1 tablespoon of the butter and 1 tablespoon of the oil. Add the onion and cook until it is soft, about 5 minutes. Do not brown.

2. Add 2 tablespoons of the butter and the remaining oil to the pan and evenly brown the quails. Season them with salt.

3. Add the tomatoes, wine, cayenne, bay leaf, and thyme and simmer, covered, for 35 minutes, or until the birds are fork-tender. Add the black olives and heat through. Remove and discard the bay leaf.

4. Chop the stuffed olives, scallions, eggs, raisins, and almonds together.

5. With a metal fork, stir the remaining butter (in small pieces) and the chopped mixture into the hot rice. Stir with the fork over heat, just until heated through, fluffing up with the fork.

6. Mound the rice in the center of a hot serving dish and arrange the birds around it. Spoon the tomato sauce over the birds and sprinkle with the parsley.

Rabbits with Olives, Anchovies, and Wild Pecan Rice

SERVES 6

We had this dish in Bologna, Italy. We continue to tell you where we enjoyed some of the dishes in this book, to point up that rice is a world traveler. In Italy, of course, this was served with their Arborio rice. Our unique Wild Pecan Rice, we believe, is better. We have more to say about this rice in the recipe for Pheasant with Wild Pecan Rice on page 120.

> *2 3-pound rabbits, cut into serving pieces*
> *Salt and freshly ground black pepper*
> *3 tablespoons butter*
> *2 tablespoons olive oil*
> *1 medium-sized onion, minced*
> *2 garlic cloves, minced*
> *1 cup dry white wine*
> *Juice of 1 lemon*
> *2 cups chicken broth*
> *1 teaspoon dried marjoram*
> *1 7-ounce package Wild Pecan Rice*
> *12 Italian black olives, pitted and sliced*
> *1 2-ounce can flat anchovy fillets, rinsed in cold*
>   *water, dried, and cut up*

1. Season the rabbit pieces with salt and pepper. In a deep nonaluminum frying pan, over medium heat, heat the butter and oil and evenly brown the rabbit. Remove and reserve.

2. Pour off all but 1 tablespoon of fat. If the rabbit has absorbed all the fat, add 1 tablespoon of butter. Stir in the onions and garlic and cook for 4 minutes, or until they are soft. Do not brown. Add the wine and lemon juice and simmer, uncovered, stirring to loosen the browned-on bits in the bottom of the pan, until the liquid has reduced by half, about 10 minutes.

3. Add the broth, marjoram, and rice and bring to a boil. Return the rabbit to the pan with the olives and anchovies. Lower the heat. Stir with a wooden fork, cover, and simmer for 25 minutes, or until the rabbit and rice are tender. If the liquid cooks off before the rice and rabbit are tender, add small amounts of hot broth or water.

Rabbit and Rice à la Roannaise

SERVES 6

The food faddists are frantically coming up with what they call "new" dishes. Right now rabbit is on their agenda of "discoveries." It's been on ours for a long time, as several of our cookbooks attest. With little fat and much flavor, and mated with rice, rabbit offers a welcome menu change. Rabbits are available frozen in some supermarkets and fresh in some larger cities.

> 1 cup long-grain brown rice
> 3 teaspoons salt
> 1 cup water
> ¾ cup all-purpose flour
> ½ teaspoon dried rosemary
> 1 teaspoon freshly ground black pepper
> 2 3-pound rabbits, cut into serving pieces
> ¼ cup olive oil
> 6 medium-sized white onions, chopped
> 3 garlic cloves, minced
> 2 cups chicken broth

1. In a saucepan, combine the rice, 1 teaspoon of the salt, and the water. Bring to a boil, stir with a wooden fork, cover, lower the heat, and simmer for 10 minutes. If the water hasn't been absorbed, drain and reserve the rice.

2. In a clean paper or plastic bag, combine the flour, rosemary, remaining 2 teaspoons of salt, and pepper. Add the rabbit pieces and shake them until they are evenly coated with the seasoned flour. In a frying pan, over medium heat, heat the olive oil and evenly brown the rabbit.

3. In a casserole, make a smooth layer of the partially cooked rice. Arrange the rabbit on top of the rice. Preheat the oven to 350 degrees.

4. In the frying pan in which the rabbit cooked, stir in the onions and garlic, adding more oil, if necessary. Cook over medium heat until the onions and garlic are soft. Gradually stir in the broth, scraping the bottom of the pan to loosen the browned-on bits. Simmer until the onion sauce is smooth and golden. Taste for seasoning, adding salt and pepper, if needed.

5. Pour the onion sauce over the rabbit and rice, cover, and bake for 30 minutes, or until the rabbit and rice are tender. If the sauce becomes too thick before the rabbit and rice are tender, add small amounts of hot broth or water. Serve right from the casserole.

Rabbit Stew with Brown Rice

SERVES 6 TO 8

We had this in Parma with Italian Arborio rice, which is not available many places in the U.S., so we've substituted brown rice, because we think it is nuttier and even better and easier to cook.

4 *tablespoons butter*
2 *tablespoons olive oil*
2 *rabbits (each weighing about 3 pounds), cut into*
  serving pieces
Salt and freshly ground black pepper to taste
3 *large shallots, chopped*
Leaves from 2 celery stalks, chopped
2 *garlic cloves, minced*
½ *teaspoon crushed dried rosemary*
1 *cup chopped prosciutto or Canadian bacon*
1 *cup dry red wine*
4 *medium-sized ripe tomatoes, peeled, seeded, and*
  chopped
3 *cups beef broth*
1½ *cups long-grain brown rice*
3 *tablespoons chopped broadleaf (Italian) parsley*
  leaves

1. Preheat the oven to 350 degrees.

2. In a large flameproof casserole, heat the butter and oil over medium heat. Evenly brown the rabbit pieces, a few at a time, seasoning them with salt and pepper. Add more butter and oil, if needed.

3. Add the shallots, celery leaves, garlic, rosemary, prosciutto, and wine. Cook until the wine has mostly evaporated.

4. Stir in the tomatoes, broth, and rice. Bring to a boil, cover, and bake for 40 minutes, or until the rabbit and rice are tender and the liquid has been mostly absorbed. If the liquid has been absorbed before the rice and rabbit are tender, add a small amount of hot broth and continue cooking. Serve right from the casserole with the parsley sprinkled over.

Rice-Stuffed Turkey Thighs

SERVES 4

4 small turkey thighs (from 6- to 8-pound birds),
    boned
4 slices bacon
4 large shallots, finely chopped
1 celery stalk, scraped and finely chopped
Salt and freshly ground black pepper to taste
3 tablespoons brandy
½ teaspoon Bell's seasoning
2 cups cooked short- or medium-grain rice
Paprika

1. Enlarge the cavity of the thighs with a knife, being careful not to cut through.

2. In a frying pan, over medium heat, cook the bacon until it is crisp and golden. Drain on paper towels, cool, and crumble. Set aside. Pour off all but 2 tablespoons of fat from the pan, reserving the remainder.

3. Add the shallots and celery to the pan and cook for 5 minutes, or until they are soft. Do not brown. Season with salt and pepper. Remove from the heat and stir in the brandy, Bell's seasoning, rice, and bacon, blending well. Preheat the oven to 450 degrees.

4. Stuff each thigh with a quarter of the mixture. Arrange, skin side up, in a shallow baking dish just large enough to snugly hold the stuffed thighs. Brush with the reserved bacon fat and sprinkle lightly with salt, pepper, and paprika. Bake for 7 minutes. Lower the oven temperature to 350 degrees and bake for 35 minutes, or until fork-tender.

Brown Rice with Turkey Giblets

SERVES 4

We had this dish for lunch one day in Louisiana, and found it so surprisingly tasty that we often prepare it. There is no problem with what to do with versatile turkey or chicken livers, but most of us are baffled when it comes to gizzards and hearts. Here's one answer.

> 4 tablespoons butter
> 3 medium-sized onions, chopped
> 1 pound turkey (or chicken) hearts and gizzards, trimmed and diced
> Salt and freshly ground black pepper to taste
> ¼ teaspoon ground nutmeg
> 1 cup long-grain brown rice
> 3 cups chicken broth
> Bouquet garni made up of 1 bay leaf, 3 sprigs fresh parsley, and 3 sprigs celery leaves tied in cheesecloth
> ¼ teaspoon dried thyme
> 3 tablespoons chopped parsley leaves

1. Preheat the oven to 350 degrees.

2. In a deep flameproof casserole, over medium heat, melt the butter. Add the onions and giblets and cook for 10 minutes, seasoning with salt, pepper, and nutmeg. Stir in the rice, coating it well.

3. Pour in the broth and add the bouquet garni and thyme. Bring to a boil, cover, and bake for 45 minutes, or until the liquid has been absorbed and the giblets and rice are tender. Discard the bouquet garni. Sprinkle with the parsley before serving.

Turkey and Rice Suprême with Italian Green Beans

SERVES 4 TO 6

3 tablespoons butter
2 medium-sized onions, chopped
½ pound small fresh mushrooms, halved, or, if larger,
     quartered
Salt and freshly ground black pepper to taste
1 cup long-grain rice
1 tablespoon curry powder, or to taste
1½ cups chicken broth
2 cups small bite-sized pieces cooked turkey
1 cup diced cooked ham
¼ cup chopped parsley leaves
1 10-ounce package frozen Italian green beans, cooked
     half of the time indicated on the package and well
     drained
6 tablespoons dry sherry
1 cup heavy cream

1. In a saucepan, over medium heat, melt the butter and cook the onions for 5 minutes, or until they are soft. Do not brown. Add the mushrooms and cook for 2 minutes. Season with salt and pepper.

2. Stir in the rice and curry powder and cook for 2 minutes. Pour in the broth and bring to a boil. Stir with a wooden fork, cover, lower the heat, and simmer for 10 minutes.

3. Stir in the turkey, ham, and parsley. Taste for seasoning, adding salt and pepper, if needed. Preheat the oven to 350 degrees.

4. Spoon half of the rice mixture into a casserole in an even layer. Arrange the beans over it in an even layer. Then spoon on the remaining rice mixture. Combine the sherry and cream and pour the mixture over the rice. Bake for 30 minutes, or until the rice is tender and the liquid has been mostly absorbed.

Venison and Wild Pecan Rice Bourguignonne

SERVES 4

Two items make this an unusual dish to offer guests: the venison—and the Wild Pecan Rice. We have special words on this rice in the Pheasant with Wild Pecan Rice recipe on page 120.

4 slices bacon, coarsely chopped
8 medium-sized fresh mushrooms, sliced medium thick
2 pounds boneless venison steak, cut into 2-inch cubes
2 tablespoons all-purpose flour, blended with 1
*   teaspoon dry mustard*
1 tablespoon sugar
1½ teaspoons salt
¼ teaspoon dried thyme
1 bay leaf
4 whole black peppercorns, crushed
¾ cup beef broth
1½ cups dry red wine
12 small white onions, root ends scored
1 7-ounce package Wild Pecan Rice
2 cups water

1. In a large heavy pot, over medium heat, cook the bacon until it is just crisp. Remove with a slotted spoon, drain on paper towels, and reserve. Cook the mushrooms in the bacon

fat for 2 minutes. Remove with a slotted spoon and reserve.

2. Add the venison cubes to the pot and brown evenly over medium heat. Stir in the sugar, ½ teaspoon of the salt, thyme, bay leaf, and the peppercorns. Pour in the beef broth and wine. Stir, cover, and simmer for 1 hour, stirring frequently.

3. Stir in the onions and bacon and simmer for 30 minutes, or until the venison and onions are tender. Add the mushrooms. Remove and discard the bay leaf. Taste for seasoning, adding salt and pepper, if needed.

4. While the venison is cooking, combine the rice, remaining 1 teaspoon of salt, and water in a saucepan. Stir well with a wooden fork. Bring to a boil, stir with a wooden fork, lower the heat, cover, and simmer for 20 minutes, or until the water has been absorbed and the rice is tender.

5. Spread the hot rice onto warm individual plates and serve topped with the venison stew. Save some red wine to sip with this special dish.

6

RICE

with MEAT and VARIETY MEATS

I t's a thousand-year-old story. The Chinese drop a few pieces of pork into a huge bowl of rice and feed a family a "meat-meal."

We didn't have to travel to China to witness that magic act. We saw it in Lake Charles, Louisiana, where Jack was interviewing Paul Faulk, a noted duck-and-goose-calling champion for a column he was writing for the *New York Herald Tribune*.

It was bayou country, and for lunch we motorboated out to the goose-caller's mother's home in the marshlands. Her house was so close to the water that it looked like an odd boat moored among the bulrushes. This is fish and shellfish country, so we expected a gumbo or jambalaya, but were pleasantly surprised.

We sat down to that region's famous dish of black beans and rice, but just before we dipped our forks into it, that lady dolloped atop it a few slices of a remarkable spicy sausage that she had left over from a batch she had made.

This was yet another example of the fact that the mating of any kind of meat with rice is one of the most graceful in the food world.

Munich Meat-Pot

SERVES 6

1½ pounds beef round steak, thinly sliced
All-purpose flour for dredging
2 tablespoons butter
2 tablespoons olive oil
Salt and freshly ground black pepper to taste
3 medium-sized onions, sliced
1 12-ounce can dark ale
1 cup beef broth
¼ teaspoon cayenne pepper
1 tablespoon dark or light brown sugar
3 small turnips, scraped and cut into ¼-inch-thick
    slices
3 cups al dente-cooked long-grain rice

1. With a meat mallet, pound the steak to tenderize it (or have your butcher do it). Cut it into 1-inch-wide strips.

2. Lightly dredge the strips of meat in the flour, shaking off any excess.

3. In a large heavy frying pan, over medium-high heat, heat the butter and oil. Evenly brown the beef, seasoning it with salt and pepper. Lower the heat, add the onions, and cook for 4 minutes.

4. Add the ale, broth, cayenne, and brown sugar. Stir well. Bring to a boil, cover, lower the heat, and simmer for 15 minutes. Add the turnips and cook for 15 minutes, or until the beef and turnips are just tender and the sauce has thickened.

5. Stir in the rice and cook for 5 minutes to heat through. Taste for seasoning, adding salt and pepper, if needed.

Burgundian Beef and Rice

SERVES 6

½ pound lean salt pork, blanched in boiling water for
    10 minutes, dried, and cut into ½-inch cubes
2 tablespoons olive oil
3 pounds lean beef (chuck or top or bottom round),
    cut into 1½-inch cubes
Salt and freshly ground black pepper
24 tiny white onions, root ends scored
1 garlic clove, minced
1 cup white Burgundy wine
3 tablespoons brandy
.Approximately 3 cups beef broth
Bouquet garni made of 2 sprigs parsley, several celery
    leaves, ¼ teaspoon dried thyme, and 1 bay leaf
    tied in cheesecloth
2 tablespoons tomato paste
2 tablespoons butter
1 cup long-grain rice

1. In a frying pan, over medium heat, cook the salt pork cubes in the olive oil until they are golden brown and crisp. With a slotted spoon transfer them to a flameproof casserole.

2. Add the beef to the frying pan (do not crowd it) and brown it evenly, sprinkling it lightly with salt and pepper. As the beef browns, transfer it to the casserole. Add the onions and garlic to the frying pan and cook until they are slightly golden. Do not brown. With a slotted spoon transfer them to the casserole. Preheat the oven to 350 degrees.

3. Pour off any fat remaining in the pan. Pour in the wine and brandy and heat, stirring, to scrape up the browned-on bits in the bottom of the pan. Pour into the casserole. Pour enough broth into the casserole to barely cover the meat. Add the bouquet garni and tomato paste. Bring to a boil on top of the stove, cover, and bake for 1½ hours, or until the beef is almost tender. If the liquid in the casserole has cooked off, add more hot broth or water, in order to have 2½ cups of liquid.

4. In the frying pan in which the beef was browned, melt the butter. Add the rice and cook, stirring, until the rice is well coated. Remove the casserole from the oven, stir in the rice, return to the oven, and bake, covered, until the beef and rice are tender and most of the liquid has been absorbed, about 25 minutes. Taste for seasoning, adding salt and pepper, if needed. Discard the bouquet garni before serving.

Stufato

A Rice and Beef Casserole

SERVES 4 TO 6

3 tablespoons olive oil
2 pounds lean beef chuck, cut into ½-inch cubes
Salt and freshly ground black pepper to taste
2 medium-sized onions, chopped
1 garlic clove, minced
3 slices lean bacon, chopped
½ cup chopped prosciutto or other ham
3 large ripe tomatoes, peeled, seeded, and chopped, or
    1 1-pound can tomatoes, drained and chopped
½ cup dry red wine
Approximately 1½ to 2 cups beef broth
3 cups al dente-cooked long-grain rice
1 cup grated Asiago or Parmesan cheese

1. Preheat the oven to 350 degrees.

2. In a flameproof casserole, heat the olive oil over medium heat and lightly brown the beef cubes, adding more oil, if needed. Season lightly with salt and pepper.

3. Add the onions, garlic, bacon, and prosciutto and cook for 5 minutes, stirring occasionally. Add the tomatoes and wine and cook, uncovered, for 10 minutes. Pour in enough of the beef broth to barely cover the meat. Bring to a boil, cover, and bake for 45 minutes, or until the beef is almost tender. Taste for seasoning, adding salt and pepper, if needed. Lower the oven temperature to 325 degrees.

4. Using a slotted spoon, remove the beef from the casserole and arrange half of it in a deep baking dish. Smooth a layer of half of the rice over the beef and sprinkle with half of the cheese. Repeat, using the remaining beef and rice. Spoon the sauce in the casserole over the top layer of rice; then sprinkle with the remaining cheese.

5. Bake, uncovered, for 30 minutes, or until the beef is tender and the liquid has been mostly absorbed.

Baked Beef and Rice

SERVES 6

3 tablespoons butter
1 tablespoon olive oil
1 large onion, finely chopped
2 celery stalks, scraped and finely chopped
1½ pounds lean ground beef (chuck, top, or bottom
   round)
2 tablespoons honey
1½ teaspoons salt
½ teaspoon freshly ground black pepper
1 teaspoon chili powder
1½ cups long-grain rice, cooked in water for 10
   minutes and drained
1 1-pound can tomatoes with their liquid (Break the
   tomatoes up with your hands.)
1 cup beef broth, heated

1. Preheat the oven to 350 degrees.

2. Over medium heat, in a large frying pan, heat the butter and oil. Add the onion, celery, and beef and cook until the beef has lost its pink color. Stir in the honey, salt, pepper, chili powder, rice, tomatoes with their liquid, and the beef broth. Taste for seasoning, adding salt and pepper, if needed.

3. Transfer to a baking dish and bake for 45 minutes, or until the rice is tender and most of the liquid has been absorbed.

Roquefort Rice Tartare Balls

SERVES ABOUT 8 TO HAVE WITH COCKTAILS

½ cup Roquefort cheese at room temperature
1 8-ounce package cream cheese at room temperature
½ cup cooked short- or medium-grain rice, cooled
2 pounds lean top or bottom round steak, finely
*   ground*
2 egg yolks
1 small white onion, grated
Salt and freshly ground black pepper to taste
Minced parsley leaves

1. Combine the cheeses and mix into a smooth paste. Blend in the rice. Refrigerate.

2. Combine and blend well the steak, egg yolks, onion, salt, and pepper.

3. Form the cheese-rice mixture into balls ½ inch in diameter. Encase them in the chopped meat, forming balls about 1 inch in diameter.

4. Roll each ball in the parsley and spear each with a toothpick. Serve with small round slices of buttered rye bread.

San Antonio Rice Hash

SERVES 6

3 tablespoons butter
2 tablespoons olive oil
6 medium-sized onions, chopped
2 sweet green peppers, seeds and ribs removed,
  chopped
2 pounds chopped beef chuck
1 1-pound, 12-ounce can tomatoes, with their liquid
  (Chop the tomatoes.)
1 cup long-grain brown rice
1 tablespoon chili powder
1 tablespoon salt
Beef broth, optional

1. Preheat the oven to 350 degrees.

2. In a flameproof casserole, over medium heat, heat the butter and oil. Add the onions and green peppers, and cook for 10 minutes, or until they are soft. Do not brown.

3. Add all remaining ingredients, except the broth, and blend well.

4. Bake, covered, for 40 minutes, or until the rice is tender and most of the liquid has been absorbed. If the rice is almost tender and there is excess liquid, remove the top and continue cooking. If the rice is not yet tender enough and the liquid has been absorbed, add a small amount of hot beef broth and continue cooking. Taste for seasoning, adding salt and pepper, if needed.

Cocido with Wild Pecan Rice

SERVES 8 TO 10

In our kitchen hang several unusual hand-carved wooden spoons that we collected from Spanish field-workers and farmers. They range from an ornately carved one, which is twice as broad as an open hand, to a delicately scrolled one the size of a serving spoon. The large one is used to dip into the boiled dinner that we detail here, and serve as the bowl for the small spoon. This system is used when Spaniards eat from the *cocido* pot while working in the field. An older woman usually tends it, keeping the lunch warm by burning straw under the blackened pot. The wooden spoons are handmade. Intricate designs and secret symbols are carved on them by the peasants. The spoons are highly prized by them—and by us. So is their boiled dinner.

2 pounds beef bones
1 3-pound beef brisket
6 quarts water
1 tablespoon salt
1 teaspoon freshly ground black pepper
3 whole onions, each nailed with 2 cloves
1½ pounds lean smoked ham
½ pound fatback
8 to 10 chorizos (Spanish sausages) or any highly seasoned smoked pork sausage
1 3-pound chicken, cut into 8 to 10 serving pieces
4 or 5 leeks (white part and some of the light green part), washed well under cool running water and cut into halves lengthwise
8 to 10 small carrots, scraped
2 garlic cloves, peeled

1 medium-sized cabbage, trimmed and cut into 8 to
*   10 wedges*
8 to 10 small potatoes
1 16-ounce can chick-peas, drained
1½ cups hot cooked Wild Pecan Rice
4 tablespoons chopped parsley leaves

1. Put the beef bones, beef brisket, water, salt, pepper, and onions into a very large deep pot. Bring to a boil, lower the heat, and simmer, partially covered, for 1 hour, skimming any scum from the top.

2. Add the ham, fatback, and sausages. Simmer for 30 minutes. Add the chicken and simmer for 30 minutes.

3. Add the leeks, carrots, garlic, cabbage, and potatoes. Simmer, partially covered, for 30 minutes, or until the meats and vegetables are fork-tender. If the chicken and vegetables are tender before the meats are, remove them and return them to the pot just before serving. Stir in the chick-peas and simmer for 10 minutes. Remove and discard the onions and bones. Taste for seasoning, adding salt and pepper, if needed.

4. Do not spoon out of the pot as the field hands do. But serve just the broth in individual bowls with the Wild Pecan Rice stirred in, sprinkled with parsley.

5. After the exceptional rice soup, present the meats (sliced), whole sausages, and chicken on a large hot serving dish, surrounded by the vegetables.

Blanquette de Veau
in a Rice Ring

SERVES 6

Here's a saucy classic French country dish that demands a rice ring. Prepare the rice ring while the veal simmers in its pot, in the second stage of preparation. Remember to use short- or medium-grain rice for the ring. The French usually use the breast of veal, cut into 1-inch pieces with bone, for this dish, but we prefer the shoulder.

We surround the ring with a green vegetable, often Brussels sprouts.

> *3 pounds boneless veal shoulder, cut into pieces 1 inch square and ½ inch thick*
> *4 medium-sized white onions, each nailed with a whole clove*
> *3 celery stalks with leaves, scraped and cut into ¼-inch slices*
> *2 medium-sized carrots, scraped and cut into ¼-inch pieces*
> *1 bay leaf*
> *½ teaspoon dried thyme*
> *1 teaspoon salt*
> *5 cups chicken broth, or enough to completely cover the veal*
> *18 small white onions, root ends scored*
> *24 small firm fresh mushrooms, halved*
> *3 tablespoons butter*
> *3 tablespoons all-purpose flour*
> *Salt and freshly ground black pepper to taste*
> *3 egg yolks*
> *½ cup heavy cream*

Juice of ½ lemon
Rice Ring (see recipes on pages 184 and 186)

1. In a deep heavy pot, blanch the veal in boiling water for 10 minutes. Drain the veal and rinse it with warm water. Return the veal to the pot and add the onions with the cloves, celery, carrots, bay leaf, thyme, salt, and broth. Cover, bring to a boil, lower the heat, and simmer for 1¼ hours, or until the veal is fork-tender. (This is the time when the rice ring can be prepared.)

2. Remove the veal with a slotted spoon and transfer it to a bowl. Strain the broth, discarding the bay leaf, and return it to the pot. Simmer the onions in the broth for 8 minutes, or until they are tender but still intact. With a slotted spoon, transfer the onions to the bowl with the veal. Cook the mushrooms in the broth for 2 minutes. With a slotted spoon transfer them to the bowl with the veal.

3. Raise the heat under the pot of broth and reduce the liquid to about 2½ cups. In a large saucepan, over medium heat, melt the butter. Add the flour and cook, stirring into a smooth paste. Gradually add the hot broth, stirring into a medium-thick, smooth sauce. Season with salt and pepper.

4. Add the veal, onions, and mushrooms to the sauce and place over low heat to warm through.

5. In a bowl, beat the egg yolks with the cream and lemon juice. Just before spooning the *blanquette* into the rice ring, stir in the egg yolk-cream-lemon juice mixture. Cook over low heat, stirring, until thickened. Do not boil or the eggs will curdle.

6. Ladle the *blanquette* into the rice ring. If the ring cannot accommodate the entire *blanquette,* serve the remainder in a bowl.

Risotto Milanese with Ossi Buchi

SERVES 6

Ossi Buchi

6 3-inch-thick meaty pieces (cut from the center) veal
　shanks with marrow
All-purpose flour for dredging
2 tablespoons butter
3 tablespoons olive oil
Salt and freshly ground black pepper to taste
⅛ teaspoon crushed dried rosemary
2 medium-sized onions, finely chopped
1 garlic clove, minced
1 large ripe tomato, peeled, seeded, and finely chopped
1 large carrot, scraped and cut into ¼-inch dice
1 large celery stalk, scraped and cut into ¼-inch dice
1½ cups dry white wine
1 cup chicken broth
Gremolata (page 148)

Risotto Milanese

8 tablespoons (1 stick) butter
1 medium-sized onion, finely chopped
1 garlic clove, minced
2 cups long-grain rice
4½ cups chicken broth
½ cup dry white wine
¼ teaspoon powdered saffron, dissolved in 1 or 2
　tablespoons chicken broth
1 cup grated Asiago or Parmesan cheese
¼ cup finely chopped broadleaf (Italian) parsley
　leaves
Salt and freshly ground black pepper to taste

1. To prepare the Ossi Buchi, dredge the shanks lightly in the flour. In a flameproof casserole (just large enough to snugly hold the shanks in a standing position), heat the butter and oil over medium heat, and brown the shanks evenly, sprinkling them with salt and pepper. Add more oil, if needed. Preheat the oven to 325 degrees.

2. Stand the shanks upright (so the bone and marrow are showing; this will prevent the marrow from falling out) in the pot. Sprinkle the rosemary and vegetables around them and pour the wine and broth over them. Bring to a boil on top of the stove; cover and bake for 1½ hours, or until the veal is very tender.

3. To prepare the Risotto Milanese, melt 4 tablespoons of the butter in a saucepan over medium heat. Add the onion and garlic and cook for 5 minutes, or until they are soft. Do not brown. Add the rice and cook for 2 minutes, stirring. Pour in the broth, wine, and saffron. Bring to a boil, stir with a wooden fork, cover, lower the heat, and simmer for 20 minutes, or until the rice is tender and almost all of the liquid has been absorbed. If the liquid has been absorbed before the rice is cooked, add a small amount of hot broth and continue cooking. If the rice is cooked and there is excessive liquid in the pan, raise heat and cook off most of the liquid. The rice should be slightly *al dente* and moist.

4. With a metal fork, stir in the cheese, the remaining butter (in small pieces), and the parsley, fluffing up the rice. Taste for seasoning and add salt and pepper, if needed. The broth may have supplied enough.

5. Serve the rice on a large hot serving dish with the shanks arranged on the rice and the *Gremolata* sprinkled on the shanks.

Note: Put small spoons or forks at each place so the marrow can be removed (and eaten!) from the shanks. Shops do sell "marrow" spoons.

Gremolata

With a fork in a small bowl, mix 1 minced garlic clove
with 3 tablespoons finely chopped broadleaf (Italian) parlsey
leaves and the grated rind of 1 lemon.

Escalopes de Veau à l'Estragon

SERVES 6

5 tablespoons butter
2 tablespoons olive oil
2 medium-sized onions, chopped
2 pounds veal, cut into 2-inch squares, ½ inch thick,
    beaten between sheets of wax paper with a mallet
    to a ¼-inch thickness
Salt and freshly ground black pepper to taste
A whole onion, nailed with 3 whole cloves
3 to 4 cups chicken broth
1½ cups long-grain rice
1 tablespoon chopped fresh tarragon, or 1 teaspoon
    dried tarragon
4 tablespoons chopped parsley leaves
2 tablespoons chopped fresh tarragon

1. Over medium heat, in a flameproof casserole, heat 2
tablespoons of the butter and 1 tablespoon of the oil. Add the
chopped onions and cook for 5 minutes, or until they are soft.
Do not brown.
2. Add the remaining butter and oil and heat. Add the
veal and brown evenly, adding more butter and oil, if needed.
Season with salt and pepper. Add the whole onion with the

cloves, cover, and cook for 20 minutes, turning the veal after 10 minutes. If the bottom of the pot starts getting too brown add a small amount of broth. Remove and discard the onion. Preheat the oven to 375 degrees.

3. Mix in the rice. Pour in enough broth to cover (about 3 cups). Add the 1 tablespoon of tarragon. Bring to a boil on top of the stove; then bake, covered, for 25 minutes, or until the rice and veal are tender and most of the liquid has been absorbed. However, the dish should be slightly moist. If the liquid is absorbed before the rice and veal are tender, add a small amount of hot broth and continue to cook. Taste for seasoning, adding salt and pepper, if needed. Stir in the parsley and remaining tarragon and serve right from the casserole.

Lamb and Rice Stew

SERVES 6

6 tablespoons butter
3 tablespoons olive oil
3 pounds lean lamb from the leg, cut into 1-inch cubes
Salt and freshly ground black pepper
4 large leeks (including some of the light green part),
    well washed and cut into ½-inch pieces
½ cup tomato purée
½ cup dry vermouth
3 cups beef broth
½ teaspoon dried oregano
¼ teaspoon ground cinnamon
1½ cups long-grain rice
1 garlic clove, minced

1. Over medium heat, in a frying pan, heat 3 tablespoons of the butter and 2 tablespoons of the olive oil. Brown the lamb evenly, seasoning it lightly with salt and pepper; transfer the lamb to a flameproof casserole.

2. Heat 1 tablespoon of the butter and the remaining oil in the frying pan. Add the leeks and cook for 5 minutes. Combine the tomato purée and vermouth and pour the mixture into the pan. Simmer for 1 minute, stirring and scraping up the browned-on bits in the pan. Pour the leeks and liquid into the casserole. Add the broth, oregano, and cinnamon and bring to a boil. Lower the heat, cover, and simmer for 30 minutes.

3. Melt the remaining butter in the frying pan and add the rice and garlic. Cook for 2 minutes, stirring. Transfer the rice to the casserole with the lamb. Cover and cook for 25 minutes, or until the rice and lamb are tender and most of the liquid has been absorbed. If the liquid is absorbed before the rice and lamb are tender, add a small amount of hot broth and continue cooking. If they are cooked and there seems to be too much liquid, remove the cover, raise the heat, and cook off the excess, being careful not to burn the rice.

Brodetto

Italian Lamb and Rice Casserole

SERVES 4 TO 6

1 cup dry white wine
3 cups water
1 teaspoon salt
½ teaspoon freshly ground black pepper
5 tablespoons chopped broadleaf (Italian) parsley
*   leaves*
6 ripe plum tomatoes, peeled, seeded, and chopped, or
*   1 1-pound can imported Italian plum tomatoes,*
*   drained and chopped*

2 *medium-sized onions, chopped*
1 *bay leaf*
½ *teaspoon dried oregano*
¼ *teaspoon dried rosemary*
2 *pounds boneless lamb, cut into large bite-sized*
    pieces
1 *cup long-grain brown rice*
4 *large eggs*
½ *cup grated Asiago or Parmesan cheese*
½ *teaspoon salt*
¼ *teaspoon freshly ground black pepper*
1 *pound fresh peas, shelled (about 1 cup), cooked in*
    water to cover until just tender, almost al dente,
    or the same amount of frozen peas, defrosted

1. Preheat the oven to 350 degrees.

2. In a flameproof casserole, combine the wine, water, 1 teaspoon salt, ½ teaspoon pepper, 3 tablespoons of the parsley, tomatoes, onions, bay leaf, oregano, rosemary, and lamb. Bring to a boil on top of the stove, cover, and bake for 45 minutes. Stir in the rice, cover, and bake for 35 minutes, or until the lamb and rice are almost tender. The rice should be *al dente,* as the lamb and rice will cook further. Check the dish as it cooks. If it seems dry, add more hot water. It should be moist but not soupy. Remove and discard the bay leaf.

3. Beat together the eggs, remaining parsley, cheese, salt, and pepper.

4. Stir the peas into the egg-cheese mixture. Pour this over the rice and lamb and bake, uncovered, for about 25 minutes, or until the eggs are set and the lamb and rice are tender.

Stuffed Leg of Lamb

SERVES 6

4 tablespoons butter
4 lamb kidneys (or chicken livers), trimmed and
    coarsely chopped
2 tablespoons brandy
1 garlic clove, minced
2 medium-sized onions, finely chopped
¾ cup long-grain rice
¼ cup of pignoli or broken up walnuts
¼ cup currants
3 tablespoons finely chopped finocchio (fennel) leaves
½ teaspoon ground allspice
¼ teaspoon ground cinnamon
1½ cups beef broth
Salt and freshly ground black pepper
1 5- to 6-pound leg of lamb, boned
1 medium-sized carrot, scraped and chopped
¼ teaspoon cayenne pepper
1 teaspoon dried rosemary
½ cup water

1. In a frying pan, over medium-high heat, melt 2 tablespoons of the butter and cook the kidneys until they are brown
on the outside but still very pink inside. Stir in the brandy and
quickly cook it off. Transfer the kidneys to a bowl.

2. In a saucepan, heat the remaining butter over medium
heat. Cook the garlic and half of the onions for 5 minutes, or
until they are soft. Do not brown. Add the rice, nuts, currants,
finocchio, allspice, and cinnamon and cook, stirring, for 1 minute. Pour in the broth. Bring to a boil, lower the heat, stir with
a wooden fork, cover, and simmer, for 15 minutes, or until the
liquid has been absorbed. The rice should still be quite al dente.

If necessary, drain before it becomes too soft. Taste for season-ing, and add salt and pepper, if needed. The broth may have supplied enough. Combine the rice mixture with the kidneys and mix well.

3. Flatten the leg of lamb, skin side down, with a meat mallet or the broad side of a knife blade. Sprinkle with salt and pepper. Spread the kidney-rice stuffing over the meat, not quite to the edge. Roll and tie to keep the stuffing intact.

4. Preheat the oven to 400 degrees.

5. Sprinkle the carrot, remaining onions, cayenne, and rosemary on the bottom of a roasting pan or casserole just large enough to hold the lamb snugly. Set lamb on top and sprinkle lightly with salt and pepper. Pour in ½ cup of water. Bake, uncovered, for 1½ hours, or until fork-tender. If necessary, add more water to the pan as the lamb cooks.

Note: To test lamb for degree of doneness, insert a narrow-bladed knife deeply into the lamb. If the juice runs pink, it is medium-rare; if the juice runs yellow, it is well-done.

Lamb Meatball Pulao

SERVES 4

While in the planning stages of an involved trip to India, where we would stay for several months in various cities and the jungles, Leela Nadhan, from the Government of India Tourist Office, visited our home in Washington, Connecticut. This is one dish she prepared, using the ingredients we had at hand. She was accustomed to first soaking and then washing the rice, but we pointed out that this wasn't necessary with American rice, that the method, in fact, washed away the important nutrients.

> 2½ cups chicken broth
> 1 cup long-grain rice
> ½ pound ground lean lamb
> ⅛ teaspoon hot red pepper flakes
> 1½ teaspoon salt
> ⅛ teaspoon ground nutmeg
> ½ teaspoon ground cumin
> ½ teaspoon ground coriander
> 1 egg, beaten
> 8 tablespoons (1 stick) butter
> 1 tablespoon olive oil
> 2 medium-sized onions, chopped
> ½ teaspoon ground cinnamon
> 1 teaspoon light brown sugar
> ½ teaspoon ground turmeric
> ½ teaspoon chili powder
> 1 small sweet red pepper, cored, seeded, and chopped
> 1 large onion, thinly sliced

1. In a saucepan, bring the chicken broth to a boil. Stir in the rice, cover, lower the heat, and simmer for 20 minutes, or until the rice is tender and the liquid has been absorbed. Reserve.

2. In a large bowl, combine and blend well (hands are good for this) the lamb, hot red pepper flakes, 1 teaspoon of the salt, nutmeg, cumin, coriander, and the egg. Form into very small meatballs (about ½ inch in diameter). In a large frying pan, over medium heat, heat 2 tablespoons of the butter and the olive oil. Brown the meatballs evenly; then remove and reserve them.

3. In the same frying pan (add 2 tablespoons of butter [not that included in the list of ingredients]), over medium heat and cook the chopped onions with the cinnamon for 3 minutes. Add the brown sugar and cook, stirring, for 1 minute. Do not burn. Stir in the turmeric, chili powder, ½ teaspoon of salt, and the chopped red pepper and cook for 5 minutes. Do not burn. With a metal fork, stir in the rice, fluffing it up and blending well. Preheat the oven to 350 degrees.

4. In a casserole, arrange half of the rice mixture in a smooth layer. Do not pack down. Arrange the meatballs on the rice in a layer, using all of them. Then arrange the remaining half of the rice on the meatballs in a smooth layer. Do not pack down. Dot with 2 tablespoons of the butter and bake for 15 minutes.

5. Meanwhile, in a frying pan, over medium heat, melt the remaining butter (at least 4 tablespoons) and cook the sliced onion until it is crisp, about 6 minutes. Do not let it burn. Drain on paper towels. Garnish the rice casserole with the crisp onion slices.

Greek Meatballs
with Piquant Sauce

SERVES 4

3 slices white bread, with crusts trimmed, soaked in
    milk
1 pound ground lean lamb
½ cup short- or medium-grain rice
1 egg, beaten
1 medium-sized onion, finely chopped
1 garlic clove, minced
¼ cup minced parsley leaves
5 fresh mint leaves, minced
½ teaspoon ground cumin
Salt and freshly ground black pepper to taste
All-purpose flour for dredging
4 cups beef broth
Piquant Sauce (see below)

1. Squeeze the milk from the bread and break the bread
up. In a large bowl, combine the bread with all of the remaining ingredients, except the flour, beef broth, and Piquant
Sauce. Mix well with a large fork (or your hands). Shape into 1-inch-diameter balls or into 1- by 1½-inch cylinders. Dredge
lightly in the flour.

2. In a large deep frying pan, heat the broth to a simmer.
With a slotted spoon, lower the balls into the liquid, cover, and
simmer for 45 minutes, turn when half of the time has elapsed.
Don't crowd. Cook in two pans, if necessary.

3. Remove the meatballs from the cooking liquid with a
slotted spoon and transfer them to a serving dish. Serve with
the Piquant Sauce spooned over them.

Piquant Sauce

MAKES ABOUT 1½ CUPS

2 tablespoons butter
2 tablespoons minced shallots or onion
2 tablespoons all-purpose flour
1 cup beef broth, heated
2 tablespoons white vinegar
½ cup bottled chili sauce
1 small sour pickle, minced
Salt and freshly ground black pepper to taste

In a saucepan, over medium heat, melt the butter. Add the shallots and cook until they are soft and slightly golden. Stir in the flour, blending well. Gradually stir in the broth, simmering and stirring until the sauce is smooth and thickened. Stir in the vinegar, chili sauce, and pickle. Taste and season with salt and pepper, if necessary.

Middle Eastern Lamb and Rice
with Apricots

SERVES 6

The Arab countries like to pair lamb with apricots, and, of course, rice. Few dishes are served without it. They have complicated ways of cooking rice, washing, then soaking, and cooking with a cloth under the cover of the pot, but we're staying with the American method, as it is easy, sure-fire, and equally delicious.

> 6 tablespoons butter
> 1½ cups long-grain rice
> 2½ cups water
> 1 teaspoon salt
> 1½ pounds boneless lamb (from the leg), cut into 1½-inch cubes
> 2 garlic cloves, minced
> Salt and freshly ground black pepper to taste
> ¼ teaspoon ground nutmeg
> 1 teaspoon ground cumin
> 1 cup dried apricots, cut into halves
> 2 tablespoons currants

1. In a saucepan, over medium heat, melt 2 tablespoons of the butter. Stir in the rice and cook for 2 minutes. Add the 2½ cups of water and the teaspoon of salt. Bring to a boil, lower the heat, stir with a wooden fork, cover, and simmer for 15 minutes, or until the rice is tender, but still somewhat *al dente* and most of the liquid has been absorbed.

2. In large heavy frying pan, over medium heat, melt the remaining butter and brown the lamb evenly. Add more butter, if needed. Add the garlic and season with salt, pepper, nutmeg, and cumin. Cook for 5 minutes. Then just barely cover with water and simmer, covered, for 20 minutes. Add the apricots and currants and cook, covered, for 20 minutes, or until the lamb is just tender. Taste for seasoning, adding salt and pepper, if needed.

3. Preheat the oven to 350 degrees.

4. In a casserole, arrange alternating layers of rice, with any of the liquid it cooked in, and the lamb mixture, with its sauce, ending with a layer of rice. Cover and bake for 15 minutes, or until bubbling and thoroughly heated. Serve from the casserole.

Baked Lamb Shoulder Chops and Brown Rice

SERVES 4

4 lean ¾-inch-thick shoulder lamb chops, trimmed
All-purpose flour for dredging
2 tablespoons olive oil
4 tablespoons butter
2 medium-sized onions, chopped
1 garlic clove, minced
6 tablespoons Madeira
3 cups beef broth
2 sprigs fresh parsley
¾ cup long-grain brown rice

1. Preheat the oven to 325 degrees.

2. Dredge the lamb with flour, shaking off any excess. Over medium heat, in a flameproof casserole just large enough to snugly hold the chops in a single layer, heat the oil and 2 tablespoons of the butter. Brown the chops on both sides. Remove from the pan. Add the onions and garlic and cook for 5 minutes, or until they are soft. Do not brown. Stir in the Madeira and cook for a minute or two, stirring up the browned-on bits in the bottom of the pan. Pour in the broth. Return the chops to the pan and add the parsley sprigs. Bring to a boil, cover, and bake for 1 hour.

3. In a saucepan, melt the remaining butter. Add the rice and cook, stirring, for 2 minutes. Add to the casserole. Cover and cook for 40 minutes, or until the lamb and rice are tender. If the liquid cooks off before they are cooked, add more hot beef broth and continue cooking. The dish should not be too dry. Taste for seasoning, adding salt and pepper, if needed. Remove and discard the parsley before serving.

Arnaki Rizi

Greek Lamb with Rice

SERVES 6

*1 5- to 6-pound leg of lamb, wiped dry with a paper
    towel*
3 garlic cloves, cut into halves lengthwise
Juice of 1 lemon, blended with ¼ cup of olive oil
1 teaspoon dried oregano
1 teaspoon dried mint
Salt and freshly ground black pepper
2 medium-sized onions, coarsely chopped
2 cups beef broth
¼ cup dry white wine
1½ cups long-grain rice

3½ cups water
½ teaspoon salt
1 cup tomato juice

1. Preheat the oven to 450 degrees.

2. Make 6 incisions in the lamb and insert a piece of garlic in each. Rub the lamb with the lemon juice-oil mixture. Place in a roasting pan or flameproof casserole just large enough to snugly hold it. Sprinkle with the oregano, mint, salt, and pepper. Sprinkle the onions around the lamb and pour in ½ cup of the broth and the wine. Roast, uncovered, for 20 minutes, basting every 5 minutes. Lower the oven temperature to 350 degrees and cook for 40 to 60 minutes, depending on how rare or well done you like lamb. It will cook more later.

3. While the lamb is roasting, cook the rice in the 3½ cups of water with the ½ teaspoon of salt, simmering for 8 minutes. Drain well.

4. Remove the roasting pan from the oven and quickly (to prevent spattering) pour in the tomato juice and the remaining broth. Bring to a boil on top of the stove, stir in the rice, return to the oven, and bake for 15 minutes, or until the rice is tender and most of the liquid has been absorbed. If the liquid cooks off before the rice is tender, add a small amount of hot broth and continue to cook. Serve the lamb sliced over the rice.

Note: To test the lamb for degree of doneness, insert a narrow-bladed knife deeply into the lamb. If the juice runs pink, it is medium-rare; if the juice runs yellow, it is well-done.

Pork and Chicken Andaluz

SERVES 6

1 cup dry red wine
2 tablespoons red wine vinegar
1 medium-sized onion, finely chopped
1 garlic clove, minced
1 teaspoon salt
½ teaspoon freshly ground black pepper
2 teaspoons ground cumin
1 bay leaf
1 pound lean pork, cut into strips ½ inch thick, ½
    inch wide, and 1½ inches long
6 chicken thighs
1 1-pound can plum tomatoes with their liquid (Chop
    the tomatoes.)
12 pimiento-stuffed olives, sliced into quarters
1 cup long-grain rice
3 tablespoons chopped parsley leaves

1. In a large bowl, combine and blend well the wine, vinegar, onion, garlic, salt, pepper, cumin, and bay leaf. Add the pork and chicken, stir, or mix with your hands to coat all well. Cover and marinate at room temperature for 1 or 2 hours, turning once or twice.

2. Preheat the oven to 350 degrees.

3. Transfer the meat with its marinade to a flameproof casserole. Mix in the tomatoes, olives, and rice. Bring to a boil on top of the stove. Cover and bake for 1 hour, or until the chicken, pork, and rice are tender and the rice has absorbed most of the liquid. If the liquid is absorbed before the meats and rice are tender, add a small amount of hot water and continue cooking. Taste for seasoning, adding salt and pepper, if needed. Sprinkle with parsley and serve from the casserole.

Pork Chops and Brown Rice Luau

SERVES 6

This has the Polynesian touch of coupling pork with pineapple.

6 slices canned pineapple (Reserve the liquid.)
12 whole cloves
4 tablespoons (½ stick) butter, or more
1 tablespoon olive oil
6 ½-inch-thick loin pork chops, trimmed
Salt and freshly ground black pepper to taste
½ cup diced sweet green peppers
1 large onion, finely chopped
2 celery stalks, scraped and finely chopped
1 cup long-grain brown rice
2½ cups chicken broth
1 bay leaf
Dark or light brown sugar

1. Arrange the pineapple slices in a shallow dish. Stud each slice with 2 cloves and pour on the pineapple liquid. Cover and let stand at room temperature until ready to use.

2. In a large flameproof casserole, heat 2 tablespoons of the butter with the olive oil over medium-high heat and brown the chops evenly, adding more butter and oil, if needed. Sprinkle the chops with salt and pepper. Remove and reserve. Preheat the oven to 350 degrees.

3. In the same pot, melt the remaining 2 tablespoons of butter. Add the green pepper, onion, and celery and cook for 5 minutes. Stir in the rice and cook for 2 minutes, stirring, until the rice is well coated with fat. Add the broth and bay leaf. Bring to a boil. Lay the browned chops on the rice. Cover tightly and bake for 1 hour, or until the chops and rice are tender and the liquid has been mostly absorbed. If they are not

tender before the liquid has cooked off, add a small amount of hot broth or water and continue to bake. Remove the bay leaf.

4. Remove the cloves from the pineapple slices and arrange the slices over the chops. Sprinkle lightly with brown sugar and bake, uncovered, for about 10 minutes, or until the sugar has melted and formed a glaze.

Hong Kong Pork and Lime Rice

SERVES 6

4 1-inch-thick loin pork chops, boned and trimmed of
    all fat, then beaten between sheets of wax paper
    with a mallet to a ¼-inch thickness
Grated rind of 1 lime (Grate before you squeeze the
    limes.)
⅓ cup soy sauce
⅔ cup fresh lime juice
2 egg whites
1 teaspoon salt
1 tablespoon cornstarch
⅓ cup peanut oil, approximately
2 medium-sized carrots, scraped and cut into julienne
1 small sweet red pepper, cored, seeded, and cut in
    half lengthwise, then into ¼-inch strips
1 celery stalk, scraped and cut into ¼-inch-wide
    diagonal slices
4 whole scallions, trimmed, cut into 2-inch lengths,
    and then cut lengthwise into julienne
1 cup chicken broth
2 tablespoons white vinegar
2 tablespoons dark or light brown sugar

1 tablespoon cornstarch, dissolved in 1 tablespoon cold
     water
3 cups cooked long-grain rice
Salt and freshly ground black pepper to taste

1. Put the pork in a single layer in a glass dish. Combine and blend the soy sauce with half the lime juice and pour the mixture over the pork. Turn to coat. Cover and marinate at room temperature for 3 hours, turning several times and spooning the marinade over the pork.

2. Combine the egg whites, salt, and cornstarch and beat well. Dip the pork into the egg white mixture, evenly coating it.

3. In a large frying pan, over medium heat, heat 3 table-spoons of the peanut oil and brown the pork evenly; then cook until it is tender, turning, about 20 minutes. Add more oil, if needed. Remove the pork and cut crosswise into ½-inch-wide strips. Reserve and keep warm.

4. If any oil remains in the pan, pour off all but about 1 tablespoon. If not, add 1 tablespoon of oil and cook the carrots, pepper, celery, and scallions for 2 minutes, or until they are crisp-tender (more crisp than tender), stirring. Add the broth, bring to a boil, and cook for 2 minutes.

5. In a small stainless steel or porcelain-lined saucepan, combine the vinegar and remaining lime juice and bring to a boil. Lower the heat, add the sugar, and simmer, stirring, for 1 minute to dissolve the sugar. Stir in the cornstarch-water blend. Add to the vegetables and bring to a boil. Lower the heat and cook just until the sauce has thickened.

6. Stir the grated lime rind and rice into the vegetables with a metal fork and cook long enough to heat through. Taste for seasoning, adding salt and pepper, if needed.

7. To serve, evenly spoon the rice-vegetable mixture onto a large hot serving dish and top with the strips of pork.

Hungarian Rice-Stuffed Pork Chops

SERVES 6

5 tablespoons butter
1 medium-sized onion, minced
1 small celery stalk, scraped and minced
½ cup short- or medium-grain rice
1½ cups chicken broth
1 tablespoon finely chopped parsley leaves
¼ cup golden raisins, halved
3 slices bacon, cooked until golden and crisp, drained
      on paper towels, and crumbled
⅛ teaspoon each ground mace, sage, and thyme
Salt and freshly ground black pepper to taste
6 1-inch-thick center-cut loin chops with a pocket cut
      for stuffing
2 tablespoons olive oil
1 cup sour cream
2 teaspoons Hungarian paprika

   1. In a saucepan, over medium heat, melt 2 tablespoons of
the butter. Add the onion and celery and cook until they are
soft. Do not brown. Stir in the rice and cook for 2 minutes.
Pour in half of the broth and add the parsley. Bring to a boil,
lower the heat, cover, and simmer for 10 minutes, or until the
rice is quite *al dente* and the liquid has been absorbed. Remove
from the heat and stir in the raisins, bacon, mace, sage, and
thyme and blend well. Taste for seasoning and add salt, if
needed.
   2. Season the chops lightly with salt and pepper. Stuff
without packing and secure with toothpicks or small skewers.
In a large frying pan, over medium-high heat, heat the remaining butter and the olive oil and carefully brown the chops on

both sides. Add the remaining broth (or substitute the same amount of dry white wine), cover, and simmer for 40 minutes, or until the chops are tender. Transfer to a hot serving dish and keep warm.

3. If there is more than ½ cup of liquid in the pan, turn up the heat to reduce it to that amount. Stir in the sour cream and paprika and heat, stirring, without boiling. Spoon the sauce over the chops.

Pork Crown with Orange Rice

SERVES 8

Here's a party dish we discovered in Spain. Crown roasts, dramatic and different, call for a number of dinner guests as spectators at the carving match. Thus, have your butcher create one with about 16 chops to serve 8: one large chop per serving, seconds, if desired.

>*1 crown roast of pork, made up of 16 ribs*
>*1 tablespoon salt*
>*½ teaspoon freshly ground black pepper*
>*¼ teaspoon ground cinnamon*
>*2 tablespoons butter*
>*3 medium-sized onions, chopped*
>*½ teaspoon ground cumin*
>*½ cup golden raisins*
>*½ cup fresh orange juice*
>*¼ cup dry sherry*
>*6 cups hot cooked long-grain rice*
>*2 tablespoons grated orange rind*
>*3 large navel oranges, peeled and sectioned, with all*
>*   membranes removed*

1. Preheat the oven to 350 degrees.

2. Sprinkle the pork with 2 teaspoons of the salt, all of the pepper, and the cinnamon. Cover the ends of the bones with aluminum foil and put the roast in a roasting pan. Roast, un-covered, for 30 to 40 minutes a pound (about 3½ to 4 hours), or until fork-tender, but not dry, basting every 20 minutes with the pan juices.

3. When the pork is nearly cooked, prepare the rice. Then melt the butter in a frying pan over medium heat. Add the onions and cook for 5 minutes, or until they are soft. Do not brown. Stir in the remaining salt, the cumin, raisins, orange juice, and sherry and simmer, covered, for 5 minutes. With a metal fork stir in the rice and 1 tablespoon of the grated orange rind, tossing and fluffing well to blend.

4. Remove the roast from the oven and stand it on a large hot serving dish. Fill the center with the orange rice, spooning any remaining rice around the roast. Sprinkle with the remaining orange rind and garnish with the orange sections.

5. Carve at the table. Each serving of pork should be lavishly accompanied by orange rice and orange sections.

New Orleans Skillet Pork Chops and Rice

SERVES 4

2 tablespoons butter
1 tablespoon olive oil
1 medium-sized onion, coarsely chopped
1 large celery stalk, scraped and chopped
4 ½-inch-thick pork chops
Salt and freshly ground black pepper to taste
1½ cups water
2 tablespoons dark or light brown sugar
2 cups tomato sauce, homemade or canned
1 cup long-grain rice
½ teaspoon fennel seeds

1. In a large heavy, deep frying pan, over medium heat, heat the butter and oil. Add the onion and celery and cook for 2 minutes, or until they are slightly soft.

2. Add the chops to the frying pan. Season with salt and pepper and brown evenly. Remove and reserve.

3. Stir the water, brown sugar, and 1½ cups of the tomato sauce into the pan. Heat, stirring and scraping up the browned-on bits in the bottom of the pan. Bring to a boil and stir in the rice and fennel seeds.

4. Return the chops to the pan, spooning the sauce and rice over them. Cover tightly and cook over medium-low heat for 30 minutes. Pour on the remaining tomato sauce, cover, and cook for 10 minutes, or until the rice and chops are tender. Taste for seasoning, adding salt and pepper, if needed.

Pork Chops
with Wined Brown Rice

SERVES 4

One of the assets of brown rice, besides its nutty flavor, is that it mates exceptionally well with baked meats, cooking in about the same time.

2 tablespoons butter
1 tablespoon olive oil
4 ¾-inch-thick loin pork chops
Bell's seasoning
Salt and freshly ground black pepper to taste
4 sweet red pepper rings
4 thick slices Bermuda onion
¾ cup long-grain brown rice
1 cup dry red wine
1 cup chicken broth

   1. In a large frying pan, over medium heat, heat the butter and oil. Season the chops lightly with Bell's seasoning, and with salt and pepper. Brown them evenly. Preheat the oven to 350 degrees.
   2. Place chops in a flameproof casserole just large enough to hold them snugly in one layer. Top each with a pepper ring and an onion slice. Sprinkle the rice around and between the chops. Combine the wine and broth and pour the mixture over all. Bring to a boil on top of the stove, cover, and bake for 1 hour, or until the chops and rice are tender and liquid has been absorbed. If the liquid cooks off before the chops and rice are tender, add more hot broth and continue cooking.

Arroz com Chourico e Paio

Portuguese Rice Stew with Sausage and Ham

SERVES 4

4 slices bacon, chopped
2 medium-sized onions, chopped
¼ pound garlic sausage, skin removed and the meat
    chopped
¼ pound lean pork sausage meat
¼ pound cooked ham, chopped
2 garlic cloves, minced
2 teaspoons ground cumin
¼ teaspoon cayenne pepper, or to taste
1 cup long-grain rice
2½ cups beef broth
Salt and freshly ground black pepper to taste

1. In a heavy saucepan, over medium heat, cook the
bacon for 5 minutes. Add the onions and cook for 5 minutes.
Do not brown. Stir in the garlic sausage, pork sausage meat,
ham, garlic, cumin, and cayenne. Simmer, stirring and breaking up the sausage meat with a fork, for 15 minutes.

2. Stir the rice and beef broth into the pan with the sausage and ham. Bring to a boil, stir with a wooden fork, lower
the heat, cover, and simmer for 20 minutes, or until the rice is
tender and most of the liquid has been absorbed. Taste for
seasoning, adding salt and pepper, if needed. The broth may
have supplied sufficient seasoning.

Glazed Ham and Rice Loaf

SERVES 6

2 tablespoons butter
1 large onion, finely chopped
1 garlic clove, minced
1 pound ground cooked ham
1 pound ground lean pork
1½ cups cooked short- or medium-grain rice
1 cup fine fresh bread crumbs
1 cup milk
3 eggs, beaten
Dark or light brown sugar (without any lumps)
1 teaspoon dry mustard
Horseradish Sauce (see following recipe)

1. In a frying pan, over medium heat, melt the butter. Add the onion and garlic and cook for 5 minutes, or until they are soft. Do not brown. Preheat the oven to 350 degrees.

2. In a bowl, combine the onion, garlic, ham, pork, rice, bread crumbs, milk, and eggs and blend well with a fork. Loosely pack into a buttered loaf pan. Smooth over the top with the back of a fork and coat it with a thin layer of brown sugar; then sprinkle on the dry mustard.

3. Set in a pan of hot water and bake for 1½ hours. Pour off the fat collected in the pan and let sit for 10 minutes before transferring to a serving dish and slicing. Serve with the Horseradish Sauce.

Horseradish Sauce

*3 tablespoons freshly grated horseradish or well-
drained bottled horseradish*
½ cup heavy cream, whipped
¼ cup mayonnaise
Salt and freshly ground white pepper to taste

Combine and blend all ingredients well.

Italian Sausage and Rice Pie

SERVES 4

1 pound Italian sausage meat
6 eggs, lightly beaten
2 cups cooked short- or medium-grain rice
1 cup grated Asiago or Parmesan cheese
¼ pound mozzarella, diced

1. In a frying pan, over medium heat, cook the sausage, stirring and breaking it up with a wooden fork, for 15 minutes, or until it loses all pink color. With a slotted spoon transfer it to a bowl. Preheat the oven to 350 degrees.

2. Add all the other ingredients to the sausage and blend well. Spoon into a well-buttered 10½-inch-square by 2½-inch-deep baking dish and bake for 40 minutes, or until golden brown and set.

Rice Planters' Risotto

SERVES 4

This is a favorite of those who work in the rice fields in Lombardy, Italy.

> 2 tablespoons olive oil
> 5 Italian sweet sausages (about 1½ pounds), casings
>   removed
> 2 medium-sized onions, chopped
> ⅛ teaspoon ground cinnamon
> 3 tablespoons butter
> 4 cups hot cooked long-grain rice (cooked in beef
>   broth)
> ½ cup grated Asiago or Parmesan cheese
> Salt and freshly ground black pepper to taste

In a large frying pan, over medium heat, heat the oil and cook the sausage and onions, breaking up the sausage with a fork as it cooks. Blend in the cinnamon and cook for 20 minutes, or until the sausage is thoroughly cooked, stirring frequently. Add the butter and stir until it is melted. With a metal fork, blend in the rice and cheese, fluffing up the rice. Taste for seasoning before adding salt and pepper, as the beef broth and cheese may have supplied enough. Spoon into a hot serving dish.

Rice Arrabiata

Raging Rice

SERVES 4

This is a dish we have eaten in Rome several times. Depending upon the amount of hot pepper in the sausages, it can raise you right out of your seat. The Romans always add extra crushed hot red pepper flakes. We don't.

With a salad and a glass of red wine, this makes an excellent lunch.

> 2 tablespoons olive oil
> 2 medium-sized white onions, finely chopped
> 8 lean Italian hot sausages, casings removed
> ½ cup dry red wine
> 1 cup long-grain rice
> 2½ cups beef broth
> ½ cup grated Asiago or Parmesan cheese
> ¼ teaspoon hot red pepper flakes
> Salt to taste

1. In a large heavy, deep frying pan, over medium heat, heat the oil and cook the onions for 5 minutes, or until they are soft. Do not brown. Stir in the sausage meat, breaking it up with a wooden fork as you brown it. Add the wine and simmer until most of the wine has evaporated.

2. Stir the rice and beef broth into the pan. Bring to a boil, stir with a wooden fork, cover, lower the heat, and simmer for 20 minutes, or until the rice is tender and the liquid has been absorbed.

3. With a metal fork, stir in the grated cheese, fluffing the rice as you do. Add the red pepper and salt, if needed.

Rice with Black Beans and Sausage

SERVES 4

>1 pound Italian hot sausages (unless you make your
>   own as the Louisiana lady did, page 134), cut into
>   ¼-inch-thick slices
>2 tablespoons olive oil (optional)
>1 medium-sized poblano pepper, cored, seeded, and
>   diced
>1 garlic clove, minced
>2 medium-sized onions, chopped
>½ cup tomato purée
>½ teaspoon salt
>½ teaspoon dried thyme
>⅛ teaspoon hot red pepper flakes, or to taste
>1½ cups chicken broth
>3 cups al dente-cooked long-grain rice
>1 1-pound can black beans (available in supermarkets'
>   Tex-Mex sections), drained

1. If the sausages appear to be fatty do not use the oil, but if they seem very lean, heat the oil in a deep frying pan and evenly brown the slices over medium heat. Remove them, drain on paper towels, and reserve.

2. Add the pepper, garlic, and onions to the frying pan and cook for 5 minutes, or until they are soft. Do not brown.

3. Stir in the tomato purée, salt, thyme, hot red pepper flakes, and broth. Bring to a boil and stir in the rice and beans, blending well. Fluff the rice with a metal fork, and place the sausage slices on top. Cover the pan and cook for 5 minutes. Remove from the heat and let sit, covered, for 10 minutes, or until the liquid has been absorbed. Taste for seasoning, adding salt and pepper, if needed. The broth may have supplied enough.

Herbed Lamb Kidneys with Rice

SERVES 4

12 lamb kidneys
1 cup chopped parsley leaves
1 tablespoon chopped fresh tarragon, or 1 teaspoon
    dried tarragon
1 small onion, minced
⅔ cup (1 stick, plus 3 tablespoons) soft butter
2 teaspoons Worcestershire sauce
Salt and freshly ground black pepper to taste
½ cup dry sherry
4 cups hot cooked long-grain rice

1. Remove the membranes from the kidneys; then cut them into halves lengthwise and remove the fatty knob inside. Wash the kidneys and pat them dry with paper towels. Preheat the broiler.

2. Combine the parsley, tarragon, onion, butter, Worcestershire sauce, salt, and pepper and blend well into a paste.

3. Coat the bottom of a shallow baking pan (just large enough to snugly hold the halved kidneys, placed side by side) with one third of the butter paste.

4. Arrange the kidneys, cut side up, in the baking pan. Dot the kidneys with the remaining butter paste. Sprinkle with sherry. Broil for 5 minutes on one side; turn, spoon the pan sauce over, and broil for 3 to 5 minutes, or until brown on the outside and pink inside. Do not overcook or they shrink and toughen.

5. Spoon a mound of rice onto each plate. Arrange the kidneys around the rice and spoon the sauce over the rice and kidneys.

Louisiana "Dirty Rice"

SERVES 4 TO 6

This dish originated with the Cajuns in the Lake Charles bayou country. We had it in the bayou home of our goose-hunting guide whose mother gave us the recipe by demonstration.

> 5 tablespoons butter
> 1 tablespoon olive oil
> 1 large onion, finely chopped
> 1 garlic clove, minced
> 1 large sweet green pepper, seeded, cored, and finely
>   chopped
> 1 celery stalk, scraped and finely chopped
> ½ pound chicken gizzards and hearts, trimmed and
>   finely chopped
> ½ pound chicken livers, trimmed and coarsely
>   chopped
> Salt and freshly ground black pepper to taste
> 1 cup long-grain brown rice
> 2½ cups chicken broth
> ⅓ cup chopped parsley leaves

1. In a deep saucepan, over medium heat, heat 2 table-spoons of the butter and the oil. Add the vegetables and cook for 10 minutes, or until they are soft. Do not brown. Add the gizzards and hearts and cook for 5 minutes. Add the livers and cook until they are no longer pink but still tender (about 5 minutes) and most of the liquid in the pan has cooked off. Do not overcook the giblets as they will toughen. Season with salt and pepper.
2. In another saucepan, heat the remaining butter. Stir in the rice and cook for 2 minutes, stirring, to coat it well. Add the broth, bring to a boil, cover, lower the heat, and simmer for

40 minutes, or until the rice is tender and the liquid has been absorbed.

3. Add the rice to the vegetable-giblet pan with half of the parsley and mix with a metal fork, fluffing the rice. Mound on a hot serving dish and sprinkle on the remaining parsley.

Pennsylvania Dutch Rice with Knockwurst and Beans

SERVES 6

6 knockwurst
1 12-ounce can beer
1 tablespoon white vinegar
2 teaspoons dark or light brown sugar
4 tablespoons (½ stick) butter
1 medium-sized onion, finely chopped
½ of a sweet green pepper, seeds and ribs removed,
    finely chopped
Salt and freshly ground black pepper to taste
1 15-ounce can red kidney beans, drained
1½ cups long-grain rice, cooked al dente
½ cup fine fresh bread crumbs

1. In a saucepan, over medium-low heat, simmer the knockwurst in the beer for 15 minutes. Remove and reserve the knockwurst. Raise the heat and reduce the beer to ¾ cup. Add the vinegar and sugar and simmer, stirring, just long enough to melt the sugar. Cut the knockwurst into ½-inch-thick slices and return them to the saucepan.

2. In a frying pan, over medium heat, melt 2 tablespoons of the butter. Add the onion and green pepper, season with salt

and pepper, and cook for 5 minutes. Do not brown. Preheat the oven to 400 degrees.

3. Combine all the ingredients, except the bread crumbs and remaining butter, in a bowl and mix carefully with a metal fork. Taste for seasoning, adding salt and pepper, if needed. Spoon into a buttered 13½- by 8¾- by 1¾-inch baking dish. Cover with the bread crumbs and dot with the remaining butter.

4. Bake for 15 minutes, or until the crumbs are golden and the dish is heated through.

Calf's Brains
with Caper and Lemon Sauce

SERVES 6

We have two favorites here. To our notion, the most delicate of the variety meats, and the nutty Wild Pecan Rice, which offers, as the best of rices do, a nice counterpoint to the somewhat tart sauce. Check the recipe for Pheasant with Wild Pecan Rice, page 120, for more on this rice.

> *3 calf's brains (about 1½ pounds)*
> *4 tablespoons white vinegar*
> *1 teaspoon salt*
> *Freshly ground black pepper*
> *All-purpose flour for dredging*
> *12 tablespoons (1½ sticks) butter*
> *2 tablespoons olive oil*
> *3 tablespoons fresh lemon juice*
> *3 tablespoons rinsed and drained capers*

*3 tablespoons chopped broadleaf (Italian) parsley
    leaves*
4 cups hot cooked Wild Pecan Rice

1. Soak the brains in cold water for 2 hours. Drain and
rinse. Soak again in fresh cold water with 2 tablespoons of the
vinegar for 1 hour. Clean the brains, removing the membranes
and blood spots. Place in a saucepan and cover with boiling
water. Add the remaining 2 tablespoons of vinegar and salt and
simmer for 15 minutes. Remove from the heat, drain, and dry.

2. Cut the brains lengthwise into ½-inch-thick slices.
Sprinkle with salt and pepper. Dredge lightly in the flour,
shaking off any excess so they are just dusted.

3. In a frying pan, over medium heat, heat 6 tablespoons
of the butter with the olive oil until the butter bubbles. Cook
the brains until golden on both sides (add more butter and oil,
if needed, in excess of that listed above).

4. In a saucepan, over medium heat, melt the remaining 6
tablespoons of the butter, stir in the lemon juice, capers, and
parsley. Blend well.

5. Arrange the hot rice in a smooth layer on individual
plates and top with the brain slices, spooning the caper sauce
over both the brains and rice.

Tripe with Wild Pecan Rice

SERVES 6

Check the recipe for Pheasant with Wild Pecan Rice on page 120 for more information on this unusual rice. One thing for sure, no European or Asian rice can compare with it for flavor and cooking ease.

As this is written, tripe, along with squid, is coming into favor with those who continue to search for something "new." We saw a sign on a pushcart in Manhattan designed for these eager searchers. The hot dog vendor had hand-lettered a sign "Hot Dogs Steamed in Perrier Water."

Actually, tripe is an old European favorite that still graces menus there—and here. We found this recipe in Spain.

What is tripe? The stomach lining of a cow, one of four, each having its own market name. The one we favor, the second stomach, is called "honeycomb tripe," which makes a surprisingly tasty dish.

3 pounds fresh white veal honeycomb tripe
3 tablespoons olive oil
3 tablespoons chopped salt pork
2 garlic cloves, minced
1 lemon, cut into 1-inch-thick slices, seeds removed
1 1-pound, 12-ounce can imported Italian plum
    tomatoes, mashed
½ teaspoon dried oregano
1 bay leaf
2 teaspoons salt
½ teaspoon freshly ground black pepper
¼ teaspoon hot red pepper flakes
1 7-ounce package Wild Pecan Rice
1 tablespoon butter
2 cups water

1. Wash the tripe carefully in four different waters. Place in a large pot, pour in 4 quarts of water, cover, and simmer for 3 hours, or until it is tender. Pour off the water twice during the cooking, replacing with fresh hot water. Drain the tripe well, cool, and cut it into ½-inch by 2-inch strips.

2. In a deep saucepan, over medium heat, heat the olive oil and sauté the salt pork and garlic for 5 minutes. Add the lemon slices, tomatoes, oregano, bay leaf, 1 teaspoon of the salt, black pepper, hot red pepper flakes, and the tripe. Simmer, uncovered, for 25 minutes. Discard the lemon slices and bay leaf.

3. While the tripe is cooking, combine the rice, the remaining 1 teaspoon of salt, the butter, and water in a saucepan over medium heat. Bring to a boil and stir with a wooden fork. Cover, lower the heat, and simmer for 20 minutes, or until the rice is tender and the water has been absorbed.

4. Spoon a bed of rice on individual hot dishes and top with generous portions of the tripe and its sauce.

A Note on Rice Rings

When cooking rice for a ring, cook enough (more than you need for the number of people being served because leftover rice makes very good croquettes). Also, it is annoying to end up with a skimpy ring. The rice should fill the ring.

Butter the ring mold well and, after the rice is cooked, stir in two or three spoonfuls of soft butter. This makes it easier to turn the ring out intact. For insurance, before turning it out, run a knife blade around the inside of the ring. Vegetables can be served on the same dish, colorfully bordering the ring.

Fill the ring with creamed mushrooms, creamed chicken, or any sauced vegetable, fish, or meat dish.

Rice Ring
with Saged Chicken Livers

SERVES 6

6 tablespoons butter
2 large shallots, or 1 small white onion, minced
2 cups short- or medium-grain rice
4½ cups chicken broth
½ cup minced parsley leaves
Saged Chicken Livers (see following recipe)

1. Melt 2 tablespoons of the butter in a saucepan, over medium heat. Add the shallots and cook for 2 minutes, or until they are soft. Do not brown. Stir in the rice and cook for 2 minutes. Stir in the broth. Bring to a boil, lower the heat, stir with a wooden fork, cover, and simmer for 20 minutes, or until the rice is tender and the liquid has been absorbed. Stir in the remaining butter and parsley.
2. Pack the rice into a buttered 6-cup ring mold, set in a pan of hot water that comes halfway up the mold, and place in a preheated 350-degree oven for 15 minutes. Carefully run a knife around the edge of the mold and turn out onto a large hot serving dish.
3. Fill the center with the Saged Chicken Livers. Serve any remaining livers in a hot serving dish. If desired, arrange your vegetable around the rice ring.

Saged Chicken Livers

5 tablespoons butter
2 large shallots, or 1 small white onion, minced
1½ pounds chicken livers, trimmed, washed, and
    thoroughly dried
All-purpose flour for dredging
1 tablespoon olive oil
Salt and freshly ground black pepper to taste
1 cup coarsely chopped prosciutto or other cooked
    ham
¼ cup brandy
¼ cup chicken broth
¾ cup heavy cream
2 tablespoons chopped fresh sage, or 1 teaspoon
    crumbled leaf sage

   1. Over medium heat, in a large frying pan, melt 2 tablespoons of the butter. Add the shallots and cook for 2 minutes,
or until they are soft. Do not brown. With a slotted spoon
transfer the shallots to a bowl.
   2. Dredge the livers in the flour, shaking off any excess.
Heat the remaining butter and the olive oil in the frying pan
over medium-high heat. Add the livers and brown them
evenly, leaving them slightly pink inside. Season with salt and
pepper. Transfer to the bowl with the shallots. Add the prosciutto to the pan and cook for 1 minute. With the slotted
spoon transfer to the bowl with the shallots.
   3. Pour the brandy into the frying pan and cook, over
medium-high heat, until half has evaporated. Stir in the broth
and cream. Cook, stirring and scraping the bottom of the pan
to release the browned-on bits, until thickened. Return the
shallots, livers, and prosciutto to the pan, stir in the sage and
heat through. Taste for seasoning, adding salt and pepper, if
needed.

Rice Ring
with Sweetbreads Veronique

SERVES 4

The sweetbreads can be blanched before you start preparing
the rice ring; then the sauce can be made while the rice ring is
baking.

> 3 tablespoons butter
> 1 medium-sized onion, finely chopped
> 2 cups short- or medium-grain rice
> 4 cups chicken broth
> 2 eggs, beaten
> 1 cup milk
> 3 tablespoons melted butter
> 1 cup grated Fontina or Gruyère cheese
> ½ cup finely chopped parsley leaves
> Salt and freshly ground black pepper to taste

1. In a saucepan, over medium heat, melt the 3 tablespoons of buttter. Add the onion and cook for 3 minutes, or
until it is soft. Do not brown. Add the rice and cook for 2
minutes, stirring. Pour in the broth and bring to a boil. Lower
the heat, stir with a wooden fork, cover, and simmer for 20
minutes, or until the liquid has been absorbed. Cool slightly.
Blend in the eggs, milk, the melted butter, cheese, and parsley.
Taste before adding salt and pepper as the broth may have
supplied enough salt. Preheat the oven to 350 degrees.

2. Spoon the rice into a buttered 8-cup mold and set in a
pan of hot water that comes halfway up the mold. Bake for 45
minutes, or until set.

Sweetbreads Veronique

2 pairs veal sweetbreads
White vinegar or fresh lemon juice
3 tablespoons butter
3 tablespoons all-purpose flour
1 cup milk
½ cup Madeira
1 cup heavy cream
1 8½-ounce can seedless white grapes, drained
1 tablespoon fresh lemon juice
Salt to taste

1. Soak the sweetbreads in cold water for 1 hour. Carefully pull off any membrane that comes off easily. Soak again in cold water with 1 tablespoon of vinegar or lemon juice for another hour. Remove the remaining membrane and the tissue connecting the lobes.

2. In a saucepan, cover the sweetbreads with water. Add 1 tablespoon of lemon juice and bring to a boil. Lower the heat and simmer for 15 minutes. Do not overcook. (They should be fairly firm but not hard.) Plunge into cold water for a few minutes, drain well, and cut into bite-sized cubes. Set aside.

3. In a saucepan, over medium heat, melt the butter. Add the flour and cook, stirring into a smooth paste. Gradually add the milk, wine, and ½ cup of the cream and cook, stirring into a smooth, medium-thick sauce. Stir in the sweetbreads, grapes, and lemon juice and heat through. Taste and add salt. Just before serving, stir in the remaining cream and heat for 1 minute.

4. Run a knife blade around the inside of the rice ring. Turn the ring out onto a hot serving dish. Fill it with the sweetbreads and grapes. If the ring doesn't accommodate all of the filling, serve the remaining in a hot serving bowl.

Rice Ring with Kidneys and Scrambled Eggs

SERVES 4 TO 6

This makes a unique brunch or late breakfast offering.

2 veal kidneys
8 tablespoons (1 stick) butter
2 tablespoons all-purpose flour
1½ cups chicken broth
⅓ cup Madeira
Salt and freshly ground black pepper to taste
¼ teaspoon ground mace
8 eggs, lightly beaten in a bowl
½ cup heavy cream
Rice Ring (see recipes on pages 184 and 186)

1. Remove the membranes from the kidneys; then cut the kidneys into thin slices, removing the fatty nugget from the center.
2. In a frying pan, over medium-high heat, melt 4 tablespoons of the butter. Cook the kidneys, turning, until they are barely golden, about 4 minutes. Sprinkle on the flour and stir.
3. Lower the heat and pour in the broth and Madeira. Add the salt, pepper, and mace and cook for 10 minutes, or until the sauce thickens. Do not overcook or the kidneys will toughen. They should be slightly pink inside.
4. Melt the remaining butter in a frying pan over medium heat and scramble the eggs, adding salt and pepper. When the eggs begin to set, stir in the cream and cook until the cream is blended with the eggs. Cook to whatever degree of firmness you prefer, but do not overcook. The eggs should be moist.
5. Turn the rice ring out onto a large hot serving dish. Fill the center with the kidneys and their sauce. Spoon the eggs around the ring.

7

RICE
with
VEGETABLES

W e were driving from New Delhi to the Nilgiri Hills, the "Blue Mountains" in the south of India, accompanied by a Government of India Tourist Officer, R. Ramaswamy, a rotund, merry man. As many are in India (it has something to do with one of their many, complicated religions, we believe), he was a vegetarian.

Late one afternoon we stopped for dinner. We ordered a crusty-moist *tandoori* chicken; he had a vegetable cutlet surrounded with lime rice. This day Ramaswamy said, somewhat vehemently, "If it weren't for rice, I think I'd give up this diet!"

We knew what he meant. During the two weeks we spent with him, he'd have a vegetable cutlet with most of his meals, but he would always have a side dish of rice, usually a different rice combination. He often toyed with the vegetable cutlet and gulped the rice, each time mixed with different vegetables. A favorite of his and ours was rice with lentils, *Kitcheri*.

Rice mates zestfully with vegetables of all kinds. Two surprises for us, however, were rice with cabbage in Germany and rice and parsnips in Hungary. With its flexibility and remarkable range, rice has a way of continually surprising. Sometimes, as with the dish of peas with rice, Risi e Bisi, it sounds like a song and tastes like a poem. Rice is one of those rare foods—a poem you eat.

Rice Parma

SERVES 4

12 tender fresh asparagus stalks
4 tablespoons butter
1 cup long-grain rice
2½ to 3 cups beef broth
1 cup fresh shelled peas or frozen, defrosted
1 cup finely diced prosciutto, fat and lean
½ cup grated Parmesan cheese

1. Snap off the tough ends of the asparagus and peel the stems. Cut the stems into ¾-inch-long pieces.

2. Separate the scaly tips and cook them in salted boiling water until crisp-tender. Set aside and keep warm.

3. Heat 2 tablespoons of the butter in a saucepan. Add the rice and cook, stirring, for 2 minutes, to coat well. Add 2½ cups of the broth, bring to a boil, stir with a wooden fork, lower the heat, cover, and simmer for 10 minutes.

4. With a wooden fork, stir in the fresh peas and the asparagus stems. Cover and simmer for 5 minutes. If using defrosted frozen peas, add them at this time and simmer for 3 minutes. Stir in the prosciutto and simmer for 5 minutes, or until the rice and vegetables are tender and most of the liquid has been absorbed. If it seems too dry, add a small amount of hot broth. It should be moist, but not soupy.

5. With a metal fork, stir in the remaining butter and half of the cheese. Garnish with the asparagus tips. Serve the remaining cheese at the table.

Rice with Cannellini Beans Cacciatore

SERVES 4 TO 6

2 tablespoons olive oil
2 slices lean bacon, chopped
1 large onion, finely chopped
1 celery stalk, scraped and finely chopped
2 large ripe tomatoes, peeled, seeded, and chopped, or
    2 cups canned imported Italian plum tomatoes,
    drained and chopped
Salt and freshly ground black pepper to taste
¼ teaspoon crumbled leaf sage
¼ teaspoon dried rosemary
2 cups cooked white beans, or a 1-pound can, drained
3 cups cooked long-grain rice
3 tablespoons butter, cut into small pieces
½ cup grated Asiago or Parmesan cheese

1. In a saucepan, over medium heat, heat the oil and cook the bacon until it is golden. Add the onion and celery and cook for 5 minutes, or until they are soft. Do not brown. Add the tomatoes, salt, pepper, sage, and rosemary. Cover, lower the heat, and simmer for 30 minutes, or until the sauce begins to thicken.

2. Stir in the beans, rice, butter, and cheese. Cook for 5 minutes, stirring with a metal fork several times, to heat through. Taste for seasoning, adding salt and pepper, if needed.

Black Beans and Rice Cuban Style

SERVES 6

1 cup dried black beans
1 sweet green pepper, halved and seeded, half left
    intact, the other half, chopped
2 medium-sized onions, 1 left whole and nailed with 2
    whole cloves, the other finely chopped
1 bay leaf
¼ teaspoon dried oregano
5 tablespoons olive oil
1 teaspoon sugar
2 tablespoons light rum, or 2 tablespoons white wine
    vinegar
Salt and freshly ground black pepper to taste
1 2-inch cube fatback, cut into ¼-inch cubes
1 garlic clove, minced
1 cup long-grain rice
2 cups hot water
1 teaspoon salt
3 tablespoons butter, cut into small pieces
1 ripe but firm avocado, peeled and cut into 6 wedges
1 lemon, cut into 6 wedges, seeds removed

1. Pick over the beans and rinse several times. Soak in
cold water for 5 hours. Drain and put the beans with the green
pepper half, the onion with the cloves, bay leaf, oregano, and 2
tablespoons of the olive oil in a heavy saucepan. Barely cover
with cold water. Bring to a boil, lower the heat, and simmer,
partially covered, for 2 hours, or until the beans are cooked but
still somewhat firm and can be mashed against the side of the
pan. If the liquid cooks off before the beans are cooked, add
small amounts of *hot* water (cold water will harden them). Re-

move and discard the green pepper half, the onion with the cloves, and the bay leaf. Mash 2 or 3 tablespoonfuls of the beans against the side of the pot. Stir in the rum, salt, and pepper.

2. In a frying pan, over medium heat, cook the fatback with the remaining olive oil until it is golden and crisp. Remove with a slotted spoon and drain on paper towels. Reserve. Add the chopped green pepper, chopped onion, and garlic to the frying pan and cook for 5 minutes, or until they are soft. Do not brown. Add the rice and cook, stirring, for 1 minute. Transfer to the bean pot. Stir in the hot water and the salt with a wooden fork. Bring to a boil, stirring, to prevent burning. Cover, lower the heat, and simmer for 20 minutes, or until the rice is tender and the liquid has been absorbed. Taste for seasoning, adding salt and pepper, if needed. Stir in the butter and the crisp fatback.

3. Transfer to a hot serving bowl and garnish with the avocado and lemon wedges.

Rice and Broccoli with Three Cheeses

SERVES 6 TO 8

2 tablespoons butter
1 garlic clove, minced
1½ cups long-grain rice
3 cups chicken broth
Salt and freshly ground black pepper to taste
1 1-pound bunch broccoli
⅓ cup crumbled blue cheese at room temperature

⅓ cup small cubes of Monterey Jack cheese at room
temperature
3 tablespoons soft butter
1 cup heavy cream, heated with ½ cup of milk
¼ cup grated Asiago or Parmesan cheese
Additional hot cream

1. In a saucepan, over medium heat, melt the 2 table-spoons of butter. Add the garlic and cook for 1 minute, or until it is soft. Do not brown. Stir in the rice and cook for 2 minutes, coating well with the butter. Pour in the broth. Heat to a boil, lower the heat, stir with a wooden fork, cover, and simmer for 15 minutes. The rice should be quite *al dente* and the liquid absorbed. Taste and add salt and pepper, if needed.

2. Trim the broccoli, dividing the flowerets and peeling the stems. Cut the stems into ½-inch diagonal pieces. Cook the stem pieces in salted boiling water for 2 minutes. Add the flowerets and cook for 2 minutes, or until they are crisp-tender (more crisp than tender as they will cook more later). Drain and set aside.

3. With a fork, mash the blue cheese and Monterey Jack cheese with the 3 tablespoons of soft butter into a semismooth paste. Preheat the oven to 350 degrees.

4. Arrange half of the rice in a loose, smooth layer in a well-buttered shallow baking dish. Do not pack the rice down. Dot with half of the cheese paste. Arrange all of the broccoli pieces on the rice. Dot with the remaining cheese paste. Spoon on the remaining rice in a smooth, loose layer. Pour over the milk-cream mixture. It should seep down through the layers. If it does not come to the top of the rice, add more cream. But it should not cover the rice. Sprinkle on the grated cheese.

5. Bake for 30 minutes, or until the top is golden and most of the liquid has been absorbed.

German Rice and Cabbage

SERVES 4 TO 6

Here's that vegetable-rice surprise we found in Munich. It makes a neat side dish when served with ham.

> 4 slices lean bacon, chopped
> 2 medium-sized onions, chopped
> 2 garlic cloves, minced
> 1 8-ounce can Hunt's tomato sauce
> 1 cup chicken broth
> 2 cups shredded cabbage
> ½ teaspoon crushed caraway seeds
> Salt to taste
> ¼ teaspoon hot red pepper flakes, or to taste
> 3 cups very al dente-cooked rice
> ¼ cup grated Emmenthal or Gruyère cheese

1. In a deep pan, over medium heat, cook the bacon until it is crisp. Remove with a slotted spoon and reserve. Pour off all but 4 tablespoons of fat. (If the bacon did not render that amount, add butter.)

2. Add the onions and garlic to the pan and cook until they are soft. Do not brown. Return the bacon to the pan. Stir in the tomato sauce, chicken broth, and cabbage and sprinkle on the caraway seeds, salt, and hot red pepper flakes. Cover and simmer for 15 minutes, or until the cabbage is tender.

3. Blend in the rice and cook, covered, until most of the liquid has been absorbed. Transfer to a hot serving dish and serve with the cheese sprinkled on top. The hot rice will melt the cheese.

Cabbage Dolmas

SERVES 4

1 large (at least 3 pounds) head cabbage
2 tablespoons butter
5 tablespoons olive oil
1 medium-sized onion, finely chopped
1 garlic clove, minced
¾ pound ground lamb, beef, or veal
¼ teaspoon ground cinnamon
½ teaspoon ground cumin
½ teaspoon dried oregano
Salt and freshly ground black pepper to taste
1 medium-sized ripe tomato, peeled, seeded, and
    chopped, or 2 tablespoons tomato purée or sauce
1 cup quite al dente-cooked rice
1 medium-sized onion, thinly sliced
1 large carrot, scraped and thinly sliced
1 lemon, thinly sliced, seeds and ends discarded
⅔ cup tomato purée or tomato sauce
1½ cups beef broth

1. Trim any imperfect leaves from the cabbage and cut out whatever part of the core you can, but leave the head intact. Immerse it in boiling water and parboil for 5 minutes. Allow to sit in the water for another 5 minutes. Remove, drain, and cool. Carefully remove the outer leaves. You'll need at least 12 large leaves. If you can, remove and stuff more, as they are even tastier as leftovers. If necessary, return the cabbage to the hot water so the leaves can be easily removed. Divide the leaves into halves, cutting along the tough spine and discarding the spine.

2. In a frying pan, over medium heat, heat the butter with 3 tablespoons of the olive oil. Add the chopped onion and garlic and cook for 5 minutes, or until they are soft. Do not brown. Add the meat and cook, breaking it up with a fork until it is just slightly pink. Stir in the cinnamon, cumin, oregano, salt, pepper, and tomato. Raise the heat and cook until most of the liquid has cooked off. Mix in the rice. Preheat the oven to 350 degrees.

3. Spread the cabbage leaves out on a large work surface and place a tablespoonful of the rice-meat mixture on each. Roll them into neat cylinders by folding the sides over the filling and then rolling away from you. Fastening them with toothpicks will help hold them together.

4. Coat the bottom of a shallow baking dish with the remaining oil. Arrange the sliced onion, carrot, and lemon on the bottom of the baking dish. As you roll the leaves arrange them, seam side down, snugly side by side on top of the lemon slices. Bake for 10 minutes.

5. Blend the tomato purée with the broth and heat to a boil. Pour the mixture over the cabbage rolls. Cover and return to the oven for 45 minutes, or until the cabbage is tender. Baste 2 or 3 times during cooking. Transfer the rolls to a hot serving dish and spoon the sauce over.

Baked Rice and Cauliflower

SERVES 4 TO 6

1 medium-sized (about 1 pound or more) firm white
cauliflower
⅔ cup medium-grain rice
1½ cups water
½ teaspoon salt
8 tablespoons (1 stick) butter
1 small onion, finely chopped
Fine fresh bread crumbs
2 cups Béchamel Sauce (page 200)
6 tablespoons grated Asiago or Parmesan cheese
Salt and freshly ground black pepper to taste

1. Break the cauliflower into flowerets. Score the stems of each floweret. Cook in salted boiling water for 10 minutes, or until they are crisp-tender. Drain.

2. Bring the 1½ cups of water to a boil in a saucepan. Add the rice and salt and bring to a boil again. Stir with a wooden fork, lower the heat, cover, and simmer for 15 minutes, or until the liquid has been absorbed.

3. In a frying pan, over medium heat, melt 4 tablespoons of the butter. Cook the onion until it is soft and golden but not brown. Add the rice. Cook, stirring, for 2 minutes. Preheat the oven to 350 degrees.

4. Butter a deep 2-quart baking dish. Sprinkle the bottom and sides with bread crumbs. Shake out any excess. Arrange layers of the rice and cauliflower. Spoon some sauce and sprinkle cheese on each layer, dotting with the remaining butter (reserve 2 tablespoons of the butter for the top). Season with salt and pepper.

5. Sprinkle bread crumbs on top and dot with the reserved 2 tablespoons of butter. Bake for 30 minutes, or until the top is golden and the sauce bubbling.

Béchamel Sauce

3 tablespoons butter
3 tablespoons all-purpose flour
2 cups milk, heated
Salt and freshly ground black pepper to taste
¼ teaspoon ground nutmeg
⅛ teaspoon cayenne pepper

1. In a saucepan, over medium heat, melt the butter. Add the flour and cook, stirring into a smooth paste.
2. Gradually stir in the milk and cook, stirring constantly into a smooth, medium-thick sauce. Season with salt and pepper. Stir in the nutmeg and cayenne.

Rice Garbanzos

SERVES 6

We like this with broiled hamburgers that have been nuggeted with blue cheese before broiling.

> 3 tablespoons butter
> 2 tablespoons olive oil
> 1 small sweet green pepper, cored, seeded, and diced
> 3 whole scallions, trimmed and finely chopped
> 1 cup long-grain rice
> 2½ cups chicken broth
> 1 1-pound can chick-peas
> Salt and freshly ground black pepper to taste
> Juice of 1 lemon

1. In a saucepan, over medium heat, heat the butter and oil. Stir in the green pepper and scallions. Cook, stirring, for 5 minutes. Do not brown. Stir in the rice and chicken broth. Bring to a boil, stir with a wooden fork, cover, lower the heat, and simmer for 20 minutes, or until the rice is tender and the liquid has been absorbed.

2. Drain the liquid from the can of chick-peas, saving one half of it. In a saucepan, combine the chick-pea liquid, the chick-peas, salt, pepper, and lemon juice. Blend and simmer for 10 minutes.

3. Spoon the hot chick-peas with the liquid over the cooked rice. Taste for seasoning, adding salt and pepper, if needed. Cover and allow to sit for 5 minutes before serving.

Cucumber Rice

SERVES 4 TO 6

This is an excellent accompaniment to fish, especially salmon.

> *2 medium-sized firm cucumbers, peeled, cut*
> *lengthwise, seeds scooped out (and discarded),*
> *and then diced*
> *1 small onion, minced*
> *2 tablespoons chopped fresh dill*
> *½ pint sour cream*
> *Salt and freshly ground black pepper to taste*
> *3 cups hot cooked long-grain rice*

1. In a bowl, blend the cucumbers, onion, dill, sour cream, salt, and pepper.

2. Spoon the hot rice into a serving dish, crown with the cucumber mixture and serve.

Neapolitan Rice and Eggplant

SERVES 6 TO 8

3 tablespoons butter
1 medium-sized onion, finely chopped
1½ cups long-grain rice
2½ to 3 cups chicken broth
2 eggplants (each about 1 pound), peeled and cut into
    ½-inch-thick slices
All-purpose flour for dredging
Salt and freshly ground black pepper
½ cup olive oil
2½ cups tomato sauce, preferably homemade
½ pound mozzarella, thinly sliced
1 cup grated Asiago or Parmesan cheese
1 teaspoon dried basil

1. In a deep saucepan, melt the butter over medium heat and cook the onion for 3 minutes, or until it is soft. Do not brown. Add the rice and cook, stirring, for 2 minutes. Pour in 2½ cups of the broth. Bring to a boil, cover, lower the heat, and simmer for 15 minutes, or until the liquid has been absorbed and the rice is just *al dente*. If the rice is too underdone, add a small amount of hot broth and continue to cook. However, the rice should be quite *al dente*.

2. Lightly salt each slice of eggplant. Arrange in 2 or 3 level stacks on several layers of paper towels, with a plate on top and a weight on the plate to allow the moisture to drain off. After 30 minutes, pat the slices dry with paper towels, lightly dredge in flour. Heat 4 tablespoons of the oil in a large frying pan, over medium heat, and brown the eggplant slices on both sides, adding more oil as needed. Lightly season with salt and pepper. Drain the browned slices on paper towels. Preheat the oven to 350 degrees.

3. Coat the bottom of a large baking dish with some of the tomato sauce. Arrange a layer of one third of the eggplant slices on the sauce, then a layer of half the rice. Cover lightly with some of the tomato sauce, a layer of mozzarella; then sprinkle with grated cheese and basil. Repeat the process, ending with a layer of eggplant, sauce, and grated cheese on top. Bake for 30 minutes, or until bubbling and golden. Allow to sit for a few minutes before serving.

Risotto with Finocchio

Risotto with Fennel

SERVES 4 TO 6

3 small firm heads finocchio (fennel)
2 tablespoons olive oil
5 tablespoons butter
2 garlic cloves, halved
1 medium-sized onion, chopped
Salt and freshly ground black pepper to taste
1 cup long-grain rice
2½ cups chicken broth
1 cup grated Asiago or Parmesan cheese

1. Trim the *finocchio*, cutting off the tops and discarding the tough outer leaves, leaving just the firm white bulb. Cut into halves lengthwise and thinly slice each half crosswise.

2. In a saucepan, over medium heat, heat the oil and 2 tablespoons of the butter. Add the garlic. Cook until it is golden; then discard the garlic. Add the onion and *finocchio,* season lightly with salt and pepper, and cook for 3 minutes, or until the fennel is just beginning to get soft but is still quite crisp.

3. Stir in the rice and cook for 1 minute, coating the grains with the butter and oil. Pour in the broth. Bring to a boil, lower the heat, cover, and simmer for 20 minutes, or until the rice is tender and the liquid has been absorbed. If the liquid is absorbed and the rice is still not cooked, add a small amount of hot broth and continue cooking; or if the rice is cooked but still liquidy, remove the cover, raise the heat, and cook until the liquid evaporates, being careful not to burn the rice. Taste for seasoning, adding salt and pepper, if needed.

4. Stir in the remaining butter (in small pieces) and half of the cheese. Let sit for 2 or 3 minutes. Pass the remaining cheese at the table.

Note: This can also be prepared with broccoli instead of *finocchio.*

Kitcheri

Indian Rice with Lentils

SERVES 4

This is served everywhere in India, sort of their French fried potatoes. It is often offered with poultry or meat. For the majority of poor, however, it is a main dish, because the lentils are very nourishing. There are several versions. This, we believe, is the most popular.

> 6 tablespoons butter
> 3 medium-sized onions, thinly sliced
> 2 garlic cloves, minced
> 1½ cups long-grain rice
> 1 cup dry lentils (try to get the orange lentils), well
>   washed, then soaked in cold water for 6 hours,
>   and well drained
> Salt
> 1 teaspoon ground turmeric
> ½ teaspoon ground ginger
> ⅛ teaspoon ground cinnamon
> 3 cups chicken broth
> Freshly ground black pepper

    1. In a large frying pan, over medium heat, melt 4 tablespoons of the butter and cook the onions for 5 minutes, or until they are deep golden in color but not brown. Remove with a slotted spoon and drain on paper towels. Set aside.
    2. Melt the remaining butter in a saucepan and stir in the garlic, rice, and lentils. Cook, stirring, for 4 minutes. Stir in ½ teaspoon salt, turmeric, ginger, and cinnamon, blending well. Pour in the chicken broth and bring to a boil. Lower the heat, stir with a wooden fork, cover, and simmer for 20 minutes, or

until the liquid has been absorbed and the rice and lentils are tender. If the rice and lentils are tender and there is still too much liquid, raise the heat, remove the cover, and cook until the liquid has evaporated, being careful not to burn. If the liquid is absorbed before the rice and lentils are cooked, add a small amount of hot broth and continue to cook. Taste for seasoning, adding salt and pepper, if needed. Serve garnished with the fried onions.

Ricealeekie

SERVES 4 TO 6

6 tablespoons butter
1 medium-sized onion, finely chopped
4 large leeks (white part only), cut into ¼-inch-thick
    slices
1 cup long-grain rice
⅛ teaspoon dried tarragon
2½ cups beef broth
Salt and freshly ground black pepper to taste

1. Preheat the oven to 350 degrees.
2. In a flameproof casserole, over medium heat, melt 3 tablespoons of the butter. Add the onion and leeks and cook for 5 minutes, or until they are soft and golden. Do not brown.
3. Stir in the rice and cook for 2 minutes. Stir in the tarragon and the broth. Bring to a boil on top of the stove, stir, cover, and bake for 20 minutes, or until the rice is tender and the broth has been absorbed. Taste before adding salt and pepper as the broth may have supplied enough seasoning. Add the remaining butter and mix with a metal fork, fluffing up the rice.

Mushroom Trifolati Risotto

SERVES 4

This technique, discovered in Milan, produces one of the most unusual of the *risotti*.

> 2 tablespoons butter
> 1 cup long-grain rice
> 2 cups chicken broth
> ¼ cup olive oil
> 4 large garlic cloves, minced
> ½ pound medium-sized fresh mushrooms, thinly sliced
> Salt and freshly ground black pepper to taste
> ¼ cup dry white wine
> Juice of 1 lemon
> 2 tablespoons chopped broadleaf (Italian) parsley
>   leaves

1. In a saucepan, over medium heat, melt the butter. Stir in the rice and cook, stirring, for 2 minutes to coat the rice. Pour in the broth. Bring to a boil, lower the heat, cover, and simmer for 20 minutes, or until the rice is tender and the liquid has been absorbed.

2. Meanwhile, in a frying pan, over medium heat, heat the oil and cook the garlic for 5 minutes, or until it is soft, stirring. Do not brown. Stir in the mushrooms, sprinkle with salt and pepper, and cook for 3 minutes. Add the wine and cook for 1 minute. Stir in the lemon juice and parsley. Cook over medium-high heat for 2 minutes, or until most of the liquid has evaporated. Remove from the heat. Blend the mushroom mixture with the hot cooked rice, fluffing it with a metal fork. Taste for seasoning. Spoon into a hot serving dish.

Louisiana Okra Rice

SERVES 4

Southerners are big on rice, with the people of Louisiana being the champions. They eat rice at least once a day, in interesting combinations.

> 2 *thick slices bacon, diced*
> 2 *medium-sized onions, chopped*
> 1 *garlic clove, minced*
> 1 *large* poblano *green pepper, or a sweet green*
>   *pepper, seeded and chopped*
> *Salt*
> 1 *cup long-grain rice*
> 2 *cups chicken broth*
> 2 *medium-sized ripe tomatoes, peeled, seeded, and*
>   *chopped*
> 1 *cup sliced okra*
> *Freshly ground black pepper*

1. In a deep saucepan, over medium heat, cook the bacon until it is golden and crisp.

2. Stir in the onions, garlic, and chopped pepper. Sprinkle on ½ teaspoon salt. Cook for 10 minutes.

3. Add the rice, blending well. Pour in the broth. Bring to a boil, lower the heat, cover, and simmer for 15 minutes.

4. With a metal fork, stir in the tomatoes and okra, fluffing up the rice. Cover and simmer for 5 minutes, or until the rice is tender and the liquid has been absorbed. Remove from the heat and let stand for 5 minutes. Taste for seasoning, adding salt and pepper, if needed. Fluff up the rice before serving.

Parsnips and Brown Rice Hungarian Style

SERVES 4

Serve hot with meat or fowl. In Rost, Hungary, this was served to us with poached fresh ham.

> *2½ cups water*
> *1 cup long-grain brown rice*
> *6 tablespoons butter*
> *Salt*
> *4 medium-sized (about 1 pound total weight)*
>   *parsnips, peeled*
> *2 medium-sized onions, chopped*
> *Freshly ground black pepper*

1. In a saucepan, bring the water to a boil. Add the rice, 2 tablespoons of the butter and 1 teaspoon salt, blending well. Cover, lower the heat, and simmer for 45 minutes, or until the rice is tender and the liquid has been absorbed.

2. While the rice is simmering, cook the parsnips in salted boiling water; then drain and mash them.

3. In a small saucepan, over medium heat, melt the remaining butter and cook the onions for 8 minutes, or until they are golden. Do not brown.

4. With all the ingredients hot, combine and blend well the rice, mashed parsnips, and the onions with their butter. Taste for seasoning, adding salt and pepper, if needed.

Rice Piselli

SERVES 4

Here's a tasty Roman number, which again proves that rice is as versatile as pasta—maybe more so.

We enjoyed this dish with a delicious and tender *scallopine* of turkey breast that the Romans prepare better than anyone.

> 1 cup long-grain rice
> 2 medium-sized ripe tomatoes, peeled, seeded, and
>   finely chopped
> 2 medium-sized onions, finely chopped
> 4 medium-sized fresh mushrooms, sliced
> 1 cup dry red wine
> 1 cup chicken broth
> ½ teaspoon salt
> ¼ teaspoon freshly ground black pepper
> 3 tablespoons butter
> 1 cup small fresh green peas, cooked and drained, or
>   use frozen tiny peas, cooked according to package
>   directions
> ½ cup grated Asiago or Parmesan cheese

1. In a large saucepan, combine the rice, tomatoes, onions, and mushrooms. Stir in the wine, broth, salt, and pepper and blend well. Bring to a boil, lower the heat, cover, and simmer for 25 minutes, or until the liquid has been absorbed and the rice is tender.

2. With a metal fork, stir in the butter and peas, also fluffing up the rice. Taste for seasoning, adding salt and pepper, if needed. Sprinkle with the cheese and serve immediately, piping hot.

Risi e Bisi

Rice and Peas

SERVES 6 TO 8

4 tablespoons butter
4 scallions, trimmed and finely chopped
2 cups long-grain rice
½ cup dry white wine
4 cups chicken broth
2 slices bacon, chopped
1 tablespoon olive oil
2 cups small fresh green peas, or 1 10-ounce package
    frozen tiny peas, defrosted
1 teaspoon sugar
½ cup water
Salt and freshly ground black pepper to taste
4 medium-thin slices prosciutto or other lean cooked
    ham, cut into small squares
¾ cup grated Asiago or Parmesan cheese

   1. In a saucepan, over medium heat, melt 2 tablespoons of
the butter. Add half of the scallions and cook for 2 minutes, or
until they are soft. Do not brown. Stir in the rice and cook,
stirring, for 2 minutes, coating the rice with the butter. Pour in
the wine and the broth. Bring to a boil, lower the heat, cover,
and simmer for 20 minutes, or until the rice is *al dente* and the
liquid has been absorbed. If the rice is not cooked before the
liquid is absorbed, add more hot broth and continue cooking.
If the rice is cooked and the liquid has not been absorbed,
remove the cover, raise the heat, and cook until the liquid has
evaporated, being careful not to burn the rice.
   2. While the rice is cooking, cook the remaining scallions
in another saucepan with the bacon and oil for 5 minutes, or

until the scallions are soft. Add the peas, sugar, and ½ cup of water. Sprinkle with salt and pepper. Cover and, if the peas are fresh, cook for 10 minutes; if they are frozen and defrosted, cook for 5 minutes, or until they are just tender. Remove with a slotted spoon and with a metal fork, mix into the rice, along with the ham, cheese, and remaining butter (in small pieces). Taste for seasoning, adding salt and pepper, if needed. Fluff up the rice before serving.

Italian Stuffed Green Peppers

SERVES 4

4 large firm sweet green peppers
3 tablespoons butter
1 medium-sized onion, finely chopped
1 garlic clove, minced
½ pound Italian sausage meat
1 cup long-grain rice
1 cup tomato juice
2 cups beef broth
½ teaspoon dried thyme
3 tablespoons chopped broadleaf (Italian) parsley
    leaves
¼ cup grated Asiago or Parmesan cheese
Salt and freshly ground black pepper to taste
4 ¼-inch-thick slices mozzarella, about 3 inches in
    diameter

1. Cut a thin slice from the top of each pepper. Remove the seeds and white ribs. Drop into boiling water and blanch for 5 minutes. Remove, invert, and drain well.

2. In a frying pan, over medium heat, melt the butter. Add

the onion and garlic and cook for 3 minutes, or until they are soft. Do not brown. Add the sausage meat and cook for 7 minutes, breaking it up with a fork. Add the rice and cook for 1 minute, stirring. Combine the tomato juice and broth. Pour 2 cups of the juice-broth mixture into the rice. Add the thyme and parsley and bring to a boil. Lower the heat, stir with a wooden fork, cover, and simmer for 15 minutes. The rice should be quite *al dente* and the liquid absorbed. If the rice is *al dente* before the liquid has been absorbed, remove the cover, raise the heat, and cook off the liquid, being careful that the rice does not burn. Remove from the heat and stir in the grated cheese. Taste for seasoning, adding salt and pepper, if needed. The broth may have supplied enough seasoning. Preheat the oven to 350 degrees.

3. Heap the stuffing into the peppers. If any remains it can be spooned into the baking dish alongside the peppers. Arrange the peppers in a baking dish just large enough to hold them. Pour the remaining juice-broth mixture around them and bake for 25 minutes. Remove from the oven and lay a slice of mozzarella over each pepper. Return to the oven and bake for 10 minutes, or until the cheese melts and is golden. Serve with the sauce spooned over.

Riz à la Basquaise

Rice Pilaf with Sweet Pepper

SERVES 4

2 tablespoons butter
1 cup long-grain rice
2½ cups chicken broth
3 tablespoons olive oil
2 medium-sized onions, chopped
1 garlic clove, minced
1 large sweet red pepper, seeded, white ribs removed,
   and coarsely chopped
Salt and freshly ground black pepper to taste
1 tablespoon white vinegar

1. In a saucepan, over medium heat, melt the butter. Add the rice and cook, stirring, for 2 minutes to coat the rice well. Add the broth. Bring to a boil, stir with a wooden fork, lower the heat, cover, and simmer for 20 minutes, or until the rice is tender and the liquid has been absorbed.
2. In a frying pan, heat the oil and add the onions, garlic, and pepper. Cook for 7 minutes, or until they are soft. Do not brown.
3. Combine the rice and vegetables and mix well, fluffing with a metal fork. Taste for seasoning, adding salt and pepper, if needed. The broth may have supplied enough seasoning. With a metal fork, stir in the vinegar.

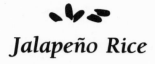

Jalapeño Rice

SERVES 4 TO 6

4 tablespoons (½ stick) butter (Mexicans use lard, but
  we prefer the flavor of butter.)
1½ cups long-grain rice
1 large onion, chopped
3 garlic cloves, minced
3 small jalapeño peppers, seeded and diced
1 teaspoon ground coriander
⅛ teaspoon ground cinnamon
2 ripe tomatoes, peeled, seeded, and chopped
3 cups beef broth
Salt to taste

1. In a flameproof casserole, over medium heat, melt the butter and add the rice, blending it well with the butter. Cook for 2 minutes, stirring. Add the onion, garlic, peppers, coriander, and cinnamon, blending well. Cook for 5 minutes. Preheat the oven to 350 degrees.

2. Stir in the tomatoes. Pour in the broth and bring to a boil.

3. Cover and bake for 20 minutes. Lower the oven temperature to 300 degrees, uncover, and cook for 10 minutes. Fluff up the rice with a metal fork. Taste before adding salt, as the broth may supply enough. At this point, the liquid should be absorbed and the rice tender. If not, return to the oven and continue baking. If the rice is tender but liquid still remains, cook, uncovered, on top of the stove until the liquid evaporates, being careful that the rice doesn't burn. Fluff up the rice with a metal fork before serving.

Note: Mexicans sometimes add a cup of briefly sautéed minced beef and stir it in during the last 10 minutes of cooking.

Peppered Rice

SERVES 4

For some reason, peppers of all kinds—hot, mild, sweet— are "in" right now. We like them, too, but not the way they are being used to excess, especially when they overwhelm delicate foods. The pepper sauce in this dish, for instance, would not be appropriate spooned over fish, which some cooks are in the habit of doing, because it would obliterate the delicate flavor of the fish. However, it is excellent on rice, which can hold its own with any flavor competition, making a snappy side dish for a bland entrée.

> 2½ cups water
> 1 cup long-grain rice
> 1 teaspoon salt
> 3 tablespoons butter
> 2 tablespoons olive oil
> 5 whole scallions, trimmed and chopped
> 2 garlic cloves, chopped
> 1 medium-sized poblano pepper, cored, seeded, and
>   chopped
> 1 medium-sized sweet red pepper, cored, seeded, and
>   chopped
> 2 tablespoons chopped jalapeño pepper
> 1 teaspoon dried thyme
> Salt to taste

1. In a saucepan, bring the water to a boil. Stir in the rice and 1 teaspoon of salt. Cover, lower the heat, and simmer for 20 minutes, or until the rice is tender and the liquid has been absorbed. Reserve the rice and keep it warm.

2. In another saucepan, over medium heat, heat the butter and oil. Stir in all the vegetables, sprinkle with thyme and salt,

and cook for 5 minutes. Cover, lower the heat, and simmer for 15 minutes, or until the vegetables are tender.

3. Purée the vegetables in a blender container or food processor. Return to the saucepan and heat through.

4. Spoon the warm rice into a hot serving dish and stir in the hot pepper purée to your taste, fluffing up the rice with a metal fork.

Iraqian Rice
with Potato Crust

SERVES 4 TO 6

This makes an excellent accompaniment to tender slices of pink roast lamb.

3 tablespoons butter
1½ cups long-grain rice
2 cups boiling water
1½ teaspoons salt
3 medium-sized potatoes, peeled and very thinly sliced
⅔ cup (1 stick plus 2 tablespoons) melted butter
2 garlic cloves, minced
½ cup toasted blanched almonds, chopped

1. In a saucepan, over medium heat, melt the 3 tablespoons of butter. Stir in the rice and cook for 1 minute. Add the water and 1 teaspoon of the salt, cover, lower the heat, and simmer for 10 minutes. Remove from the heat and drain. Reserve the rice.

2. In a large bowl, toss the potato slices with half of the melted butter and the remaining salt. In a heavy-bottomed pot with a tight-fitting cover, arrange the potato slices, overlapping (using all the butter they were tossed in) in 2 or 3 layers covering the bottom of the pot. Sprinkle with the garlic. Evenly spoon the half-cooked rice on top of the potatoes and garlic, and spoon the remaining melted butter over the rice.

3. Cover the pot with aluminum foil and then the cover. Cook over very low heat for 45 minutes, or until the rice is tender. Sprinkle with the almonds, gently stirring them into the rice with a metal fork. Be careful not to touch the bottom potato layer while you fluff the rice.

4. Serve on warm plates with spoons of rice side-by-side with a scoop of the crisp garlic-potatoes.

Potatoes and Rice

SERVES 4

The potato is probably our most popular vegetable, but rice is closing in on it fast. We discovered this unique coupling of the two winners in Frankfurt.

> 7 tablespoons butter
> ½ cup long-grain rice
> 2 medium-sized potatoes, peeled and cut into ½-inch cubes
> 1 cup water
> ½ teaspoon salt
> ¼ teaspoon freshly ground black pepper
> ½ teaspoon ground allspice
> 3 whole scallions, trimmed and thinly sliced

1. In a saucepan, over medium heat, melt 2 tablespoons of the butter. Add the rice and cook, stirring, for 1 minute. Add the potatoes and water and stir in the salt, pepper, and allspice.

Bring to a boil, lower the heat, cover, and simmer for 15 minutes, or until the rice and potatoes are tender and the liquid has been absorbed.

2. In a frying pan, melt 2 tablespoons of the butter. Cook the scallions for about 2 minutes, or just until they are crisp-tender. With a metal fork, mix them and the remaining butter (in small pieces) with the rice and potatoes, fluffing as you mix. Taste for seasoning, adding salt and pepper, if needed.

Rice and Sauerkraut Bake

SERVES 6

This was served with roast pork at the elegant Schloss Fuschl near Salsburg, Austria.

> 2½ cups water
> 1 teaspoon salt
> 1 cup long-grain rice
> 4 tablespoons grated sharp Cheddar cheese
> 2 tablespoons chopped broadleaf (Italian) parsley
>   leaves
> ½ teaspoon freshly ground black pepper
> 3 tablespoons butter
> 1 large onion, chopped
> 2½ pounds sauerkraut, well drained
> 1 teaspoon caraway seeds
> 1 cup milk
> 3 eggs

1. In a saucepan, bring the water to a boil. Stir in the salt and rice. Cover, lower the heat, and simmer for 20 minutes, or until the rice is tender and the liquid has been absorbed. If the rice is cooked before the liquid is absorbed, remove the cover, raise the heat, and cook until the liquid evaporates, being careful that the rice does not burn. If the liquid is absorbed and the rice is not yet tender, add a small amount of hot water and continue cooking. Stir in the cheese, parsley, and pepper with a metal fork. Reserve.

2. In a deep saucepan, over medium heat, melt the butter. Cook the onion for 5 minutes, or until it is soft. Do not brown. Stir in the sauerkraut and caraway seeds, blending well. Sauté for 15 minutes. Preheat the oven to 350 degrees.

3. Lightly butter a casserole and alternate layers of sauerkraut and rice, starting and ending with a layer of sauerkraut.

4. In a small bowl, beat the milk and eggs together and pour the mixture over the sauerkraut. Bake, uncovered, for 25 minutes, or until the top is set and golden.

Spanakorizo

SERVES 6

In Athens, the old section of the city is an area called the *Plaka*. It is filled with gay *tavernas* and the throbbing music of the guitar-like *bouzoukis,* making it popular with tourists and Greeks alike. We had this rice dish in one of the little restaurants there, oddly enough, with a highly spiced ground lamb dish that we think is Turkish, *kadm budu* (lady's thigh).

> 2 tablespoons olive oil
> 4 whole scallions, trimmed and chopped
> 2 pounds fresh spinach, washed, drained, and finely
>   chopped
> 1½ cups long-grain rice
> 3 cups tomato juice
> 6 ripe plum tomatoes, peeled, seeded, and chopped
> 1 teaspoon salt
> ¼ teaspoon freshly ground black pepper
> ½ teaspoon ground cinnamon

1. In a large heavy saucepan, over medium heat, heat the oil. Add the scallions and cook for 3 minutes. Make an even layer of the spinach over the scallions. Cover with an even layer of the rice.

2. In a bowl, blend the tomato juice, tomatoes, salt, and pepper and spoon the mixture over the rice. Sprinkle with the cinnamon. Bring to a boil; then turn the heat very low, cover, and simmer for 20 minutes, or until the rice is tender. Remove from the heat and let sit, covered, for 10 minutes before serving.

Brown Rice and Spinach

SERVES 4

4 tablespoons olive oil
4 large shallots, chopped
2 garlic cloves, minced
1 cup long-grain brown rice
2 medium-sized ripe tomatoes, peeled, seeded, and
    diced
Salt and freshly ground black pepper to taste
2½ cups water
2 10-ounce packages fresh spinach, trimmed, washed,
    drained, and chopped

1. In a deep saucepan, over medium heat, heat the olive oil and cook the shallots and garlic for 5 minutes, or until they are soft. Do not brown.

2. Stir in the rice and cook for 2 minutes, stirring. Add the tomatoes, salt, pepper, and water. Bring to a boil, cover, lower the heat, and simmer for 35 minutes.

3. Quickly stir in the spinach, cover again, and cook for 10 minutes, or until the rice is tender and the liquid has been absorbed. Fluff up with a metal fork. If the liquid is absorbed before the rice is tender, add more hot water and continue cooking. If the rice is cooked before the liquid is absorbed, remove the cover, raise the heat, and cook until the liquid evaporates, being careful not to burn the rice.

Riso al Forno

SERVES 4

2 cups al dente-*cooked long-grain rice* (*It should be quite firm.*)
1 1-pound can *imported Italian plum tomatoes with their liquid* (*Chop the tomatoes.*)
1 medium-sized *onion, sliced*
Salt and freshly ground black pepper to taste
3 tablespoons *butter*

1. Preheat the oven to 350 degrees.
2. In a buttered baking dish, combine and blend well all the ingredients, except the butter.
3. Dot with the butter and bake, uncovered, for 30 minutes, or until bubbling and most of the liquid has been absorbed.

Tomatoes Antalya Irfan

SERVES 6

We enjoyed these tomatoes when they were served to us with calf's liver at Antalya, called the Turkish Riviera. The chef gladly gave us the recipe, but asked that his first name be attached. It is.

> 6 medium-sized firm ripe tomatoes
> Salt and freshly ground black pepper
> 2 tablespoons olive oil
> 1 medium-sized onion, finely chopped
> 1 garlic clove, minced
> 1 cup long-grain rice
> ½ teaspoon ground turmeric
> ⅛ teaspoon ground cinnamon
> ½ teaspoon dried oregano
> 1½ cups chicken broth
> ¼ cup dry white wine
> 3 tablespoons finely chopped broadleaf (Italian)
>   parsley leaves
> ½ cup pignoli
> ¼ cup tomato purée
> ¼ cup olive oil
> ½ cup chicken broth

1. Cut a thin slice from the stem ends of the tomatoes. Remove the seeds and center pulp, leaving firm shells. Discard the seeds and chop the pulp and the tops. (Peel the tops before chopping.) Sprinkle the inside of the tomatoes with salt and pepper and invert to drain.

2. In a saucepan, over medium heat, heat the 2 tablespoons of olive oil. Add the onion and garlic and cook for 2 minutes, or until they are soft. Do not brown. Stir in the rice

and cook for 2 minutes, coating with the oil. Stir in the turmeric, cinnamon, and oregano. Pour in the broth and wine and bring to a boil. Lower the heat, cover, and simmer for 10 minutes, or until the liquid has been absorbed and the rice is *al dente*. If the rice is not cooked before the liquid has been absorbed, add more hot broth and continue cooking. If the rice is cooked and the liquid has not been absorbed, remove the cover, raise the heat, and cook off the liquid, being careful not to burn the rice. Taste and season. Add the chopped tomato pulp and tops. Preheat the oven to 350 degrees.

3. Stir the parsley and *pignoli* into the rice, mixing with a metal fork. Fill the tomato shells with the rice mixture, dividing it equally. Place the stuffed tomatoes in a baking dish just large enough to hold them snugly. If there is too much filling, spoon it around the tomatoes.

4. Combine the tomato purée, ¼ cup olive oil, and the chicken broth and pour the mixture around the tomatoes. There should be about ½ inch of liquid in the bottom of the pan. Bake for 20 minutes (basting 2 or 3 times), or until the rice is tender.

Stuffed Tomatoes Creole Style

SERVES 6

6 medium-sized firm ripe tomatoes
3 tablespoons butter
1 medium-sized onion, finely chopped
1½ cups al dente-cooked long-grain rice
1 cup shelled and deveined shrimp, cut into cubes
    slightly smaller than ½ inch
½ cup cooked corn kernels
¼ teaspoon cayenne pepper
Salt to taste
3 tablespoons bread crumbs

1. Cut a thin slice from the stem ends of the tomatoes. Remove the seeds and center pulp, discarding the seeds and chopping the pulp and the tops (peel the tops before chopping), leaving firm shells. Sprinkle the inside of the shells with salt and invert them to drain.

2. Melt the butter over medium heat in a frying pan. Add the onion and cook for 3 minutes, or until it is soft. Do not brown. Combine the rice, shrimp, corn, onion, cayenne, and salt and stir with a fork. Taste and season. Add the chopped tomato pulp and tops. Preheat the oven to 400 degrees.

3. Divide the stuffing equally and fill the tomatoes, mounding it, if necessary. Cover the tops with bread crumbs. Arrange the stuffed tomatoes in a baking dish just large enough to hold them snugly. Pour ½ cup water into the baking dish and bake, uncovered, for 20 minutes, or until the tops are golden and the rice stuffing heated through. At this time the shrimp should be pink.

Risotto Estivo

A Summertime Risotto

SERVES 6 TO 8

2 tablespoons butter
2 tablespoons olive oil
4 whole scallions, trimmed and cut into ¼-inch
    lengths
2 celery stalks, scraped and coarsely chopped
1½ cups long-grain brown rice
3½ cups chicken broth
4 ripe but firm plum tomatoes, peeled, seeded, and
    coarsely chopped
1 bay leaf
1 cup shelled fresh peas, cooked al dente, or frozen,
    defrosted
¼ pound small fresh mushrooms, sliced and cooked in
    3 tablespoons of butter until brown but still firm
½ cup chopped broadleaf (Italian) parsley leaves
5 fresh basil leaves, chopped
Salt and freshly ground black pepper to taste
¼ pound prosciutto, cut into slivers
1 cup grated Asiago or Parmesan cheese

1. In a large saucepan, over medium heat, heat the butter
and oil. Add the scallions and celery and cook for 6 minutes, or
until they are slightly soft. Do not brown.

2. Stir in the rice and cook for 2 minutes, stirring to coat
the rice well with the fat. Add the broth, tomatoes, and bay
leaf. Bring to a boil, lower the heat, stir with a wooden fork,
cover, and simmer for 35 minutes, or until the rice is *al dente*
and most of the liquid has been absorbed. The rice should be
moist but not soupy. Remove and discard the bay leaf.

3. Stir in the peas, mushrooms, parsley, and basil and cook for 3 minutes, or to heat through. Taste for seasoning, adding salt and pepper, if needed. The broth may have supplied enough.

4. Remove from the heat and stir in the prosciutto and half of the cheese with a metal fork, fluffing up the rice. Pass the remaining cheese at the table.

Risotto Legumi Misti

Rice with Mixed Vegetables

SERVES 6 TO 8

6 slices bacon
2 medium-sized onions, chopped
2 garlic cloves, minced
2 medium-sized parsnips, scraped and diced
2 medium-sized carrots, scraped and diced
2 small (about 4 inches by 1 inch) zucchini, cut into
    ½-inch-thick slices
2 cups fresh baby lima beans
1½ cups long-grain rice
3½ cups beef broth
Salt to taste
¼ teaspoon hot red pepper flakes
1 cup grated Romano cheese

1. In a large saucepan, over medium heat, cook the bacon until it is crisp and golden brown. Drain on paper towels; then cool and cut into ½-inch pieces. Reserve.

2. Stir the onions, garlic, parsnips, carrots, zucchini, and lima beans into the pot with the bacon fat. Cook for 15 minutes, stirring occasionally. Do not brown.

3. Stir in the rice, broth, salt, and hot red pepper flakes. Bring to a boil, stir with a wooden fork, lower the heat, cover, and simmer for 20 minutes. Remove from the heat and let sit for 5 minutes, covered. The rice should be slightly *al dente* and moist, but not soupy. Taste for seasoning, adding salt and pepper, if needed.

4. Sprinkle the rice and vegetables with the bacon and half of the cheese. Toss with a metal fork, fluffing up the rice. Serve the remaining cheese at the table.

Armenian Rice-Stuffed Zucchini

SERVES 4

These go very nicely with slices of pink roasted leg of lamb.

> *4 zucchini, about 2½ inches by 6 inches*
> *3 tablespoons olive oil*
> *2 medium-sized onions, finely chopped*
> *1 garlic clove, minced*
> *Salt and freshly ground black pepper to taste*
> *3 cups al dente-cooked long-grain rice (cooked in chicken broth)*
> *6 medium-sized fresh mushrooms, chopped*
> *2 tablespoons minced broadleaf (Italian) parsley leaves*
> *5 fresh mint leaves, minced*
> *½ teaspoon ground cumin*
> *½ cup grated Asiago or Parmesan cheese*
> *1 1-pound, 12-ounce can imported Italian plum tomatoes*
> *½ cup beef broth*

1. Cut the zucchini into halves lengthwise; scoop out the pulp, leaving a shell about ¼ inch thick. Lightly salt the zucchini shells and invert them on paper towels to drain. Chop one third of the pulp and discard the remainder. In a frying pan, over medium heat, heat the oil and cook the onions, garlic, and zucchini pulp for 5 minutes, or until the onion is soft, seasoning with salt and pepper. Remove from the heat and blend in the rice, mushrooms, parsley, mint, cumin, cheese, and 2 of the canned tomatoes, chopped.

2. Preheat the oven to 375 degrees.

3. Place the zucchini halves in a baking dish or casserole just large enough to hold them snugly. Divide the rice mixture, mounding it in the shells. Chop the remaining tomatoes and blend them and their liquid with the beef broth. Season with salt and pepper. Spoon this mixture over and around the stuffed zucchini.

4. Tightly cover the baking dish with foil or the casserole with its cover and bake for 15 minutes. Baste with the sauce in the pan, return to the oven, and bake, covered, for 30 minutes, or until the zucchini shells are tender. Serve with the tomato sauce spooned over.

Parsleyed Zucchini Rice

SERVES 4 TO 6

4 *small (about 4 inches by 1½ inches) zucchini, cut into ¼-inch-thick slices*
3 *tablespoons butter*
1 *small onion, finely chopped*
1 *garlic clove, minced*
1 *cup long-grain brown rice*
1 *bay leaf*

2½ cups chicken broth
Salt and freshly ground black pepper to taste
¾ cup chopped broadleaf (Italian) parsley leaves
2 tablespoons fresh lemon juice
1 cup ricotta
½ cup grated Gruyère or Fontina cheese
¼ cup grated Asiago or Parmesan cheese

1. Cook the zucchini slices in just enough salted boiling water to cover until they are crisp-tender. Drain well.

2. In a saucepan, over medium heat, melt the butter. Add the onion and garlic and cook for 3 minutes, or until they are soft. Do not brown. Stir in the rice and cook for 1 minute, coating the rice well with the butter. Add the bay leaf and broth and bring to a boil. Stir with a wooden fork, lower the heat, cover, and cook for 40 minutes, or until the rice is tender but still slightly *al dente* and the liquid has been absorbed. Discard the bay leaf. Taste for seasoning, adding salt and pepper, if needed. Preheat the oven to 350 degrees.

3. With a metal fork, mix the parsley and lemon juice with the rice.

4. Butter a shallow baking dish. Arrange the rice in a smooth layer on the bottom. Cover the rice with a layer of the ricotta and an overlapping layer of the zucchini slices. Sprinkle the zucchini with the grated cheeses and bake for 25 minutes, or until the cheese has melted and the dish is heated through.

Zucchini Rice alla Parma

SERVES 6

Just about everything (except stuffing for poultry and some meats) that is rice to Italians is *risotto*. They like it soupy, not so soupy that it must be eaten with a spoon, but often a little too moist for our taste. But here's one we discovered in Parma (with, what else, Parmesan cheese!) that we often enjoy when that ubiquitous, do-everything zucchini is dominating our garden.

> 3 tablespoons butter
> 2 tablespoons olive oil
> 3 slices panchetti (this is Italian bacon and delicious; but if you can't find it, use bacon), diced
> 2 medium-sized onions, chopped
> 2 garlic cloves, minced
> 5 small (about 4 inches by 1 inch) zucchini, cut into ¼-inch-thick slices
> 1½ cups long-grain rice
> 3 cups chicken broth
> Salt and freshly ground black pepper to taste
> ½ cup grated Parmesan cheese

1. In a flameproof casserole, over medium heat, heat the butter and olive oil. Add the *panchetti* and cook for 5 minutes. Add the onions, garlic, and zucchini and cook, stirring, for 10 minutes. Preheat the oven to 350 degrees.

2. Stir in the rice, blending it with the fat and vegetables. Add the broth and bring to a boil. Cover the casserole and bake for 25 minutes, or until the rice is tender and the liquid has been absorbed. Taste before seasoning, as the broth may have supplied enough. Fluff the rice with a metal fork and serve with a generous spoonful of the cheese on top of each portion.

8
RICE
SPECIALTIES
and
SIDE DISHES

One of our several idiosyncrasies regarding food is a dislike for the word "leftover." Thus, we have no chapter on that category.

Instead, convinced that rice is surely the most versatile of all accompaniments, we offer the following recipes, with rice given a starring role. Even if it only has a walk-on part in the drama of dinner, rice usually steals the show.

We still remember a dinner for which we prepared a perfectly cooked whole filet of beef and served it with its own delicious juices. With it we offered Riz Bourguignonne—rice with egg, wine, cream, and cheese. Remarks on the rice ran around the table among our guests, but the filet was not commented on at all.

Chinese Eight-Jewel Rice

SERVES 4 TO 6

Other than several simple versions of fried rice, the Chinese do not do anything spectacular with rice, except eat it—about three times a day. But it usually is a side dish, to be mixed by the diner with other foods, or simply eaten as an accompaniment. There is nothing wrong with this technique. In fact, the Chinese know more about eating and cooking rice than anyone. But we're partial to this fancier version that we discovered in Hong Kong. Either a wok or frying pan can be used to cook this dish. The finest Chinese cooks we know, the Wah Chins, don't even own a wok.

3 tablespoons peanut oil
4 eggs, beaten
4 whole scallions, trimmed and cut into ½-inch
    lengths
2 lean loin pork chops (all fat removed), diced
½ cup diced smoked ham
½ chicken breast, boned and diced
4 water chestnuts, thinly sliced
4 large fresh mushrooms, thinly sliced
8 medium-sized shrimp, shelled, deveined, and diced
4 cups cooked long-grain rice
1 tablespoon soy sauce, blended with 3 tablespoons
    chicken broth
Salt to taste

1. In a wok or large frying pan, over medium heat, heat 1 tablespoon of the oil and lightly scramble the eggs, until they are just barely set. Remove and set aside.

2. Add the remaining oil to the pan and, over medium heat, stir-fry the scallions for 20 seconds. Stir in the pork and stir-fry for 4 minutes. Add the ham, chicken, and water chestnuts. Stir-fry for 1 minute. Add the mushrooms and shrimp and stir-fry for 1 minute, or until the shrimp just turn pink.

3. Stir in the cooked rice and the soy sauce-chicken broth blend and stir-fry for 2 minutes, or until the rice is heated through. Return the scrambled eggs to the pan and carefully stir-fry for 30 seconds. Taste and add salt, if needed. Serve immediately.

Apple-Time Rice

SERVES 6 TO 8

This is a rice dish that we like to serve with pork or ham in October, when we can pick apples from our tree. It's unusual—and taste tempting.

> *2 tablespoons butter*
> *1½ cups long-grain rice*
> *Salt*
> *1 cup cranberry juice*
> *2 cups unsweetened apple juice*
> *2 tablespoons fresh lemon juice*
> *2 teaspoons dark or light brown sugar*
> *½ teaspoon ground cinnamon*
> *1 tablespoon chopped raisins*
> *2 small tart apples, peeled, cored, and coarsely*
> *   chopped*
> *2 whole small scallions, trimmed and cut into ¼-inch*
> *   lengths*
> *Freshly ground black pepper*

1. In a saucepan, over medium heat, melt the butter. Stir in the rice and 1 teaspoon salt and cook, stirring, for 2 minutes to coat the rice. Add the cranberry, apple, and lemon juices, sugar, cinnamon, and raisins and bring to a boil. Stir with a wooden fork, lower the heat, cover, and simmer for 20 minutes, or until the rice is tender and the liquid has been absorbed.

2. Stir in the apples and scallions with a metal fork and heat through. Do not cook, as the apples and scallions should be crunchy counterpoints to the rice. Taste for seasoning, adding salt and pepper, if needed.

Arroz Alentejo

Portuguese Rice and Pea Pudding

SERVES 6

5 tablespoons butter
2 medium-sized onions, chopped
1½ cups long-grain brown rice
3½ cups chicken broth
Salt and freshly ground black pepper to taste
1 10-ounce package frozen tiny peas, cooked slightly
     less than the package directs and then drained
¼ pound smoked ham or prosciutto, minced
3 large eggs, beaten

1. In a saucepan, over medium heat, melt 3 tablespoons of the butter. Cook the onions for 5 minutes. Do not brown. Stir in the rice, coating it well with the butter.

2. Pour in the chicken broth and bring to a boil. Stir with a wooden fork, lower the heat, cover, and simmer for 35 minutes, or until the rice is *al dente*. Taste and season with salt (remember, the ham is salty, as is the broth) and pepper, if needed. Remove from the heat. Preheat the oven to 400 degrees.

3. Stir the peas and remaining butter into the rice with a metal fork. Add the ham and beaten eggs, blending well.

4. Spoon into a buttered 8-inch-square by 2-inch-deep baking dish. Bake, uncovered, until the eggs are set, about 20 minutes.

Avocado Rice

SERVES 4

We had this in Florida with pompano that had been baked in parchment; it was a delicious and exotic combination. We've also enjoyed a similar dish, served with broiled sea trout in the Bahamas, where mango was substituted for the avocado.

> 2 cups water
> ½ cup unsweetened pineapple juice
> 1 cup long-grain rice
> 1 teaspoon salt
> 3 tablespoons butter, cut into small pieces
> 1 large ripe but firm avocado, peeled, coarsely
>   chopped, and mixed with 2 tablespoons pineapple
>   juice

1. In a saucepan, bring the water and pineapple juice to a boil. Stir in the rice and salt, cover, lower the heat, and simmer for 20 minutes, or until the rice is tender and the liquid has been absorbed.

2. With a metal fork, stir in the butter; then carefully blend in the avocado and cook for 1 or 2 minutes to heat through. Fluff up the rice with a metal fork before serving.

Au Gratin Rice

SERVES 4

This is an excellent plate-mate for a nice juicy piece of roast chicken.

> 3 cups hot cooked seasoned long-grain rice
> 1 cup grated Monterey Jack cheese with jalapeño
>   pepper
> 2 tablespoons melted butter
> ½ cup fine dry bread crumbs
> 2 tablespoons grated Parmesan cheese

1. Preheat the oven to 350 degrees.
2. In a bowl, with a metal fork, toss the rice with half of the Monterey Jack cheese. Spoon evenly into a buttered baking dish. Sprinkle with the remaining Monterey Jack cheese.
3. Bake, uncovered, for 10 minutes, or until the cheese melts.
4. With a fork, blend the butter, bread crumbs, and Parmesan cheese together. Sprinkle evenly on the rice dish. Return to the oven and bake until the crumbs are crusty.

Bacon and Chives Toss-Up

SERVES 4

This is a taste-enlivening dish to serve with something simple, such as broiled fish.

> *3 slices bacon, cooked until crisp and crumbled (Save the drippings.)*
> *3 cups cooked long-grain rice*
> *3 tablespoons chopped fresh chives*
> *4 tablespoons bacon drippings (If the bacon does not render that amount of fat, add butter to make that amount of fat.)*
> *Salt and freshly ground black pepper to taste*
> *⅛ teaspoon Tabasco sauce, or to taste*

In a bowl, combine the bacon, rice, chives, and bacon drippings and toss. Taste and season with salt and pepper. Sprinkle on the Tabasco and toss again. Transfer to a saucepan and heat thoroughly on top of the stove, fluffing up the rice with a metal fork as you heat it.

Bacon-and-Egg Fried Rice

SERVES 4

2 tablespoons peanut oil or light vegetable oil
2 slices lean bacon, coarsely chopped
4 whole scallions, trimmed and chopped
3 eggs, lightly beaten with ½ teaspoon of salt
4 cups cooked long-grain rice
2 tablespoons soy sauce
¼ teaspoon sugar
Salt and freshly ground black pepper to taste
3 tablespoons butter, cut into small pieces
½ cup cooked tiny peas, fresh or frozen

1. In a wok or deep frying pan, over medium heat, heat the oil. Add the bacon and cook for 2 minutes. Add the scallions and cook for 1 minute.

2. Pour in the eggs, covering the bottom of the pan, and cook until the eggs are almost set. Quickly stir the eggs into a coarse, soft scramble. With a metal fork quickly stir in the rice, soy sauce, and sugar. Heat through. Taste for seasoning before adding salt and pepper. Just before serving, stir in the butter and the peas.

Deep-Fried Rice Balls

SERVES 4 TO 6

Serve as a hot hors d'oeuvre or to accompany a main course.

> 2 cups cooked short- or medium-grain rice, seasoned
> with salt and pepper and blended with ½ cup
> grated Asiago or Parmesan cheese and ¼ cup soft
> butter
> 2 eggs, beaten in a large bowl
> About 12 ½-inch cubes mozzarella
> Fine dry bread crumbs for dredging
> Fat for deep-frying

1. Mix the rice with the beaten eggs.

2. Scoop about 2 tablespoonfuls of the mixture into your hand, push a cube of mozzarella into it, molding the rice around it into a ball to enclose the cube. Holding the ball in your hand, sprinkle it with bread crumbs until it is evenly covered. Pat the crumbs onto the rice. Refrigerate the completed balls, not touching, for 1 hour or more.

3. Heat the fat to 375 degrees, or until a 1-inch cube of bread becomes golden brown in 40 to 50 seconds. Cook a few balls at a time (lowering them into the hot fat with a slotted spoon), until they are golden brown. (Do not crowd them.) Remove with a slotted spoon and drain on a baking sheet lined with paper towels. The rice balls may be kept warm in a 200-degree oven while the others are being fried.

Riz Bourguignonne

SERVES 4 TO 6

This is a good accompaniment for Beef Bourguignonne.

>2 tablespoons butter
>1 cup long-grain rice
>2¼ cups water
>1 teaspoon salt
>Freshly ground black pepper to taste
>1 egg, beaten
>½ cup grated Gruyère cheese
>¼ cup grated Asiago or Parmesan cheese
>2 tablespoons dry white wine
>¾ cup heavy cream
>¼ cup fine fresh bread crumbs
>2 tablespoons melted butter

1. In a saucepan, over medium heat, melt the 2 tablespoons of butter. Add the rice and cook, stirring, for 2 minutes. Stir in the water and salt. Bring to a boil, lower the heat, stir with a wooden fork, cover, and simmer for 20 minutes, or until the rice is *al dente* and the liquid has been absorbed. Remove from the heat. Taste and add salt and pepper, if needed. Beat in the egg. Preheat the oven to 400 degrees.

2. Spread the rice in a 1½-inch-thick layer in a shallow baking dish. Smooth the top but do not pack it down. Combine and blend the cheeses, wine, and cream and spoon the mixture over the rice. Sprinkle with the bread crumbs and melted butter. Bake for 15 minutes, or until golden.

Fried Rice Cakes Italiano

SERVES 4

8 tablespoons (1 stick) butter
2 cups cold leftover Risotto Milanese (page 146),
    mixed with 1 beaten egg
¼ pound mozzarella, cut into small pieces

1. Over medium heat, melt 2 tablespoons of the butter in a small (4 to 5 inches in diameter) shallow frying pan. When hot, stir in one quarter of the rice mixture. Mix it with the butter. Before it starts to cook, press with a spatula into a cake, covering the bottom of the pan. Continue to pat as it cooks. Shake the pan gently from time to time to keep the rice from sticking but do not break up the cake.

2. When the rice cake is golden brown on the underside, place a plate, larger than the frying pan, over the pan, turn the pan over so the rice cake falls onto the plate, browned side up. Slide the cake back into the pan, browned side up and pat it flat.

3. Put one quarter of the mozzarella on the top, cover, and cook for 3 to 4 minutes to brown the bottom. Slide out onto a small hot serving plate (see Note). Cover and keep warm in a 250-degree oven while cooking the others. Serve each right on the hot plate on which you kept it warm.

Note: You'll need 4 small hot plates. This prevents the cakes from being broken up while being transferred from one plate to another.

Rice with Four Cheeses

SERVES 6 TO 8

1 cup heavy cream
2 ounces Fontina cheese, cut into small, less than ½
   inch, cubes
2 ounces Gouda cheese, cut into small, less than ½
   inch, cubes
2 ounces mozzarella, cut into small, less than ½ inch,
   cubes
3 tablespoons butter, cut into small pieces
Freshly ground black pepper to taste
4 cups hot cooked long-grain rice
1 cup grated Asiago or Parmesan cheese

1. In a saucepan, over medium heat, heat the cream just to a simmer. Remove from the heat and stir in the cubed cheeses.

2. Mix the butter and pepper with the rice, stirring and fluffing up with a metal fork.

3. Return the cheese sauce to the heat and heat until the cheese is very nearly melted, but the cubes still have some shape.

4. Place the rice in a hot serving bowl. Pour on the cheese sauce and mix with a metal fork. Serve the grated cheese at the table.

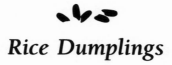

Rice Dumplings

SERVES 6

These dumplings can be served with any stew.

1 egg, beaten
½ cup milk
1½ cups sifted all-purpose flour (Sift the flour before
*   measuring it.)*
2½ teaspoons baking powder
1 teaspoon salt
¼ teaspoon ground nutmeg
1 cup cooked short- or medium-grain rice
2 tablespoons finely minced parsley leaves
2 tablespoons melted butter
Additional milk, if needed

1. In a large bowl, blend the egg and milk. Sift the flour, baking powder, salt, and nutmeg together and add to the egg-milk bowl. With a metal fork, stir in the rice, parsley, and butter. Blend well. If the batter seems too heavy, add a small amount of milk. It should be just thick enough to hold its shape on a spoon.

2. Drop by tablespoonfuls onto barely simmering stew. Cover tightly and cook for 15 minutes. Test for doneness by inserting a toothpick. If it comes out clean, the dumplings are ready.

Indian Egg Rice

SERVES 4

The Indian version of fried rice, which also has eggs, is softer than Chinese fried rice and has a different taste texture.

> *1½ cups long-grain rice*
> *1 teaspoon salt*
> *⅛ teaspoon hot red pepper flakes*
> *2 whole cloves*
> *⅛ teaspoon ground nutmeg*
> *3 cups boiling water*
> *Salt and freshly ground black pepper to taste*
> *4 tablespoons (½ stick) butter*
> *1 large garlic clove, minced*
> *4 eggs, beaten*

1. In a saucepan, combine the rice, salt, hot red pepper flakes, cloves, and nutmeg. Stir in the boiling water. Over high heat, keep at a boil for 1 minute. Lower the heat, cover, and simmer for 20 minutes, or until the rice is tender and the liquid has been absorbed. Remove and discard the cloves. Taste for seasoning, adding salt and pepper, if needed.

2. In a large deep frying pan, over medium heat, melt the butter. Add the garlic and cook until it is soft. Do not brown. Stir in the eggs and cook, stirring, for 1 minute, or until they are set. Do not overcook. Blend in the hot cooked rice. Remove from the heat and serve immediately.

Turkish Egg-Sauced Rice

SERVES 4

This simple, but extremely tasty, dish was served in Istanbul, with *shish kebab,* its usual accompaniment, but it is excellent with any meat or chicken dish. In fact, we also had it with swordfish, another specialty of that city.

> 2½ cups beef broth
> 1 cup long-grain rice
> Salt and freshly ground black pepper to taste
> 3 tablespoons soft butter
> 1 large raw egg yolk at room temperature (Carefully separate the yolk in order not to break it and save half of the shell to serve it in.)

1. In a saucepan bring the broth to a boil. Slowly pour the rice into the broth, stirring and keeping the broth at a boil until all of the rice has been poured in. Lower the heat, cover, and simmer for 20 minutes, or until the rice is tender and the broth has been absorbed. Taste before adding salt and pepper, as the broth may have had enough.

2. With a metal fork, stir in the butter, fluffing up the rice. Spoon into a hot serving dish. Make a small depression in the center of the rice. Set the egg yolk in the shell in it. At the table, just before serving, stir the egg yolk into the hot rice with a metal fork.

Kasha-Rice Pilaf

SERVES 6

3 tablespoons butter
1 cup buckwheat groats
1 cup long-grain rice
4½ cups beef broth
Salt and freshly ground black pepper to taste
½ teaspoon powdered saffron, or to taste
2 tablespoons melted butter
¼ cup fresh lemon juice

1. In a deep saucepan, over medium heat, melt the 3 tablespoons of butter. Add the buckwheat groats and rice and cook for 2 minutes, stirring, until they are well coated with the butter.

2. Pour in the broth, bring to a boil, and stir with a wooden fork. Lower the heat, cover, and simmer for 20 minutes, or until the grains are tender and the liquid has been absorbed. Taste for seasoning, adding salt and pepper, if needed. The broth may have supplied enough.

3. With a metal fork, stir in the saffron, melted butter, and lemon juice, tossing to fluff.

4. Cover, place over high heat for 1 minute. Remove from the heat and let sit, covered, for 5 minutes, before serving.

Rice with Harlot Sauce
Napolitano

SERVES 4 TO 6

This quick spicy sauce is said to have been originated by the
loose ladies of Naples, who prepared it between assignments.

The rice does not need additional seasoning; the sauce
handles that nicely. We like to serve this with veal or chicken
breast *scallopine*.

> 2 tablespoons olive oil
> 2 garlic cloves, minced
> 1 2-ounce can flat anchovy fillets, drained and broken
>   into pieces
> 1 1-pound, 12-ounce can imported Italian plum
>   tomatoes (Place the tomatoes in a bowl and crush
>   them by hand into small pieces.)
> 8 pimiento-stuffed olives, sliced
> 8 pitted black "Greek" olives, sliced
> 1 teaspoon capers, drained
> 1 teaspoon dried basil
> ⅛ teaspoon hot red pepper flakes, or to taste
> 3 cups water
> 1½ cups long-grain rice
> 1 teaspoon salt
> 4 tablespoons (½ stick) butter

1. In a deep saucepan, over medium heat, heat the olive
oil and cook the garlic for 2 minutes, or until it is soft. Do not
brown. Add the anchovies and cook until they have disin-
tegrated.

2. Stir in the tomatoes, olives, capers, basil, and hot red
pepper flakes, blending well. Lower the heat and simmer, un-

covered, stirring occasionally, for 25 minutes, or until the sauce has thickened.

3. Meanwhile, in a saucepan, bring the water to a boil and stir in the rice and salt. Lower the heat, cover, and simmer for 20 minutes, or until the rice is *al dente* and the water has been absorbed. Serve with the sauce spooned on top.

Irish Ricejacks

SERVES 4

Serve with melted butter and warm syrup. We like these with "honey butter."

> *1½ cups all-purpose flour*
> *½ teaspoon salt*
> *1½ teaspoons baking powder*
> *1½ cups milk*
> *1½ cups cooked short- or medium-grain rice*
> *1½ tablespoons melted butter*
> *1 egg, beaten*

1. Sift the flour, salt, and baking powder into a bowl. Pour in the milk and stir just to blend. Add the remaining ingredients and stir until blended.

2. Drop by tablespoonfuls onto a very hot, lightly oiled griddle. Cook until holes appear on the surface of the cakes. Turn and brown the other side.

Bombay Lime Rice

SERVES 4 TO 6

In India there are many unique rice dishes that exist in no other area. Most cities there have a different version of this recipe, but this one we enjoyed in a friend's home in Bombay. It is especially good with broiled lamb chops.

> 4 cups water
> 1½ cups long-grain rice
> Salt
> ¼ cup sweet butter (In India they use ghee, butter
> made from buffalo milk. Clarified by boiling, it
> resembles oil in consistency. We think American
> butter has superior flavor.)
> ½ teaspoon mustard seeds, preferably black
> 1 cup halved cashews
> ½ tablespoon minced fresh ginger, or ¼ teaspoon
> ground ginger
> ⅛ teaspoon cayenne pepper, or to taste
> 2 tablespoons chopped fresh coriander leaves, or 1
> tablespoon chopped fresh parsley leaves and 1
> tablespoon chopped fresh chives
> ½ teaspoon ground turmeric
> ½ cup chopped unsweetened fresh coconut
> ½ cup fresh lime juice
> 1 cup chicken broth

1. Bring the water to a boil in a deep saucepan over medium-high heat. Stir in the rice and 1 teaspoon salt and simmer for 10 minutes, stirring once or twice. Drain. Preheat the oven to 350 degrees.

2. Melt the butter in a flameproof casserole with a tight-fitting cover. Add the mustard seeds and cook until they start popping. Add the nuts, ginger, and cayenne and cook for 2 minutes, stirring constantly.

3. Stir in the drained rice, coriander, turmeric, coconut, lime juice, and broth. Bring to a simmer, cover tightly, and bake for 20 to 30 minutes, or until the rice is tender and the liquid has been absorbed. Taste for seasoning, adding more salt, if needed. Fluff with a metal fork before serving.

Maria Cifelli's Limone Riso

SERVES 4 TO 6

This is excellent with a broiled swordfish steak.

> *3 tablespoons butter*
> *3 cups hot cooked long-grain rice*
> *Juice of 1 lemon*
> *3 eggs*
> *½ cup grated Asiago or Parmesan cheese*
> *Salt and freshly ground black pepper to taste*

1. In a saucepan, over medium heat, melt the butter. With a metal fork, stir in the rice, fluffing it up. Lower the heat.

2. In a bowl, beat the lemon juice, eggs, and cheese together. Blend this mixture thoroughly with the hot rice. Cook, stirring with a metal fork until the eggs are set. Taste for seasoning, adding salt and pepper, if needed.

Po Valley Rice Omelet

SERVES 3 OR 4

¾ cup cooked long-grain rice
½ cup grated Provolone
½ cup pepperoni cut into ¼-inch cubes
8 eggs
Salt and freshly ground black pepper to taste
3 tablespoons butter

1. In a bowl with a fork, blend the rice, Provolone, and pepperoni.

2. Beat the eggs in a bowl just long enough to mix the whites and yolks; then season lightly with salt and pepper.

3. In a large frying pan or omelet pan, over medium-high heat, melt the butter, being sure the entire bottom of the pan is coated. Pour the eggs into the pan and cook as for an omelet, lifting the cooked part of the eggs to allow the uncooked part to run under and shaking the pan when the bottom starts to set.

4. While the top is still moist, spoon the rice filling down the center of the omelet. Fold over and cook just long enough to heat the filling and melt the cheese. Or, if you prefer, cook individual omelets, using 2 or 3 eggs per person and divide the filling among the omelets.

Madras Spicy Rice

SERVES 4 TO 6

We were taught to make this simple but tasty Indian dish by the Nadhans, friends from Madras, who also taught us to make delicious vegetable and ground lamb cutlets. For this dish, they used the whole spices (obtainable in Indian and Middle Eastern grocery stores), but we find that the ground spices found in supermarkets also work fine. We like this rice with a simple lightly seasoned fish or chicken dish.

1½ cups long-grain rice
4 cups water
1 teaspoon salt
1 bay leaf
3 whole cloves
½ teaspoon ground cinnamon
1 teaspoon ground cardamom
3 tablespoons butter
2 teaspoons light brown sugar
1 teaspoon cumin seeds

1. In a large saucepan, combine the rice, water, salt, bay leaf, cloves, cinnamon, and cardamom. Stir well; then set aside.

2. In a small frying pan, over medium-low heat, melt the butter and stir in the sugar and cumin seeds, stirring until the sugar has caramelized, about 1½ minutes. Stir into the pan with the rice.

3. Bring the water in the rice pan to a boil, stir with a wooden fork, and cover. Lower the heat and simmer for 20 minutes, or until the rice is tender and the liquid has been absorbed. Let sit, covered, for 10 minutes. Taste for seasoning, adding salt and pepper, if needed. Remove the cloves, if you can find them, and the bay leaf. Fluff the rice up with a metal fork before serving.

Rice Pancakes

SERVES 4

These nifty little cakes are an excellent way to use leftover rice. They can be served as a breakfast cake with eggs or as a side dish for lunch or dinner.

3 cups cooked short- or medium-grain rice
Salt to taste
3 medium-sized eggs, beaten
5 slices bacon

1. Put the rice in a bowl and season it lightly with salt; then stir in the beaten eggs, blending well.

2. In a large frying pan, over medium heat, cook the bacon until it is crisp and golden brown. Drain on paper towels and save the bacon fat. Cool the bacon; then finely crumble half of it. (Save the remaining bacon to use for some other purpose or eat it in a bacon roll. Five slices were cooked, as their fat was needed to fry the rice pancakes.)

3. Blend the crumbled bacon with the rice-egg mixture. Heat the fat in the frying pan in which the bacon cooked over medium heat. Drop heaping tablespoons of the rice mixture into the hot fat, leaving a space between each spoonful. With a spatula, flatten each spoonful of rice into a flat cake. Fry until crisp and golden; turn over and repeat. Serve immediately.

Note: Serve with apricot jam thinned with some lemon juice.

Stir-Fried Pepper Rice

SERVES 4

3 tablespoons peanut oil or light vegetable oil
5 scallions, trimmed and cut into ½-inch-thick slices,
    using all but the last inch of the dark green part
1 medium-sized sweet green pepper, seeded, cored,
    and cut into pieces the same size as the scallions
1 garlic clove, minced
1 ¼-inch-thick slice boiled or other cooked ham, cut
    into ½- by 1-inch strips
4 cups cooked long-grain rice
3 tablespoons soy sauce
1 egg, beaten
Salt to taste
½ cup chopped fresh coriander or parsley leaves

In a wok or large deep frying pan, over medium heat, heat the peanut oil. Stir in the scallions, green pepper, garlic, and ham and cook for 2 to 3 minutes, stirring. Stir in the rice and soy sauce. Cook for 5 minutes, stirring, until heated through. Stir in the egg and cook just long enough to set the egg. Taste for seasoning, adding salt, if needed. Stir in the coriander and serve.

Small Fried Rice "Pies" with Gorgonzola Cheese Sauce

SERVES 6

3 cups cooked seasoned short- or medium-grain rice
1 whole egg and 1 egg yolk, beaten together in a large
* bowl*
Fine fresh unseasoned bread crumbs for dredging
6 tablespoons butter
1½ cups heavy cream
½ cup crumbled Gorgonzola cheese
½ cup grated Asiago or Parmesan cheese

1. Add the rice to the bowl with the egg and mix well with a fork.

2. Form 6 neat patties approximately ¾ inch thick. Dredge in the bread crumbs.

3. In a large frying pan, over medium-high heat, melt 3 tablespoons of the butter. Cook the "pies" on one side until they are golden brown. Add the remaining butter to the pan and cook the "pies" on the other side until golden brown. Transfer to a hot serving dish and keep warm while making the sauce.

4. In a saucepan, over low heat, heat the cream and cheeses, stirring, until the cheeses have melted and the sauce is reasonably smooth. Serve at the table to be spooned onto the "pies."

Note: The rice mixture can also be baked in well-buttered 3-inch tart tins. Sprinkle the top with the crumbs and dot with butter. Bake in a preheated 375-degree oven until they are golden on top. Run a knife around the inside edges of the tins to make it easier to turn them out.

Greek Pilaf

SERVES 4 TO 6

This is a dish we had on the Greek island of Lesbos. It was served with cold poached sea bass, which was dolloped with a nut sauce, probably made from walnuts.

> 4 tablespoons (½ stick) butter
> 1 cup long-grain rice
> ½ teaspoon salt
> 1 cup broken up (¼-inch pieces) vermicelli
> 2 medium-sized onions, minced
> 2¼ cups chicken broth
> ¼ cup dry white wine
> 1 tablespoon tomato purée
> Salt and freshly ground black pepper to taste

In a saucepan, over medium heat, melt the butter. Stir in the rice, coating it well with the butter. Stir in the salt, noodles, and onions. Combine the broth, wine, and tomato purée and add the mixture to the pan. Stir, bring to a boil, cover, lower the heat, and simmer for 20 minutes, or until the rice is tender and the liquid has been absorbed. Taste for seasoning before adding salt and pepper. Fluff up with a metal fork before serving.

Note: The Greeks place a towel over the pot, then replace the cover and let the rice sit for 5 minutes. This technique is supposed to make certain that all moisture is absorbed and each grain of rice is separate. But with U.S. converted rice, this is unnecessary.

Roman Pilaf

SERVES 4 TO 6

This dish, discovered in Rome, was not called a *risotto*. Why, we never discovered. The restaurant chef gave us the recipe, a confusing one that we believe we have clarified. The Italians cook rice differently, using a lot of water (usually after first soaking the rice) and a short cooking time. But, as we have stated, the recipes in this book are cooked with American rice, using our techniques.

In Rome, this was served to us with a delicious turkey breast cutlet, which was topped with ham and cheese—a dish created in that city.

> 6 tablespoons butter
> 2 medium-sized onions, chopped
> 2 garlic cloves, minced
> 1½ cups long-grain rice
> ½ teaspoon salt
> Freshly ground black pepper to taste
> ⅛ teaspoon ground cinnamon
> 3½ cups chicken broth
> ⅓ cup golden raisins, halved
> 2 tablespoons chopped toasted almonds (see Note)

1. In a saucepan, over medium heat, melt 3 tablespoons of the butter and stir in the onions, garlic, rice, salt, pepper, and cinnamon. Cook for 5 minutes, stirring, blending the rice with the onions, garlic, and butter.

2. Stir in the broth and bring to a boil. Stir with a wooden fork, cover, lower the heat, and simmer for 20 minutes, or until the rice is just tender, *al dente,* and the liquid has been mostly absorbed. (The Italians seem to like their rice a little more moist.) Taste for seasoning, adding salt and pepper, if needed.

3. With a metal fork stir the remaining butter (in small pieces), the raisins, and almonds into the rice, fluffing it up.

Note: To prepare unblanched almonds, drop them into boiling water. Allow to stand for a minute or two; then drain and slip off the skins. Dry thoroughly and place in a shallow pan in a preheated 300-degree oven, turning frequently to avoid burning. They should be golden, not brown.

Rice O'Brien

SERVES 4

5 tablespoons butter
6 whole scallions, trimmed and chopped
1 medium-sized sweet green pepper, seeded, cored,
    and chopped
3 cups cooked long-grain rice
3 tablespoons chopped pimientos
Salt and freshly ground black pepper to taste

In a frying pan, over medium heat, melt 2 tablespoons of the butter. Add the scallions and green pepper and cook for 3 minutes, or until they are just crisp-tender. Blend in the rice, pimientos, and remaining butter (in small pieces). Season with salt and pepper. Heat through, fluffing up the rice with a metal fork.

Turkish Pilaf Nuyam Yigit

SERVES 6

We've named this one after Turkish journalist, Nuyam Yigit, who introduced it to us in Istanbul, along with the best piece of swordfish we've ever tasted.

> *8 tablespoons (1 stick) butter*
> *2 medium-sized onions, chopped*
> *1½ cups long-grain brown rice*
> *3½ cups chicken broth*
> *Salt and freshly ground black pepper to taste*
> *⅓ cup golden raisins*
> *⅓ cup pignoli or broken up walnuts*

1. In a saucepan, over medium heat, melt 3 tablespoons of the butter. Stir in half of the onions and cook for 3 minutes, or until they are soft. Add the rice and cook, stirring, for 2 minutes. Stir in the broth and bring to a boil. Lower the heat, cover, and simmer for 35 minutes, or until the rice is *al dente*. Taste before adding salt and pepper.

2. Cook the raisins, remaining onions, and nuts separately, in 1 tablespoon of butter each, until the raisins are plump, the onions golden, and the nuts crisp. Stir them into the rice along with the remaining butter using a metal fork. Set over low heat for 1 or 2 minutes, fluff up with a metal fork, and serve.

Rice Pommarola

SERVES 4 TO 6

We like to serve this as an accompaniment to broiled sirloin steak.

1 cup tomato juice
2½ cups water
1 teaspoon salt
1½ cups long-grain rice
3 tablespoons butter
1 large ripe tomato, peeled, seeded, and chopped
3 fresh basil leaves, chopped

1. In a saucepan, bring the tomato juice and water to a boil. Stir in the salt and rice, cover, lower the heat, and simmer for 20 minutes, or until the rice is *al dente* and the liquid has been absorbed. With a metal fork, stir in the butter. Preheat the oven to 350 degrees.

2. With a metal fork combine and blend the rice, tomato, and basil. Lightly spoon into a well buttered casserole. Bake, uncovered, for 10 minutes.

Rijsttafel

The most popular dish of Holland isn't Dutch, it's Indonesian, originating in that former possession of Holland. We don't suppose that Dutch families are big on *rijsttafel,* the "rice table," but visitors are always taken to a restaurant that serves it. When we were in Amsterdam, we had it six times in one week (out of politeness we didn't say we'd had the menu), and each restaurant had a different version. It's sort of an Eastern smorgasbord. Thus, one can set a rice table limited only by the imagination. At one restaurant in Amsterdam, forty items were offered to be spread upon hot rice which is evenly layered on large individual warm plates (which become the base or "table") on which the sauced food and condiments are spooned or sprinkled.

Classically, a rice table is laid with at least twenty dishes, which are chosen to offer a variety, and at the same time, a taste symphony of different flavor textures, always with a *saté,* sort of an Oriental *shish kebab,* of pieces of broiled pork, beef, or chicken, a heavily-spiced fish dish, vegetables fried with rice, shrimp, and pieces of chicken, and, always a very hot curry. Small dishes of fried bananas, pineapple slices, grated fresh coconut, peanuts, pistachios, cashews, cucumbers, gherkins, and various chutneys are also offered.

To Americanize it, use little sausages, sliced hard-cooked eggs, toasted almonds, raisins, kumquats, and fried onion rings. Once you get into the mood, the little extra dishes will be fun to dream up.

Rijsttafel is definitely a party dish (increase the ingredients according to the number of guests), perfect for dramatically different entertaining. It hasn't yet caught on in the United States, but with rice's current popularity, *rijsttafel* may soon be with us.

We have two dishes we favor for the rice table, a shrimp curry and a saté of chicken. We also make our own chutney, so we'll offer all here.

First on the agenda for a rice table is the rice. Cook plenty as it not only is the flavor conveyor, but the tastemaker.

Rice for Rijsttafel

SERVES 8

7½ cups water
3 cups long-grain rice
1½ tablespoons salt
4 tablespoons (½ stick) butter

In a large saucepan, over high heat, bring the water to a boil, stir in the rice, salt, and butter. Cover, lower the heat, and simmer for 25 minutes, or until the rice is tender and the water has been absorbed. Fluff the rice up with a metal fork and keep it warm in a very low oven.

Curry of Shrimp for Rijsttafel

SERVES 8

2½ pounds medium-sized shrimp, shelled and
   deveined
6 tablespoons butter
5 large scallions (white part only), minced
1 bay leaf
1½ tablespoons curry powder, or to taste (See our
   curry powder, page 86.)
3 tablespoons all-purpose flour
3 cups clam juice, warmed
½ cup heavy cream
½ tablespoon dried dill
Salt to taste

1. Bring a large pot of water to a boil. Add the shrimp and cook for 2 minutes, or until they just turn pink. Do not overcook. Immediately remove from the water.

2. In a large saucepan, over medium heat, melt the butter and cook the scallions for 3 minutes. Do not brown. Add the bay leaf and stir in the curry powder and flour, blending well. Simmer, stirring, for 3 minutes. Gradually add the clam juice, stirring into a smooth, medium-thick sauce. Stir in the cream and dried dill. Simmer, stirring, for 3 minutes. Remove and discard the bay leaf. Taste for seasoning before adding salt.

3. Add the shrimp, heat for 1 minute, and serve immediately.

Saté of Chicken Breast for Rijsttafel

SERVES 8

2½ pounds skinned and boned chicken breasts, cut into 1-inch cubes
¼ cup olive oil
3 tablespoons minced scallions
¼ cup fresh lemon juice
3 garlic cloves, minced
½ teaspoon ground ginger
½ teaspoon ground cumin
⅛ teaspoon cayenne pepper
1 teaspoon salt
½ teaspoon freshly ground black pepper

1. In a large bowl, combine and mix well all ingredients. Marinate for 3 hours. Preheat the broiler.

2. Using skewers, spear 5 or 6 pieces (or more, depending

upon the length of the skewer used) of chicken. Broil the *satés* 5 inches from the heat, turning several times to brown evenly. Do not overcook. A total cooking time of 7 minutes should do it.

Fruit Chutney for Rijsttafel

MAKES ABOUT 3 CUPS

5 tablespoons butter
1 tablespoon curry powder
½ cup dark brown sugar
4 cups fresh fruit, such as apples, peaches, pineapple,
    pears, and dark cherries (canned fruits can be
    used, but fresh are better), peeled and cut into
    chunks and the cherries pitted

1. In a saucepan, over medium heat, melt the butter. Add the curry powder and sugar and blend well. Preheat the oven to 350 degrees.

2. Arrange the fruit chunks in a deep baking dish. Pour the curry-sugar mixture over the fruit and bake, uncovered, for 45 minutes. Stir once, halfway through the cooking period. This can be jarred and frozen.

Riso all'Onda

SERVES 4

This is what the Italians call "rippling rice," a *risotto* that bubbles just before it is served. Actually, this recipe, called *insaporito* (tasty), is a base for various *risotti*, but, as we are anchovy fans, we often serve it as is.

> 3 tablespoons olive oil
> 2 medium-sized onions, finely chopped
> 2 garlic cloves, minced
> 1 2-ounce can (or 2 cans, if you are an anchovy fan)
>   flat anchovy fillets, drained
> 1 cup long-grain rice
> 2 cups chicken broth, heated
> 3 tablespoons chopped broadleaf (Italian) parsley
>   leaves
> Salt and freshly ground black pepper to taste

1. In a saucepan, over medium heat, heat the oil and cook the onions and garlic for 5 minutes, or until they are soft. Do not brown. Add the anchovies and cook for 1 minute.
2. Stir in the rice and cook for 1 minute, or until it is well coated with the oil. Pour in 1 cup of the broth and simmer, uncovered, for 10 minutes, or until the rice has absorbed the liquid. Add the remaining broth, and again cook until the rice expands and absorbs nearly all of the broth. The rice should be moist when served and *al dente,* with a small amount of liquid still bubbling when it is taken off the heat. Taste before seasoning, as the anchovies and broth may have supplied enough seasoning. Stir in the parsley and spoon into a hot serving dish.

Note: Sometimes we can't resist stirring in a cup of hot cooked shrimp and using the rippling rice as a light supper.

Risotto in Cagnone

SERVES 4

2½ cups water
1 cup long-grain rice
1 teaspoon salt
8 tablespoons (1 stick) butter
2 garlic cloves, crushed and peeled
1 tablespoon chopped fresh sage, or 1 teaspoon leaf
*   sage, crumbled*
½ cup grated Asiago or Parmesan cheese

1. In a pot, bring the water to a boil. Stir in the rice and salt. Lower the heat, cover, and simmer for 20 minutes, or until the rice is tender and the liquid has been absorbed.

2. In a saucepan, over medium heat, melt the butter. Add the garlic and sage and cook until the garlic is golden brown. Remove and discard the garlic. Pour half of the butter-sage sauce over the rice and mix it in well with a metal fork, fluffing up the rice. Taste for seasoning, adding more salt, if needed. Transfer to a hot serving dish. Pour the remaining sauce over the rice. Sprinkle on 2 tablespoons of the cheese and serve the remaining cheese at the table.

Risotto alla Genovese

SERVES 4

Risotti bases are created in various ways. One we favor is this vegetable mixture, with main ingredients, such as Genoa salami in this recipe, added after the rice has cooked.

> 2 *tablespoons olive oil*
> 5 *tablespoons butter*
> 1 *small white onion, finely chopped*
> 1 *garlic clove, minced*
> 1 *small carrot, scraped and finely chopped*
> 1 *small celery stalk, scraped and finely chopped*
> 1 *cup long-grain rice*
> 2½ *cups chicken broth, heated*
> 3 *tablespoons tomato sauce (homemade or canned)*
> 4 *medium-sized fresh mushrooms, thinly sliced*
> 4 *½-inch-thick slices Italian Genoa salami, skin*
>   *removed, diced*
> ¼ *cup grated Parmesan cheese*
> *Salt and freshly ground black pepper to taste*

1. In a saucepan, over medium heat, heat the oil and 2 tablespoons of the butter. Add the onion, garlic, carrot, and celery and cook for 7 minutes, or until the vegetables are soft. Do not brown. Stir in the rice and cook, stirring, for 2 minutes. Pour in 1 cup of the broth and simmer, uncovered, for 10 minutes, stirring frequently with a wooden fork, until the liquid has been absorbed.

2. Add the tomato sauce, mushrooms, and the remaining broth. Cook, uncovered, stirring several times, for about 10 minutes, or until the rice is *al dente* and the liquid has been mostly absorbed. With a metal fork, stir in the salami and cheese, fluffing up the rice. Taste for seasoning before adding salt and pepper.

3. Top with the remaining butter (in small pieces). Remove from the heat and keep covered until the *risotto* is served.

Baked Green Risotto

SERVES 6

2 tablespoons butter
1 small onion, minced
1 garlic clove, minced
1 celery stalk, scraped and minced
2 whole eggs plus 1 egg yolk
1½ cups milk
½ cup finely chopped spinach leaves
½ cup finely chopped watercress leaves
1 cup finely chopped broadleaf (Italian) parsley leaves
3 cups al dente-cooked long-grain rice (cooked in
    chicken broth)
1 cup grated Gruyère or Fontina cheese
Salt and freshly ground black pepper to taste

1. Melt the butter in a saucepan, over medium heat. Add the onion, garlic, and celery and cook for 5 minutes, or until they are soft. Do not brown. Preheat the oven to 350 degrees.

2. Beat the eggs with the egg yolk in a large bowl. Add the milk, spinach, watercress, parsley, rice, cheese, salt, pepper, and the onion-garlic-celery mixture and blend well.

3. Spoon into a buttered baking dish and bake for 35 minutes, or until puffed, golden, and set.

Risotto Piemontese

SERVES 6

Risotti are all alike and yet they are all different—like the Italians themselves, a race of individuals, if there ever was one. The rices are alike because mostly they are cooked in the same, or almost the same, manner, but ingredients vary according to the region from which they originate.

Italians insist that a *risotto* must be stirred almost constantly, adding hot broth as the rice absorbs it, then adding more, and so on until the rice is tender. The rice, they also insist, must be moist, never dry.

We've run numerous tests and find that all this isn't necessary; techniques in various countries differ, mainly because of the variety and quality of the rices. Anyway, this is a favorite *risotto* of northern Italy—cooked our way. We served it to an Italian friend from Milan, and he pronounced it perfect. But maybe he was hungry.

> *1 3-inch-long piece beef or veal shank bone with*
> *   marrow*
> *3 tablespoons butter*
> *1 medium-sized onion, finely chopped*
> *½ teaspoon salt*
> *1½ cups long-grain rice*
> *¾ cup dry red wine*
> *2½ to 3 cups chicken broth*
> *Pinch of powdered saffron (less than ¼ teaspoon)*
> *Salt and freshly ground black pepper to taste*
> *½ cup grated Parmesan cheese*

1. Poach the shank in water until the marrow is barely cooked, pinkish, but can be easily pried out of the bone. Chop and reserve the marrow.

2. In a deep saucepan, over medium heat, melt the butter and stir in the onion and salt. Cook, stirring, for 3 minutes. Do not brown. Stir in the rice, coating it well with the butter. Stir in the marrow, the wine, 2½ cups of the broth, and the saffron. Stir well with a wooden fork, bring to a boil, lower the heat, cover, and simmer for 17 minutes, or until the rice is tender, but still slightly *al dente,* and the liquid has been mostly absorbed. If the liquid is absorbed before the rice is tender, add a small amount of hot broth so that the rice will be slightly moist while the cooking is finished. Taste for seasoning, adding salt and pepper, if needed.

3. With a metal fork, stir in the cheese, fluffing up the rice. Serve immediately.

Chicken Risotto

SERVES 6

5 fresh ripe plum tomatoes, peeled, seeded, and
    chopped
8 tablespoons (1 stick) butter
3 small shallots, finely chopped
½ chicken breast, skinned, boned, and cut into
    julienne
4 chicken livers, trimmed and each cut into 6 pieces
4 medium-sized fresh mushrooms, chopped
Salt and freshly ground black pepper to taste
1½ cups long-grain rice
3½ to 4 cups chicken broth
¾ cup grated Asiago or Parmesan cheese
3 tablespoons chopped broadleaf (Italian) parsley
    leaves

1. In a saucepan, over medium heat, cook the tomatoes until most of the liquid has evaporated, about 15 minutes.

2. In a frying pan, over medium heat, melt 3 tablespoons of the butter. Add the shallots and cook until soft, about 2 minutes. Do not brown. Add the chicken breast strips and cook, stirring occasionally, for about 5 minutes, or until the pieces start to become firm. Add the chicken livers and mushrooms and cook until the livers are brown on the outside and pink inside. Add the tomatoes and cook for 5 minutes. Season with salt and pepper.

3. In a deep saucepan, melt 3 tablespoons of the butter. Add the rice and cook, stirring, for 1 or 2 minutes to coat it well. Add 3½ cups of the broth, bring to a boil, and stir with a wooden fork. Lower the heat, cover, and simmer for 15 minutes, or until most of the liquid has been absorbed and the rice is tender but slightly *al dente*. If the liquid is absorbed before the rice is cooked, add a small amount of hot broth. The rice should be slightly moist.

4. With a metal fork, stir in the remaining butter, 4 tablespoons of the cheese, half of the chicken-liver-tomato sauce, and half of the parsley. Cook for 5 minutes over low heat, fluffing up the rice with a metal fork. Transfer to a hot serving dish and spoon the remaining sauce on top. Sprinkle with the remaining parsley and pass the remaining cheese at the table.

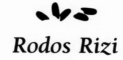

Rodos Rizi

SERVES 6

This was served to us with broiled fish on the Greek Island of Rhodes. It may seem odd to blend rice cooked in fish stock with cheese, but the Greeks believe that their feta cheese mates with everything. This combination proves their point.

> 6 tablespoons butter
> 1½ cups long-grain rice
> 3½ cups fish stock (page 51)
> 1½ cups crumbled feta cheese
> 5 fresh basil leaves, chopped
> Salt and freshly ground black pepper to taste

1. In a saucepan, over medium heat, melt 3 tablespoons of the butter. Stir in the rice and cook, stirring, for 2 minutes, or until the rice is well coated with butter. Stir in the stock and bring to a boil. Lower the heat, stir with a wooden fork, cover, and simmer for 20 minutes, or until the rice is tender and the liquid has been absorbed.

2. In another saucepan, melt the remaining butter. Add the cheese and stir just long enough to melt the cheese and blend well. With a metal fork, blend the butter-cheese mixture and basil with the rice, fluffing up the rice. Taste before adding salt and pepper.

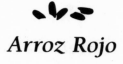

Arroz Rojo

SERVES 6

6 slices bacon
1 large onion, finely chopped
1 celery stalk, scraped and finely chopped
½ cup finely chopped sweet green pepper
1½ cups long-grain rice
⅛ teaspoon cayenne pepper, or to taste
1 teaspoon sugar
3 medium-sized ripe tomatoes, peeled, seeded, and
    chopped
¼ teaspoon dried thyme
2½ cups chicken broth
Salt to taste

1. In a deep frying pan over medium heat, cook the bacon until it is crisp and golden brown. Remove and drain on paper towels. Pour off all but 4 tablespoons of fat. (If the bacon hasn't rendered that amount, add butter.) Add the onion, celery, and green pepper and cook for 5 minutes, or until the onion is soft. Do not brown.

2. Stir in the rice and cook, stirring, for 2 minutes, or until the rice is well coated with fat. Stir in the cayenne pepper, sugar, tomatoes, thyme, and broth. Bring to a boil, lower the heat, stir with a wooden fork, cover, and simmer for 20 minutes, or until the rice is tender and the liquid has been absorbed. If the liquid has been absorbed before the rice is tender, add a small amount of hot broth (or water) and continue to cook. Taste for seasoning before adding salt.

3. Crumble the bacon and, just before serving, use a metal fork to mix half of it with the rice, fluffing up the rice. Sprinkle the remainder on top.

Deep-Fried Rice Rolls

SERVES 4 TO 6

3 cups cooked short- or medium-grain rice
1 cup grated Swiss cheese
½ teaspoon ground mace
Salt and freshly ground black pepper to taste
1 egg beaten (to be mixed with the rice)
1 egg (for dipping the rice rolls before frying)
Fine dry unseasoned bread crumbs for dredging
Fat for deep-frying

1. In a large bowl, combine and mix well the rice, cheese, mace, salt, pepper, and the beaten egg.

2. Form the rice mixture into rolls, 1 inch in diameter and 2 inches long.

3. Beat the remaining egg in a shallow bowl. Dredge the rice rolls in the bread crumbs, dip into the beaten egg, and dredge again in the bread crumbs. Place in the refrigerator for 3 hours to set, removing about 1 hour before cooking.

4. Heat the fat to 370 degrees, or until a 1-inch cube of bread dropped into it becomes golden in 40 to 50 seconds. Lower the rolls into the hot fat with a slotted spoon a few at a time and cook until golden. Drain on paper towels and serve immediately.

Croquettes

Prepare as above but shape the rice mixture into oval patties instead of rolls.

Tromso Scallion Rice

SERVES 4

3 tablespoons butter
8 scallions, trimmed and chopped
1 cup long-grain rice
2½ cups beef broth
Salt and freshly ground black pepper to taste
1 teaspoon Worcestershire sauce
3 tablespoons chopped parsley leaves

1. In a large saucepan, over medium heat, melt the butter. Add the scallions and cook for 3 minutes, stirring.
2. Add the rice to the saucepan and cook for 1 minute, stirring, until the rice is well coated with butter.
3. Pour in the broth and bring to a boil. Stir with a wooden fork, lower the heat, cover, and simmer for 20 minutes, or until the rice is tender and the liquid has been absorbed. Taste for seasoning, adding salt and pepper, if needed.
4. Stir in the Worcestershire and fluff up the rice with a metal fork. Sprinkle with the parsley before serving.

Soubise

SERVES 4 TO 6

This purée of onions and rice is a famous French dish, found nowhere but in France. At least we have never encountered it in French restaurants in the United States. This method was taught us by our mentor, Antoine Gilly, one of the four greatest living French chefs. We like to serve it with a nice rare filet of beef.

> 6 tablespoons sweet butter
> 1 pound Bermuda onions, thinly sliced
> 1 cup long-grain rice
> 3 cups chicken broth
> ⅛ teaspoon ground nutmeg
> Bouquet Garni made up of a sprig fresh parsley, 1 bay
>   leaf, 1 teaspoon of chopped fresh thyme (or ⅓ of
>   dried), and a few celery leaves tied in cheesecloth
> Salt and freshly ground black pepper to taste
> ½ cup heavy cream, beaten with 2 eggs

1. In a flameproof casserole, over medium-low heat, melt the butter and cook the onions for 15 minutes, or until they are soft. Do not brown. Preheat the oven to 350 degrees.

2. Stir in the rice and cook for 2 minutes, stirring. Then gradually stir in the broth. Add the nutmeg and the bouquet garni. Bring to a boil. Cover with aluminum foil and then a cover and bake for 25 minutes, or until the rice is tender and the liquid has been absorbed. Raise the oven temperature to 450 degrees.

3. Remove the rice from the oven and discard the *bouquet garni*. Put the rice and onions in a fine sieve, pushing them through into a bowl. Or use your blender to purée them. Taste before adding salt and pepper, as the broth may have supplied enough seasoning.

4. Stir in the cream-egg mixture.

5. Lightly butter a 1½-quart soufflé dish and pour in the mixture. Place in a pan of boiling water that comes halfway up the side of the dish. Bake, uncovered, for 20 minutes, or until the top is crusty and light brown and the *soubise* is set. Serve immediately.

Sesame Rice

SERVES 4 TO 6

Many of us haven't discovered the culinary value and unique flavor of sesame seeds. Native to Asia, and cultivated extensively in China and India, the seeds are the dried, hulled fruit of a tropical annual herb. Creamy white and oval-shaped, the flavor is delicate, somewhat like that of toasted almonds. The seeds are a natural rice plate-mate. Here's a dish with an Asian touch. We like to serve this with a poached chicken with velouté sauce.

3½ cups water
1½ teaspoons salt
1½ cups long-grain rice
2 medium-sized onions, chopped
4 tablespoons sesame seeds
½ teaspoon ground cumin
5 tablespoons butter
1 tablespoon mustard seeds, preferably black

1. In a deep saucepan, bring the water to a boil. Stir in the salt, rice, and onions. Lower the heat, cover, and simmer for 20 minutes, or until the rice is tender and most of the liquid has been absorbed. The rice should still be moist. Remove from the heat and reserve.

2. In another saucepan, over medium heat, shaking the pan, heat the sesame seeds until they are golden and stop popping and sputtering. With a metal fork, stir the sesame seeds and cumin into the rice.

3. Over medium heat, in the pan the sesame seeds were toasted in, melt 2 tablespoons of the butter. Add the mustard seeds, and cook for a minute or two, or until they start to crackle. Stir the seeds, the butter they cooked in, and the remaining butter into the rice. Heat the rice, fluffing it up with a metal fork and serve.

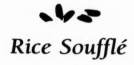

Rice Soufflé

SERVES 4

2 tablespoons butter
3 scallions, trimmed and finely chopped
1 tablespoon all-purpose flour
¾ cup milk
1½ cups cooked short- or medium-grain rice
½ cup chopped parsley leaves
½ cup grated Gruyère cheese
½ cup grated Parmesan cheese
3 egg yolks, beaten
3 egg whites, stiffly beaten
Salt and freshly ground black pepper to taste

1. Preheat the oven to 350 degrees.
2. In a saucepan, over medium heat, melt the butter. Add the scallions and cook for 2 minutes. Do not brown. Stir in the flour, blending well. Gradually add the milk, stirring into a smooth sauce.
3. Remove from the heat and stir in the rice, parsley, cheeses, and egg yolks. Fold in the egg whites and season with salt and pepper.
4. Pour into a buttered 1½-quart soufflé dish and bake for 30 minutes, or until set. A knife blade inserted just off center will come out clean.

Rice Stuffings and Dressings

Rice is a stuffing's star, second to none in this role that enhances other food, be it just a festive plate-mate, dressing up a serving of sliced turkey, chicken, or fish, or a major part of a holiday or special-occasion meal, stuffing a bird or a leg of lamb. (We show rice in action in this regard on pages 117, 128, 152, 166, and 167.)

If used as a dressing, that is as an accompaniment, long-grain rice can be used and it should be cooked the full length of time. If, however, it is being used to stuff poultry or meats, short- or medium-grain rice should be used, because they hold together better than long grain.

Also, the stuffing rice should be cooked *al dente,* less than the normal time, as the rice will have further cooking. Two further points: Use less liquid in this shorter cooking. For example, rather than 2½ cups, use 2 cups and cook for 15 minutes rather than 20 minutes. If the liquid hasn't been absorbed in that length of time, drain the rice.

Rice starts right off better than bread as a spectacular stuffer. Run a simple test: Cook some rice, place it hot on a plate with a dab of butter; then taste it. Then cut some bread into cubes and repeat the process. Without the addition of a single other ingredient, the flavor of rice is superb. Bread needs all the help it can get. Rice responds with stuffing mixtures by magnifying and enhancing other flavors.

Besides, it's innovative, and will delight many of your dinner guests. Rice, as we hope this book exemplifies, is full of surprises, as you will see on the following pages.

Almond-Rice Dressing

SERVES 6

We like to serve this with *goujonettes* (slender strips) of sole sautéed in butter.

> 3 tablespoons butter
> 2 medium-sized onions, finely chopped
> 2 celery stalks, scraped and finely chopped
> 1 cup finely chopped celery leaves
> 1 cup long-grain rice
> ¾ teaspoon Bell's seasoning
> 2 cups boiling chicken broth
> 8 medium-sized fresh mushrooms, sliced
> Salt and freshly ground black pepper to taste
> ½ cup chopped toasted almonds

1. In a saucepan, over medium heat, melt the butter. Add the onions, celery, celery leaves, rice, and Bell's seasoning, blending well. Cook for 5 minutes, stirring. Preheat the oven to 350 degrees.

2. Transfer the rice mixture to a buttered shallow 2-quart casserole. Stir in the boiling broth. Cover and bake for 10 minutes. Remove from the oven and stir in the mushrooms. Return to the oven for 10 minutes, or until the rice is tender and the liquid has been absorbed. Taste for seasoning, adding salt and pepper, if needed. The broth may have supplied enough.

3. Sprinkle with the almonds before serving as an accompaniment.

Bacon-Chestnut Stuffing

MAKES APPROXIMATELY 5 CUPS

We favor this simple stuffing, with surprisingly excellent flavor, for a small turkey that we stuff, truss, butter well, and roast in foil. We roast an 8- to 12-pound bird for 3 to 4 hours, the first hour in a preheated 350-degree oven; the remaining time at 300 degrees. A meat thermometer in the thigh should register 180 degrees when the bird is done.

> *6 slices bacon, chopped*
> *3 medium-sized onions, finely chopped*
> *3 cups al dente-cooked short- or medium-grain rice*
> *1 pound chestnuts, peeled, cooked, and chopped*
> *1 teaspoon salt*
> *½ teaspoon ground sage*
> *½ cup chicken broth*

1. In a deep saucepan, over medium heat, cook the bacon and onions for 5 minutes. With a metal fork stir in the rice, chestnuts, salt, sage, and chicken broth, tossing as you mix. Taste for seasoning, adding salt and pepper, if needed.

2. Loosely stuff the bird. The rice will expand as the bird cooks. Any extra stuffing can be wrapped in foil and cooked with the bird.

Brown Rice Stuffing

MAKES APPROXIMATELY 4½ CUPS

We use this to stuff a capon, but you can stuff anything from a chicken to a goose with this combination.

> *5 tablespoons butter*
> *1 cup medium-grain brown rice*
> *2 cups chicken broth*
> *1 medium-sized onion, chopped*
> *3 tender (inside) celery stalks, scraped and chopped*
> *1 cup chopped cooked chestnuts*
> *½ teaspoon leaf sage, crumbled*
> *½ teaspoon dried thyme*
> *1 teaspoon salt*
> *¼ teaspoon freshly ground black pepper*
> *½ cup heavy cream*

1. In a saucepan, over medium heat, melt 2 tablespoons of the butter. Stir in the rice and cook, stirring, for 1 minute. Pour in the broth, stir with a wooden fork, cover, lower the heat, and simmer for 35 minutes, or until the rice is *al dente*.

2. In a frying pan, over medium heat, melt the remaining 3 tablespoons of butter. Stir in the onion and celery and cook until they are just crisp-tender. Stir in the chestnuts, sage, thyme, salt, and pepper. Add the cooked rice and cream and mix thoroughly. Taste for seasoning, adding salt and pepper, if needed.

3. Loosely stuff the bird. The rice will expand as the bird cooks. Any extra stuffing can be wrapped in foil and cooked with the bird.

Chili-Rice Stuffing

MAKES APPROXIMATELY 4½ CUPS
(AMPLE FOR 4 GAME HENS)

We find this gives Cornish game hens a dash of personality.

4 tablespoons (½ stick) butter
2 onions, finely chopped
1 garlic clove, minced
1 cup Wild Pecan Rice
2 cups chicken broth
1½ cups chopped cooked ham
2 tablespoons chopped broadleaf (Italian) parsley
*   leaves*
2 teaspoons chili powder, or to taste
½ teaspoon ground cumin
1 egg, beaten
¼ cup melted butter
Salt and freshly ground black pepper to taste

1. In a saucepan, over medium heat, melt the butter. Add the onions, garlic, and rice and cook for 4 minutes, stirring. Pour in the chicken broth and bring to a boil. Stir with a wooden fork, cover, lower the heat, and simmer for 15 minutes. The rice should be *al dente*.
2. In a bowl, combine and blend well the rice mixture with the ham, parsley, chili powder, cumin, egg, and butter. Taste for seasoning before adding salt or pepper, as the broth and ham may have supplied enough.
3. Loosely stuff the birds; the rice will expand as the birds cook. Any extra stuffing can be wrapped in foil and cooked with the birds.

Italian Po Valley
Rice Stuffing for Poultry

MAKES ENOUGH TO STUFF A 5- TO 6-POUND BIRD

We discovered this in northern Italy, the same area where Thomas Jefferson risked his life by stealing a handful of rice. Rice is used in this region instead of pasta and the innovations are all unique. This stuffing is a good example, giving poultry a new taste dimension.

> 2 Italian sweet sausages, casings removed
> 3 tablespoons butter
> 2 medium-sized onions, finely chopped
> 3 cups al dente-cooked short- or medium-grain rice
>   (cooked in chicken broth)
> ¼ cup grated Asiago or Parmesan cheese
> 2 eggs, beaten
> ¼ teaspoon dried oregano
> ⅛ teaspoon dried basil
> Salt and freshly ground black pepper to taste
> Soft butter to rub on the outside of the bird

In a frying pan, over medium heat, cook the sausage meat for 10 minutes, breaking the meat up with a fork. Drain off any fat. Transfer the sausage to a large bowl. Add the butter to the frying pan and cook the onions until they are soft. Do not brown. Add the onions to the sausage along with all other ingredients. Mix well, but lightly, with a fork. Loosely spoon the stuffing into the cavity of the bird. Do not pack it in. Truss the bird, rub with soft butter, and sprinkle with salt and pepper. Roast by any method you prefer.

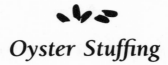

Oyster Stuffing

MAKES APPROXIMATELY 5 CUPS

We use this to stuff a large chicken, a capon, or a small turkey.
For larger birds just increase the amount of rice.

> *4 tablespoons (½ stick) butter*
> *2 medium-sized onions, chopped*
> *3 celery stalks, scraped and chopped*
> *Salt and freshly ground black pepper*
> *1 teaspoon Bell's seasoning*
> *3 cups al dente-cooked short- or medium-grain rice*
> *2 tablespoons chopped broadleaf (Italian) parsley*
> *   leaves*
> *¼ cup grated Asiago or Parmesan cheese*
> *2 beaten eggs*
> *1 pint fresh oysters with their liquor*

1. In a deep saucepan, over medium heat, melt the butter.
Add the onions and celery and cook for 4 minutes, or until
they are crisp-tender. Remove from the heat and season with 1
teaspoon salt, ½ teaspoon pepper, and Bell's seasoning.

2. In a large bowl, combine and blend well the onions and
celery with the rice, parsley, cheese, and eggs. Taste for seasoning, adding salt and pepper, if needed.

3. Carefully mix in the oysters with their liquor.

4. Loosely stuff the bird. The rice will expand as the bird
cooks. Any extra stuffing can be wrapped in foil and cooked
with the bird.

Piquant Turnip Stuffing

MAKES APPROXIMATELY 4 CUPS

This is one we created for squab, our all-time favorite bird. This will handle six of those delicious, butter-tender baby pigeons. The turnips offer a delightfully different taste change.

> 5 tablespoons butter
> 3 small turnips, peeled and finely chopped
> 1 cup finely chopped celery hearts with leaves
> 4 shallots, minced
> 1 teaspoon salt
> ⅛ teaspoon ground allspice
> ⅛ teaspoon ground nutmeg
> 3 cups al dente-cooked short- or medium-grain rice
> Salt and freshly ground black pepper to taste

1. In a deep saucepan, over medium heat, melt the butter and cook the turnips, celery, and shallots, for 5 minutes. Stir in the remaining ingredients, blending lightly with a metal fork. Cook for 5 minutes. Taste for seasoning, adding salt and pepper, if needed.

2. Loosely stuff the squabs, game hens, or whatever birds you prefer (or can obtain). The rice will expand as the bird cooks. Any extra stuffing can be wrapped in foil and cooked with the birds.

Wild Pecan Rice Stuffing with Pecans

MAKES APPROXIMATELY 7½ CUPS

This will stuff a 15-pound turkey.

> 4 tablespoons (½ stick) butter
> 2 medium-sized onions, chopped
> 2 celery stalks, scraped and chopped
> 2 tablespoons broadleaf (Italian) parsley leaves
> 1 turkey liver, chopped
> Salt and freshly ground black pepper
> 1 teaspoon dried thyme
> 1 teaspoon leaf sage, crumbled
> 6 cups al dente-cooked Wild Pecan Rice
> 2 eggs, beaten
> ½ cup grated Asiago or Parmesan cheese
> 1 cup chopped pecans
> ¼ cup brandy

1. In a saucepan, over medium heat, melt the butter. Add the onions and celery and cook for 5 minutes. Add the parsley, liver, 1 teaspoon salt, ½ teaspoon pepper, thyme, and sage, blending well. Cook for 1 minute.

2. In a large bowl, combine and blend well with a metal fork, the rice, eggs, cheese, pecans, and brandy. Blend in the onions, celery, parsley, and liver. Taste for seasoning, adding salt and pepper, if needed.

3. Loosely stuff the bird. The rice will expand as it cooks. Any extra stuffing can be wrapped in foil and cooked with the bird.

Wild Rice as a Garnish or Stuffing for Game

SERVES 6 TO 8

Wild rice (as we've pointed out, is not rice at all) is very expensive, but it also is impressive when served as a garnish or stuffing for game, pheasant, quail, partridge, or duck. Game itself is expensive, not an everyday meal, so pairing it with wild rice is most appropriate. Here's a garnish with a French touch, in what is called a *mirepoix*.

> *3 quarts water*
> *1 tablespoon salt*
> *2 cups wild rice*
> *5 tablespoons butter*
> *4 large scallions (white part only), minced*
> *3 small carrots, scraped and minced*
> *1 large celery stalk, scraped and minced*
> *½ teaspoon dried marjoram*
> *1 bay leaf*
> *3 cups beef broth*

1. Bring the water to a boil in a large pot. Stir in the salt and rice, lower the heat, and simmer for 10 minutes. Drain. Preheat the oven to 325 degrees.

2. In a flameproof casserole, over medium heat, melt the butter and cook the scallions, carrots, and celery for 5 minutes. Stir in the drained rice and simmer, stirring, until the rice has absorbed the butter.

3. Stir in the marjoram, bay leaf, and beef broth. Bring to a simmer. Cover and bake for 1 hour, or until the rice is tender and the liquid has been absorbed. If the rice is cooked before the liquid has been absorbed, quickly cook off the excess liquid on top of the stove, being careful not to burn the rice. If the liquid has cooked off before the rice is tender, add a small amount of hot broth or water and continue to cook. Be careful: The rice should be quite dry and the grains separate. Do not overcook or it will be mushy. Discard the bay leaf.

Note: If you are using this for stuffing, cook the rice in 2½ cups of beef broth instead of 3 and cook for 45 minutes instead of 1 hour. The rice should be slightly underdone.

Rice Texakana

SERVES 4 TO 6

2¼ cups water
1 teaspoon salt
1 tablespoon butter
1 cup long-grain rice
½ cup sour cream
2 teaspoons chili powder
1 cup grated Monterey Jack cheese

1. In a saucepan, over medium heat, combine the water, salt, butter, and rice and bring to a boil. Stir with a wooden fork, lower the heat, cover, and simmer for 20 minutes, or until the rice is tender, but still a little *al dente,* and the liquid has been absorbed. Preheat the oven to 350 degrees.

2. Combine the rice with the sour cream, chili powder, and half of the cheese. Blend with a metal fork and spoon into a buttered, shallow baking dish.

3. Sprinkle with the remaining cheese and bake for 20 minutes.

Swiss Baked Rice
with Cheese and Tomatoes

SERVES 4 TO 6

We had this in a restaurant by the lake in Geneva and wheedled the chef out of his recipe. As he was Italian, it wasn't too difficult; if he had been French, it would have been impossible.

4 tablespoons (½ stick) butter
4 small white onions, minced
1 garlic clove, minced
2 cups long-grain rice
2 large ripe tomatoes, peeled, seeded, and chopped
1 teaspoon salt
¼ teaspoon dried thyme
1 small bay leaf
3½ cups chicken broth
½ cup grated Swiss cheese
¼ cup grated Parmesan cheese
Salt and freshly ground black pepper to taste

1. In a flameproof casserole, over medium heat, melt the butter. Add the onions and garlic and cook for 5 minutes, or until they are soft. Do not brown. Stir in the rice, blending it well with the onion, garlic, and butter. Stir in the tomatoes, salt, thyme, and bay leaf, blending well. Preheat the oven to 350 degrees.

2. Stir in the chicken broth and bring to a boil. Cover and bake for 25 minutes, or until the rice is tender and the liquid has been absorbed. If the liquid is absorbed before the rice is tender, add a small amount of hot broth and continue to cook. If the rice is tender but the liquid has not been absorbed, remove the cover and cook on top of the stove until the liquid evaporates. Watch carefully and do not burn the rice. Taste for seasoning, adding salt and pepper, if needed.

3. Remove from the oven, discard the bay leaf, and, with a metal fork, stir in the cheeses. Return to the oven for 5 minutes, or until the cheeses have melted.

Tomato Rice with Mornay Sauce

SERVES 4 TO 6

> 6 slices lean bacon, cooked until golden brown and
>   crisp, saving the fat; drain, cool, and crumble the
>   bacon
> 1 medium-sized onion, finely chopped
> 1 1-pound can imported Italian plum tomatoes with
>   their liquid (Chop the tomatoes.)
> 1½ cups chicken broth
> 1 teaspoon sugar
> 1 cup long-grain rice
> Salt and freshly ground black pepper to taste
> Mornay Sauce (see below)

1. In a saucepan, over medium heat, heat 2 tablespoons of the bacon fat. (If the bacon was too lean to yield this amount of fat, add some butter.) Add the onion and cook for 3 minutes, or until it is soft. Do not brown. Add the tomatoes with their liquid, the broth, and sugar. Simmer for 2 minutes.

2. Stir in the rice and bring to a boil. Lower the heat, stir with a wooden fork, cover, and simmer for 20 minutes, or until the rice is tender and the liquid has been absorbed. If the liquid is absorbed before the rice is tender, add a small amount of hot broth or water and continue to cook until the rice is cooked.

Taste for seasoning, adding salt and pepper, if needed. Preheat the broiler.

3. Transfer to a buttered, shallow casserole. Spoon on the Mornay Sauce and place under the broiler until the top is golden. Sprinkle with the crumbled bacon and serve immediately.

Mornay Sauce

MAKES APPROXIMATELY 1½ CUPS

1½ tablespoons butter
1½ tablespoons all-purpose flour
1 cup milk, heated
⅛ teaspoon cayenne pepper
½ cup grated Gruyère or Cheddar cheese
¼ cup grated Asiago or Parmesan cheese
Salt to taste

1. In a saucepan, over medium heat, melt the butter. Add the flour and stir into a smooth paste. Gradually stir in the milk and cook, stirring constantly into a smooth sauce.

2. Stir in the cayenne and the cheeses and cook just long enough to melt the cheese, making a smooth sauce. Taste for seasoning, adding salt, if needed.

Aromatic Stuffed Grape Vine Leaves

MAKES ENOUGH TO STUFF APPROXIMATELY 34 LEAVES

These little morsels can be served hot or cold. The Greeks like to offer them cold as an appetizer.

> *40 or more, vine leaves, fresh, or preserved (Vine leaves are available in 1-pound jars containing 40 to 50 leaves.)*
> *4 tablespoons olive oil*
> *2 tablespoons butter*
> *1 large onion, finely chopped*
> *½ cup long-grain rice*
> *1¼ cups water*
> *2 tablespoons* pignoli *or chopped walnuts*
> *2 tablespoons currants*
> *2 teaspoons ground allspice*
> *¼ teaspoon ground cinnamon*
> *1 teaspoon chopped fresh mint leaves*
> *Salt and freshly ground black pepper to taste*
> *1 cup chicken broth*
> *Juice of 1 lemon*
> *1 cup plain yogurt*
> *Lemon wedges*

1. If fresh leaves are used, bring a large pot of water to a boil. Drop the leaves in, a few at a time, and blanch them for 5 minutes. Carefully remove with a slotted spoon or skimmer and plunge into cold water. Remove and drain on paper towels. If preserved leaves are used, rinse well, but carefully, in cold water and drain. Cut off the stems.

2. In a saucepan, over medium heat, heat 3 tablespoons of the oil and 1 of the butter and cook the onion for 3 minutes, or until it is soft. Do not brown. Add the rice and cook, stirring, for 2 minutes. Add the water and bring to a boil. Cover, lower the heat, and simmer for 15 minutes, or until the rice is *al dente* and the liquid has been absorbed. Transfer to a mixing bowl.

3. Heat the remaining oil and butter in a frying pan and cook the *pignoli* until they are golden. Do not brown. Remove with a slotted spoon and add to the rice bowl. Add the currants to the frying pan and cook for 1 minute, or until they are slightly plumped. Transfer to the rice bowl. Add the allspice, cinnamon, mint, salt and pepper to the bowl and mix well with a metal fork.

4. Line the bottom of a flameproof casserole with 6 leaves. Arrange the remaining leaves, a few at a time, on a flat surface, rough side down. Place a heaping teaspoonful (or more, depending on the size of the leaf) on the stem side of the leaf. Fold the sides of the leaf over the filling, then roll, fairly tightly, from the stem side to the end of the leaf, without breaking the leaf. Do not roll too tightly as the rice may expand.

5. Arrange the stuffed leaves, seam side down, side by side in snug layers in the leaf-lined casserole.

6. Pour on the broth and lemon juice. Lay a plate on top of the leaves, cover the pot with aluminum foil, and then with its cover. Bring to a boil, lower the heat, and simmer for 45 minutes. Remove the cover and let the rolls cool. Lift them out with a slotted spoon onto a serving dish and serve with the yogurt and/or lemon wedges.

Rice Timbales

SERVES 4

Under the section on Rice Molds (page 16), we've pointed out how interesting and decorative offerings of rice can dress up a meal. Here's one, made slightly spicy with watercress, that we like to serve with a piece of fish or a *scallopine* of chicken or veal.

> *6 medium-sized fresh mushrooms*
> *2½ cups beef broth*
> *2 tablespoons butter*
> *1 medium-sized onion, finely chopped*
> *1 cup short- or medium-grain rice*
> *Salt and freshly ground black pepper to taste*
> *½ cup finely chopped watercress*
> *2 tablespoons melted butter*

1. In a saucepan, combine the mushrooms and beef broth. Bring to a boil, lower the heat, and simmer for 5 minutes. With a slotted spoon remove the mushrooms, cool, and finely chop them. Reserve the broth.

2. In another saucepan, over medium heat, melt the 2 tablespoons of butter. Stir in the onion and rice and pour in the broth in which the mushrooms cooked. Bring to a boil, stir with a wooden fork, cover, lower the heat, and simmer for 20 minutes, or until the rice is tender and the liquid has been absorbed. Taste for seasoning, adding salt and pepper, if needed. The broth may have supplied enough.

3. Combine and blend well the rice, mushrooms, watercress, and melted butter. Butter four 5-ounce timbale molds. Fill with the rice mixture, pressing it into the molds. You'll be

tempted to unmold these on a large platter, centered with the entrée. Don't do it. The molds can break up when served. Unmold them on the individual plates.

Rice Waffles

SERVES 4 TO 6

These are excellent served with creamed chicken, tuna, or other sauced foods.

> 2 cups sifted all-purpose flour (sifted before
>   measuring)
> 1 tablespoon baking powder
> ½ teaspoon salt
> 3 egg yolks, beaten
> 1¾ cup milk
> 4 tablespoons butter, melted
> ¾ cup cooked short- or medium-grain rice
> 3 egg whites, stiffly beaten

1. Sift the flour, baking powder, and salt into a large bowl. Combine the egg yolks, milk, melted butter, and rice in another bowl. Add the egg yolk-milk-rice mixture to the flour bowl and mix thoroughly. Fold in the egg whites.

2. Pour a little batter into a hot, greased waffle iron and cook according to the manufacturer's directions, usually about 4 minutes.

9

RICE
SALADS

Time was when salads, especially potato salads, were considered suitable only as picnic fare. Today salads have become so popular and so exotic that they're running away with many menus. Now some cookbooks have made salads so complicated that a number of the recipes may take over an hour to prepare. This is nonsense. One of the virtues salads always had (and should have) is their simplicity.

In this regard, rice has always ruled supreme throughout the world. Rice salads are also light, easily digested, attractive to the eye, and, as some devotees claim, seductive. They come cold or hot with a "dress up" or presentation advantage that few other foods have. We doubt that any other salad could so successfully combine all of these assets as do Dilled Shrimp and Rice Salad, Tomato-Stuffed Eggplant Rice Salad, or a Rice-Crab Meat Salad.

For all rice salads, be sure to use parboiled or converted rice. Rice grains for salads should be firm, fluffy, and separate, never sticky or gummy. Parboiled or converted rice ensures perfect salad rice every time.

Rice and Beet Salad

SERVES 6

3 cups cooked long-grain rice, cooled
2 cups cubed cooked beets
1 7-ounce can tuna, drained and broken into bite-
    sized pieces
2 scallions (white part only), minced
1 cup cubed heart of fennel
12 black "Greek" olives, pitted and halved
5 tablespoons olive oil
1 tablespoon red or white wine vinegar
½ cup mayonnaise
Salt and freshly ground black pepper to taste
Boston lettuce leaves
1 hard-cooked egg, sliced
6 anchovy fillets
6 cooked asparagus spears

1. In a large bowl, combine the rice, beets, tuna, scallions, fennel, and olives. Combine the olive oil, wine vinegar, mayonnaise, salt, and pepper and add to the rice bowl. Toss with two metal forks. Taste for seasoning, adding salt and pepper, if needed.

2. Line a salad bowl with the lettuce leaves. Spoon in the salad. Garnish with the egg slices in the center, like the hub of a wheel and the asparagus and anchovy fillets like the spokes.

Rice-Crab Meat Salad

SERVES 6

1½ cups cooked long-grain rice, cooled
1 pound fresh cooked crab meat, or 2 7½-ounce cans,
    picked over to remove any cartilage or shell
1 4-ounce can water chestnuts, drained and sliced
2 small tender (inside) celery stalks, scraped and
    chopped
2 whole scallions, trimmed and thinly sliced
¼ cup mayonnaise
¼ cup sour cream
3 tablespoons fresh lemon juice
1 teaspoon salt
¼ teaspoon cayenne pepper
6 ¾-inch-thick slices ripe firm large tomatoes (use just
    the center portion of the tomatoes), seeds scooped
    out
6 lettuce leaves
3 tablespoons chopped fresh dill
2 hard-cooked eggs, yolks and whites sieved separately

1. In a large bowl, combine the rice, crab meat, water chestnuts, celery, scallions.

2. Combine the mayonnaise, sour cream, lemon juice, salt, and cayenne and blend well. Fold two thirds of the salad dressing into the salad, mixing well but gently. Taste and add more dressing, if desired.

3. Lay a slice of tomato on a lettuce leaf on individual plates, or on one large flat serving dish. Spoon on the salad, dividing it equally. Sprinkle on the dill, the sieved egg white, and then the sieved egg yolk. Serve any remaining salad dressing at the table.

Rice and Ham Salad

SERVES 6

3 cups cooked long-grain rice, cooled
2 cups cubed cooked ham
2 hard-boiled eggs, coarsely chopped
½ cup black "Greek" olives, halved
4 tender (inside) celery stalks, scraped and cut into
    small dice
3 scallions (white part only), thinly sliced
¾ cup mayonnaise, blended with 3 tablespoons lemon
    juice, 2 tablespoons honey, and salt and pepper to
    taste
6 large Boston lettuce leaves
3 ripe tomatoes, peeled and each cut into 6 wedges

1. In a large bowl, combine and mix well with a metal fork the rice, ham, eggs, olives, celery, and scallions.

2. Spoon half of the mayonnaise onto the rice mixture and mix with a metal fork. Taste and add more mayonnaise, salt, and pepper, if needed.

3. Spoon the salad onto the lettuce leaves on one large serving dish or individual plates. Garnish with the tomato wedges.

Mussel and Rice Salad

SERVES 4

30 mussels, scrubbed and beards removed
2 shallots, chopped
Leaves from 2 celery stalks
½ bay leaf
4 tablespoons (½ stick) butter
½ cup water
1½ cups dry white wine
3 tablespoons white wine vinegar
¾ cup olive oil
½ teaspoon each fresh tarragon, fresh chives, fresh
    basil, and fresh thyme, or use one-third that
    amount of dried herbs
Salt and freshly ground black pepper to taste
¾ cup long-grain rice
Salt to taste
3 tablespoons chopped broadleaf (Italian) parsley
    leaves

1. In a large saucepan, combine the mussels, shallots, celery leaves, bay leaf, butter, water, and wine. Bring to a boil over high heat. Cover, and cook for 2 minutes, stir and cook for another 2 minutes, or until the mussels open. Discard any that do not. Drain the mussels, saving the liquid they cooked in. Reduce the liquid to ¾ cup over high heat. Strain through a double thickness of cheesecloth.

2. Combine the wine vinegar, olive oil, tarragon, chives, basil, thyme, salt, and pepper and blend well.

3. Shell the mussels and set them aside in a bowl. Mix with ⅓ cup of the salad dressing. Set aside.

4. In a saucepan, heat to a boil ¾ cup of water with the ¾ cup of reduced liquid the mussels cooked in. Add the rice and

bring to a boil. Lower the heat, stir with a wooden fork, cover, and cook for 15 minutes, or until the rice is tender and the liquid has been absorbed. Taste for seasoning, adding salt, if needed. Cool.

5. Mix the rice with one third of the salad dressing. Taste and add more dressing, if desired.

6. Arrange the mussels in the center of a serving bowl. Surround them with the rice. Sprinkle the rice with parsley. Pass the remaining dressing at the table.

Cold Chicken Salad

SERVES 6 TO 8

3 cups cooked long-grain rice, cooled
3 cups cubed cooked chicken breast
1 large firm ripe tomato, peeled, seeded, and diced
1 cup scraped and diced celery heart
½ cup diced pimiento
2 whole scallions, trimmed and diced
1 cup mayonnaise (homemade or a good commercial
*   one), blended with 2 tablespoons lemon juice and*
*   ¼ teaspoon ground cumin*
Salt and freshly ground black pepper to taste
6 to 8 Boston lettuce leaves

1. In a large bowl, combine and blend well the rice and chicken, using two metal forks. Add the tomato, celery, pimiento, scallions, and two thirds of the mayonnaise, mixing well but carefully. Season with salt and pepper. Taste, adding more mayonnaise, if desired.

2. Spoon onto the lettuce leaves on individual plates and serve, passing any remaining mayonnaise at the table.

Hot Rice Salad

SERVES 4 TO 6

4 slices lean bacon
4 cups cooked warm long-grain rice
3 tender (inside) celery stalks, scraped and chopped
8 to 10 large black "Greek" olives, pitted and halved
1 dill pickle, chopped
¼ cup hot chicken broth
2 tablespoons dry white wine
½ cup Vinaigrette Sauce (see String Beans Vinaigrette,
    page 311)
Salt and freshly ground black pepper to taste
Boston or Bibb lettuce leaves
1 teaspoon chopped fresh chives
1 tablespoon chopped parsley

1. Cook the bacon until it is crisp and golden; then drain and cool. Crumble the bacon and reserve it.

2. The rice should be warm and all the other ingredients at room temperature. Combine the rice, celery, olives, pickle, broth, wine, and half of the Vinaigrette Sauce. Blend with a metal fork, fluffing as you mix. Taste and add more sauce, if desired, and salt and pepper.

3. Spoon the salad into a lettuce-lined salad bowl. Sprinkle with the bacon, chives, and parsley. Serve while still tepid. Pass any remaining sauce at the table.

Rice Rex

SERVES 6 TO 8

This superb summer salad could be the king of the rice salads, combining cold meat, seafood, and vegetables. Actually it is also a unique cold "casserole."

> 3 cups al dente-*cooked long-grain rice, cooled*
> 1 cup Vinaigrette Sauce (*see String Beans Vinaigrette, page 311*)
> 1 cup chopped scallions (*including some of the green stems*)
> 2 tender (*inside*) celery hearts, scraped and chopped
> 2 small cucumbers, peeled, halved lengthwise, seeds scooped out, and sliced
> 1 cup thinly sliced radishes
> 3 or 4 baby carrots, scraped and blanched in boiling water; then cooled and thinly sliced
> 1 4-ounce jar pimientos, drained and cut into julienne
> 2 tablespoons rinsed and drained capers
> 1 7½-ounce can red salmon, drained and flaked
> 12 medium-sized cooked shrimp, halved lengthwise
> 1 cup diced pickled lamb's tongue
> Salt and freshly ground black pepper
> Boston lettuce leaves

1. Put the rice in a large bowl. It is important that the rice be cooked *al dente,* with the grains separate and firm.

2. Pour on the Vinaigrette Sauce, a tablespoonful at a time, tossing well with a metal fork as each spoonful is added.

3. Add all remaining ingredients, except the lettuce, blending and tossing well with one or two forks. The ingredients should not be stirred together or mashed. Taste for seasoning, adding salt and pepper, if needed. Serve on lettuce leaves.

Ricotta-Rice-Vegetable Salad

SERVES 4 TO 6

3 cups cooked long-grain brown rice, cooled
1 cup ricotta, set in a sieve over a bowl to drain
1 cup broccoli flowerets, cooked tender-crisp
½ cup julienne carrots, cooked tender-crisp
2 whole scallions, trimmed and cut into ¼-inch
    lengths
6 tablespoons olive oil
3 tablespoons fresh lemon juice
Salt and freshly ground black pepper to taste
Bibb or Boston lettuce leaves
⅓ cup drained small capers

Combine the rice with all ingredients, except the lettuce and capers, and mix with a metal fork, fluffing up the rice as you mix. Taste for seasoning, adding whatever your taste demands. Spoon into a bowl lined with the lettuce leaves and sprinkle with the capers.

Rice-Stuffed Pimientos

SERVES 4 TO 6
(depending on the size of the pimientos)

1 cup cooked long-grain rice, cooled
½ cup finely diced Italian Genoa salami
½ cup finely diced Swiss cheese
½ cup finely diced radishes
2 scallions (white part only), minced

½ *cup mayonnaise*
2 *tablespoons olive oil*
2 *tablespoons white vinegar*
1 *tablespoon chopped fresh tarragon, or 1 teaspoon*
    dried
Salt and freshly ground black pepper to taste
4 *to 6 large whole canned pimientos*
½ *pound String Beans Vinaigrette (see below)*
4 *to 6 Boston lettuce leaves*

1. In a bowl, combine and mix well the rice, salami, cheese, radishes, and scallions.

2. In another bowl, combine the mayonnaise, olive oil, vinegar, tarragon, salt, and pepper and blend well. Add this salad dressing to the bowl with the rice and blend well with a fork. Taste for seasoning, adding more vinegar, salt, pepper, or whatever your taste demands.

3. Divide and fill the pimientos, handling the pimientos gently, as they are very fragile.

4. Set each stuffed pimiento on a lettuce leaf and arrange the string beans around each pimiento.

String Beans Vinaigrette

½ *pound young, tender string beans, trimmed*
3 *tablespoons olive oil*
1 *tablespoon wine vinegar*
Salt and freshly ground black pepper to taste
1 *shallot, minced*
3 *tablespoons chopped parsley leaves*

1. Cook the beans in salted boiling water for 5 minutes, or until they are tender but still slightly crisp. Plunge in cold water to cool and drain well. Cut into 1-inch lengths.

2. In a bowl, combine the remaining ingredients and blend well. Pour this salad dressing over the beans and toss to coat.

Dilled Shrimp and Rice Salad

SERVES 4 TO 6

1 pound medium-sized shrimp, shelled and deveined
½ cup olive oil
3 tablespoons fresh lemon juice
⅛ teaspoon cayenne pepper, or to taste
Salt to taste
½ garlic clove, minced
2 tablespoons chopped fresh dill, or 2 teaspoons dried
    dill
1½ cups cooked long-grain rice, cooled
Bibb or Boston lettuce leaves
1 tablespoon chopped fresh dill, or 1 teaspoon dried
    dill or chopped parsley leaves
4 hard-cooked eggs, quartered

1. Cook the shrimp in salted boiling water for 3 minutes, or until they just turn pink and become firm. Do not overcook as they will toughen. Immediately drain and cool. Cut into halves lengthwise.

2. Combine the olive oil, lemon juice, cayenne pepper, salt, garlic, and the 2 tablespoons of dill and blend well.

3. In a large bowl, combine the shrimp, two thirds of the salad dressing, and the rice. Mix with a metal fork, lifting as you mix. Taste and add more lemon juice, pepper, or salt to taste.

4. Line a salad bowl with the lettuce leaves and spoon the salad into it. Or serve on individual salad plates on a lettuce leaf. Garnish the top with the 1 tablespoon of dill or parsley and arrange the egg quarters on the salad. Serve the remaining salad dressing at the table.

Stella Insalata

SERVES 4

1½ cups cooked long-grain rice, cooled
¼ cup quartered pimiento-stuffed olives
¼ cup scraped and chopped celery
¼ cup scraped and shredded carrots
⅓ cup small Provolone cubes
1 teaspoon chopped chives
½ cup olive oil
2 tablespoons red wine vinegar
⅛ teaspoon dried oregano
Salt and freshly ground black pepper to taste
4 large ripe but firm tomatoes
4 rolled anchovies
1 tablespoon chopped broadleaf (Italian) parsley
    leaves

1. In a bowl combine and blend with a metal fork the rice, olives, celery, carrots, cheese, and chives.

2. In a measuring cup, combine and blend well the oil, vinegar, oregano, salt, and pepper. Pour half of the dressing over the rice mixture and toss with a fork. Taste for seasoning. Add more salad dressing to taste. Chill for 30 minutes.

3. Set the tomatoes stem side down. Cut each tomato nearly through forming 6 wedges held together by the stem end. Carefully open each tomato to form a star. Spoon one quarter of the rice mixture into each tomato. Top each with a rolled anchovy. Sprinkle on the parsley and pass any remaining salad dressing at the table.

Singapore Rice Salad

SERVES 6 TO 8

6 tablespoons peanut oil or light vegetable oil
3 eggs, lightly beaten, seasoned with salt and black
    pepper
1 cup tiny fresh peas or frozen peas, defrosted
1 cup fresh corn kernels or frozen corn, defrosted
1/4 pound small firm fresh mushrooms, quartered
1/2 cup currants
1/2 cup rich chicken broth
4 cups cooked long-grain rice, cooled
2 crisp lettuce leaves (the heart of romaine is good),
    shredded
1/2 of a medium-sized cucumber, peeled, seeded, and
    cut into bean-sized pieces
3 tablespoons soy sauce
2 tablespoons sesame oil
1/2 teaspoon salt
1 teaspoon sugar
2 tablespoons dry sherry
3 whole scallions, trimmed and finely chopped

1. In a wok or frying pan over medium heat, heat 3 tablespoons of the oil. Pour in the eggs and cook much like an
omelet, until the eggs have set. Remove and cut into 1/2- by 1-
inch strips. Set aside.

2. Heat the remaining oil in the wok or frying pan. Stir in
the peas and corn and cook for 2 minutes. Add the mushrooms
and currants and cook for 1 minute, or until the currants are
somewhat plump. Add the chicken broth and bring to a boil.

3. Spoon the vegetable mixture, including its liquid, over
the rice. Mix with a fork. Add the egg, lettuce, and cucumber

and mix well. Combine the soy sauce, sesame oil, salt, sugar, and dry sherry and blend well. Pour the mixture over the salad and mix thoroughly. Sprinkle the scallions on top. Serve hot or cold.

Rizi Tabbouleh

SERVES 4 TO 6

4 cups cooked long-grain rice, cooled
½ cup finely chopped fresh mint leaves
1 large Italian red onion, coarsely chopped
¼ cup olive oil
3 tablespoons fresh lemon juice
Salt and freshly ground black pepper to taste
1 large ripe firm tomato, peeled and cut into 4 or 6
*   wedges*
Blanched grape vine leaves (see Note below) to line the
*   salad bowl (optional)*

1. In a bowl, combine and blend well all the ingredients, except the tomato and vine leaves. Taste, then add more oil, lemon juice, etc., if needed.

2. Line a glass salad bowl with the grape leaves, rough side against the glass. Spoon the rice salad into the bowl and garnish with the tomato wedges.

Note: To blanch vine leaves, wash the leaves and drop them into boiling water. Blanch for 3 minutes. Lift out with a large fork and plunge into cold water. Drain well on paper towels.

Tomatoes Stuffed with Eggplant-Rice Salad

SERVES 6

6 large ripe firm tomatoes
1 eggplant, weighing about 1 pound, peeled and cut
    into cubes slightly smaller than ½ inch
3 tablespoons olive oil
1 garlic clove, minced
½ cup chopped tender celery
1½ cups cooked long-grain rice, cooled
¼ cup chopped black olives (the plump, "Greek" ones)
¼ cup chopped pimiento-stuffed green olives
6 anchovy fillets, chopped
1 tablespoon drained capers
2 tablespoons cider vinegar
½ cup olive oil
2 scallions (white part only), minced
1 hard-cooked egg yolk, sieved
Freshly ground black pepper to taste

1. Peel the tomatoes, dipping them in hot water, if necessary. Cut a slice from the stem end and scoop out the inside, leaving a firm shell. Invert on a plate to drain.

2. Sprinkle the eggplant with salt; set it in a strainer over a bowl and allow to stand for 30 minutes to drain. Rinse and pat dry.

3. In a frying pan, over medium heat, heat the 3 tablespoons of olive oil. Add the eggplant, garlic, and celery and cook for 5 minutes, or until they are tender, but still slightly crisp. Cool.

4. Combine the eggplant mixture, rice, olives, anchovies, and capers in a bowl and blend well with a metal fork. Combine the vinegar, ½ cup olive oil, scallions, sieved egg yolk, and black pepper and blend well. Pour over the salad and mix thoroughly. Taste for seasoning and add more of whatever your taste demands.

5. Divide the mixture equally and mound it in the tomatoes. Serve on lettuce leaves.

Baked German Rice Salad

SERVES 6

3 cups al dente-cooked long-grain rice
4 knockwurst, cut into ¼-inch-thick slices
2 celery stalks, scraped and diced
1 small onion, finely chopped
½ cup mayonnaise
1 teaspoon prepared mustard
Salt and freshly ground black pepper to taste
½ cup heavy cream
2 hard-cooked eggs, sliced
3 tablespoons chopped parsley leaves

1. Preheat the oven to 350 degrees.
2. Combine the rice, knockwurst, celery, and onion in a large bowl.
3. Combine and blend into a salad dressing the mayonnaise, mustard, salt, pepper, and cream.
4. Stir the salad dressing into the rice bowl.
5. Spoon into a buttered shallow baking dish. Cover and bake for 30 minutes. Garnish with the egg slices, each topped with a dab of mayonnaise and then sprinkled with parsley.

Valencia Salad

SERVES 6

½ pound shrimp, peeled and deveined
3 cups al dente-cooked long-grain rice, cooled
1 6½-ounce can minced clams, drained
1½ cups diced cooked chicken
1 cup sliced celery heart (Scrape the celery before
    slicing it.)
1 cup cut up small cooked string beans
1 medium-sized red onion, thinly sliced and separated
    into rings
1 tablespoon fresh chopped mint leaves
1 cup mayonnaise
3 tablespoons dry white wine
3 tablespoons rinsed and drained capers
Salt and freshly ground pepper to taste
2 medium-sized ripe firm tomatoes, peeled and each
    cut into 6 wedges

1. Cook the shrimp in salted boiling water, just until they turn pink. Do not overcook. Cut into halves, lengthwise.
2. In a large glass bowl, combine the shrimp, rice, clams, chicken, celery, string beans, onion, and mint.
3. Combine the mayonnaise, wine, capers, salt, and pepper and blend well. Spoon over the salad and mix well but carefully with a metal fork. Taste for seasoning. Chill.
4. Garnish with the tomato wedges.

Wild Rice Salad
with Aïoli Sauce

SERVES 4 TO 6

3 cups cooked wild rice
½ pound small white fresh mushrooms, sliced
3 tablespoons olive oil
2 tablespoons fresh lemon juice
2 hard-cooked eggs, coarsely chopped
1 small sweet green pepper, chopped
2 cups cooked bay scallops or shrimp (If you are using
    the scallops, slice them, but cut the shrimp in half
    lengthwise.)
1 cup Aïoli Sauce (see below)

1. In a large bowl, combine all the ingredients, except the
Aïoli Sauce.
2. Spoon in half of the Aïoli Sauce and mix well, but carefully, with a metal fork, fluffing.
3. Taste and add more sauce, if desired. Serve the remaining sauce at the table.

Aïoli Sauce

1 cup mayonnaise
3 garlic cloves, minced
½ teaspoon dry mustard
½ teaspoon paprika
1 tablespoon fresh lemon juice

Combine and blend all the ingredients well.

Summer Rice Salad

SERVES 6

4 cups cooked long-grain rice, cooled
4 scallions (white part only), thinly sliced
½ cup finely chopped sweet pickles
1 small pimiento, cut into short strips
4 hard-cooked eggs, chopped
1 cup mayonnaise, blended with 1 teaspoon Dijon
*   mustard*
Salt and freshly ground black pepper to taste
2 bunches watercress
1 ripe but firm avocado, cut into 6 wedges
2 ripe firm tomatoes, peeled and each cut into 6
*   wedges*

1. In a large bowl, combine and blend well, but gently, with a metal fork the rice, scallions, pickles, pimiento, eggs, and two thirds of the mayonnaise. Add salt and pepper. Taste and add more mayonnaise to taste.

2. Serve on a bed of watercress, garnished with the avocado and tomato wedges.

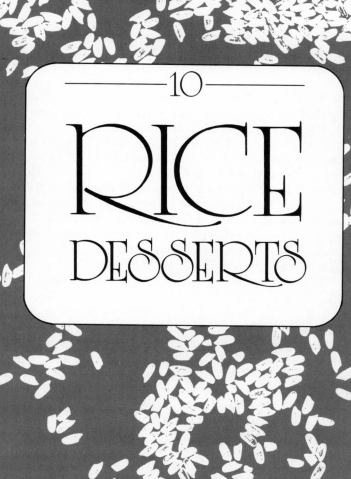

10

RICE

DESSERTS

Antoine Gilly, one of the greatest of the French chefs, once observed, "It probably isn't fair, but one of the strongest and very often the most favorable impressions of a dinner is the last course. Maybe we have short taste memories.

"I still remember," he went on, "serving the Maharaja of Bharatpur one of my own favorites, smoked salmon wrapped around caviar, pheasant under feather, and several other offerings, including barquettes of crayfish. It was, admittedly, a rather full meal, so, for dessert, I served another favorite of mine, something light, cool, and refreshing—a goblet of orange sherbet topped with light rum. *That* got the applause."

At many a state dinner, the White House chefs must have been less than gratified when a beaming President Eisenhower remarked upon how delicious the rice pudding was. It was his favorite dessert, and it was served often.

That was a president with excellent taste.

Rice surprises many of us when it appears as a dessert. We once forgot all that went before (at a remarkable dinner of smoked trout followed by quail) when Strawberry Rice Custard Pie was served. As rice often does, it stole the show.

In cooking the following desserts, we've run tests with various rices and found that short- or medium-grain rice worked best. We also checked many markets and found that medium grain is available just about everywhere. In testing and assembling these recipes, with some of them, we worked with Rae Hartfield, R. D., Director of Nutrition of The Rice Council, a master of rice desserts.

Almond-Date Cream

SERVES 4

2 whole eggs plus 1 egg yolk
1½ cups milk
1½ cups cooked short- or medium-grain rice
¼ cup firmly packed light brown sugar
⅛ teaspoon salt
3 tablespoons butter
½ cup chopped pitted dates
½ teaspoon pure vanilla extract
⅓ cup chopped blanched and toasted almonds
¼ teaspoon cream of tartar
4 tablespoons granulated sugar
½ teaspoon pure almond extract

1. Separate the whole eggs. In a bowl, beat the 3 egg yolks slightly; stir in the milk, rice, brown sugar, salt, butter, and dates. Transfer to a deep saucepan and cook over medium-low heat, stirring constantly, until thickened. Do not overcook. Stir in the vanilla extract. Preheat the oven to 350 degrees.

2. Butter a shallow baking dish. Sprinkle the almonds on the bottom. Then spoon in the custard.

3. Beat the egg whites until frothy. Beat in the cream of tartar. When stiff, add the granulated sugar, a small amount at a time, and continue beating after each addition. Beat until the mixture holds its shape. Beat in the almond extract.

4. Spread the meringue over the rice custard. Bake for 20 minutes, or until the top is golden brown. Serve warm or cold.

Algarve Rice Pudding

SERVES 4

We call this excellent dessert the "Algarve" pudding, for it was in that southern province, Portugal's Riviera, that we found it.

1 cup short- or medium-grain rice
2½ cups water
Peel of 1 lemon, cut into strips
2 cups of medium cream or half-and-half
2 egg yolks
¼ cup sugar
1 teaspoon ground mace

1. In a saucepan, combine the rice, water, and lemon peel. Bring to a boil, stir well with a wooden fork, lower the heat, cover, and simmer for 15 minutes, or until the rice is tender. Drain any liquid that remains. Discard the lemon peel.

2. In a bowl, combine and beat well the cream, egg yolks, and sugar. Stir this mixture into the rice and simmer over low heat, until the rice is very soft, of pudding consistency, and the custard is creamy. Serve warm in bowls, sprinkled with the mace.

Apricot Twist

SERVES 6 TO 8

3 cups cooked short- or medium-grain rice
2½ cups milk
⅔ cup sugar
1 tablespoon butter
3 egg yolks beaten with ½ cup milk
1 teaspoon pure vanilla extract
3 egg whites beaten with ¼ teaspoon cream of tartar
    and ⅛ teaspoon salt until stiff but not dry
¾ cup well-drained and chopped cooked dried apricots
2 teaspoons brandy

1. Combine the rice, milk, ⅓ cup of the sugar, and the butter in a saucepan. Cook over low heat until thick and creamy, about 20 minutes, stirring occasionally.

2. Stir the egg yolk mixture into the rice mixture and cook for 2 or 3 minutes. Stir in the vanilla. Turn into a buttered 1½-quart baking dish. Preheat the oven to 350 degrees.

3. A tablespoonful at a time, beat the remaining ⅓ cup of sugar into the egg whites.

4. Fold the apricots and brandy into the egg whites. Spread over the pudding in little twists or swirls, completely covering it. Bake for 10 minutes, or until golden brown. Serve immediately.

Apple-Walnut Crisp

SERVES 6

2 cups cooked short- or medium-grain rice
2 cups thinly sliced tart apples
1 tablespoon fresh lemon juice
1 cup firmly packed light brown sugar
½ teaspoon ground cinnamon
¼ teaspoon salt
¾ cup all-purpose flour
6 tablespoons butter
½ cup chopped walnuts
1 cup heavy cream, whipped

1. In a bowl combine and mix well, but carefully, the rice, apples, lemon juice, ½ cup of the brown sugar, cinnamon, and salt. Transfer to a buttered shallow baking dish. Preheat the oven to 350 degrees.

2. Mix the flour and remaining sugar together. With a pastry cutter, cut in the butter until the mixture is crumbly. Stir in the nuts. Evenly spoon over the rice and bake for 30 minutes, or until the top is crispy and golden brown. Serve warm or cool, topped with the whipped cream.

Apple-Rum Pudding

SERVES 6

1 cup cooked short- or medium-grain rice
2 cups light cream or half-and-half
⅓ cup sugar

½ *teaspoon salt*
1 *envelope (1 tablespoon) unflavored gelatin*
¼ *cup water*
2 *tablespoons light rum*
1 *cup sour cream*
Apple-Rum Topping (see below)

1. Combine the rice, cream, sugar, and salt in a saucepan. Bring to a boil, stir with a wooden fork, lower the heat, and cook, stirring occasionally, until creamy, about 20 minutes.

2. Soften the gelatin in the water. Heat the mixture over hot water until it is clear and liquid. Add to the rice mixture and stir to blend well. Cool until thickened but not set.

3. Fold in the rum and sour cream. Spoon into individual 1-cup molds. Chill until firm. Unmold and serve with the hot Apple Rum Topping spooned on top.

Apple-Rum Topping

½ *cup firmly packed light brown sugar*
2 *teaspoons cornstarch*
¼ *teaspoon salt*
½ *teaspoon ground cinnamon*
½ *cup water*
2 *cups coarsely chopped tart apples*
3 *tablespoons butter*
2 *tablespoons light rum*

Combine and blend well the sugar, cornstarch, salt, cinnamon, and water in a saucepan. Add the apples. Bring to a boil, lower the heat, and simmer, stirring occasionally, for 15 to 20 minutes, or until the apples are tender. Remove from the heat and stir in the butter and rum.

Apple-Ricot Soufflé

SERVES 4 TO 6

3½ cups light cream or half-and-half
1¼ cups short- or medium-grain rice
2 eggs, separated
6 tablespoons superfine sugar
6 tablespoons apricot jam
4 tablespoons applesauce
¼ teaspoon cream of tartar
½ teaspoon pure almond extract
1 tablespoon light rum (optional)

1. In a saucepan, over medium heat, bring the cream to a boil. Stir in the rice, turn the heat to the lowest setting, cover, and simmer, stirring frequently, for 30 minutes, or until the rice is very tender and most of the liquid has been absorbed. Remove from the heat.

2. Beat the egg yolks with 3 tablespoons of the sugar and stir into the rice. Preheat the oven to 350 degrees.

3. Butter a 2-quart soufflé dish and spread a layer of rice over the bottom. Spread a thin layer of jam over the rice. Repeat until the rice is used, ending with a layer of jam. The number of layers depends on the size of the dish. Spread the applesauce over the last layer of jam.

4. Beat the egg whites until they are frothy. Add the cream of tartar and beat until stiff enough to form peaks. Add the remaining sugar in small amounts, beating after each addition. Beat in the almond extract. Spread over the applesauce and bake for 20 minutes, or until golden. Just before serving, spoon the rum over the top and ignite it.

Dolce Budino Velluto con Salsa di Fragole

SERVES 6 TO 8

1½ cups ricotta
2 cups milk
3 cups cooked short- or medium-grain rice
½ cup sugar
½ teaspoon salt
1 tablespoon grated lemon rind
2 eggs, beaten in a bowl
1 teaspoon pure vanilla extract
1 quart fresh strawberries, hulled, rinsed, and sliced
½ cup red currant jelly

1. Mash or process the cheese in a blender or food processor until it is smooth. Transfer to a deep saucepan; stir in the milk, rice, sugar, salt, and lemon rind, blending well. Cook over low heat, stirring frequently, until thick and creamy, about 20 minutes.

2. Stir a small amount of the hot mixture into the eggs; return all to the saucepan. Cook, stirring constantly, until the eggs have set, about 1 minute. Stir in the vanilla. Cool.

3. Meanwhile, to make the sauce, mash 1 cup of the strawberries. Combine with the jelly and a dash of salt in a saucepan. Heat to boiling. Stir in the remaining berries and cook for about 1 minute. Chill.

4. Spoon the pudding into serving dishes and cover with the strawberry sauce.

Danish Rice Cream

SERVES 4 TO 6

While staying at the Terminus, an elegant small hotel near the railway station in Copenhagen, we heard that cooking classes were being conducted in a nearby building that we believe was called The National House. We think that was the name because the classes were offered free by the Danish government.

Four pink-cheeked, robust ladies in aprons worked on a platform, the wall behind them mirrored so spectators could observe the hands of the skilled cooks at work. One lady explained the actions in Danish, another in English, while the other two cooked. We learned how to cook Danish chickens in nothing but "the world's best butter," and lemon, with a currant jelly-cheese-mustard sauce, and the following rice dish. The dessert is varied with different nuts and sometimes tart wild "cloudberries."

> 1 quart milk
> 4 tablespoons superfine sugar
> ¾ cup short- or medium-grain rice
> 1 large egg yolk, beaten
> ½ cup chopped walnuts
> 1 teaspoon pure vanilla extract
> 1 cup heavy cream, whipped
> 1 1-pound can pitted Bing (black) cherries with their liquid
> 1 tablespoon cornstarch, dissolved in 1 tablespoon cold water
> 1 tablespoon Crème de Cassis (black currant liqueur)

1. Pour the milk into a deep saucepan, stir in the sugar, and bring to a boil. Stir in the rice, lower the heat, and simmer, uncovered, for 20 minutes, or until thick and creamy. Stir frequently.

2. Remove the rice from the heat and stir in the egg yolk, walnuts, and vanilla extract. Pour the rice mixture into a chilled mixing bowl and let sit at room temperature until it cools. Fold in the whipped cream. Cover and refrigerate.

3. Pour the cherries and the liquid from the can into a saucepan with the Cassis. Simmer, stirring, for 5 minutes. Add the cornstarch mixture and cook, stirring, for 30 seconds, or until thickened and clear.

4. Transfer the rice to a fairly shallow serving dish, smooth the top, and evenly spoon on the cherry mixture. Refrigerate for 2 hours before serving.

President Grant's Rice Pudding

SERVES 8

1 tablespoon butter, softened
3 cups hot cooked short- or medium-grain rice
4 egg yolks, beaten in a large bowl
2 cups light cream or half-and-half
2 cups milk
½ cup sugar
1 tablespoon grated lemon rind
1 teaspoon pure vanilla extract
⅛ teaspoon salt
4 egg whites, beaten until stiff but not dry
Lemon Sauce (see below)

1. Preheat the oven to 350 degrees.
2. Stir the butter into the rice. Add the rice, cream, milk,

sugar, lemon rind, vanilla extract, and salt to the bowl with the beaten egg yolks and blend well. Fold in the beaten egg whites.

3. Turn into a buttered shallow 2½-quart baking dish. Set in a pan of hot water. Bake for 1 hour, or until a knife blade inserted just off center comes out clean. Serve warm with Lemon Sauce.

Lemon Sauce

½ cup sugar
1 tablespoon cornstarch
⅛ teaspoon salt
1 cup boiling water
1 tablespoon butter
1 tablespoon grated lemon rind
1 tablespoon fresh lemon juice

1. Combine and blend well the sugar, cornstarch, and salt in a saucepan. Gradually stir the hot water into the sugar-cornstarch mixture.

2. Cook over medium-low heat, stirring constantly, until it thickens, about 5 minutes. Blend in the butter, lemon rind, and lemon juice.

Cherries Jubilee Pudding

SERVES 6

1 recipe for rice pudding, as prepared for Raspberry Parfait (page 349). Do not use the fruit for that recipe but do use the almonds, if desired.
Cherries Jubilee Sauce (see below)

1. Prepare pudding and cool.
2. Serve in individual dessert dishes, spooning Cherries Jubilee Sauce over each serving.

Cherries Jubilee Sauce

1 1-pound can pitted Bing (black) cherries, drained, reserving syrup
1 tablespoon sugar
1 tablespoon cornstarch, blended with 1 tablespoon cold water
¼ cup kirsch, heated

1. In a saucepan, combine and blend well the sugar and cornstarch mixture. Gradually stir in the reserved syrup. Cook over low heat, stirring constantly, until the sauce starts to thicken, about 2 minutes. Add the cherries and heat through.
2. Pour over the kirsch and ignite it (stand back as it will flare).
3. Spoon the sauce over the pudding.

Cream Mold

SERVES 4 TO 6

¼ cup short- or medium-grain rice
½ cup water
½ teaspoon salt
2 cups milk
1 tablespoon butter
1½ envelopes (1½ tablespoons) unflavored gelatin
6 tablespoons sugar
2 teaspoons grated lemon rind
1 teaspoon pure vanilla extract
1 cup heavy cream, whipped

1. Combine the rice, ¼ cup of the water, and the salt. Heat to boiling, stir with a wooden fork, lower the heat, cover, and cook for 5 minutes. Add the milk and butter and return to a boil. Lower the heat, cover, and simmer until the rice is tender, about 20 minutes, stirring occasionally.

2. Soften the gelatin in the remaining water; stir over hot water until it is dissolved, clear, and liquid. Stir into the rice mixture. Stir in the sugar, lemon rind, and vanilla. Remove from the heat and cool until it just starts to set. Fold in the whipped cream.

3. Pour into a 1-quart mold. Cover and chill until the mixture sets.

4. Unmold and serve with a raspberry, strawberry, peach, or other fruit sauce.

Flan de Arroz

SERVES 6

4 cups (1 quart) light cream or half-and-half
⅓ cup short- or medium-grain rice
Thin strips of rind from 1 large lemon, colored part
only (not any of the white)
9 tablespoons sugar
6 egg yolks

1. Heat the cream in the top of a double boiler. Stir in the rice and lemon rind. Bring the water in the bottom of the double boiler to a boil, lower the heat, and cook the rice over the simmering water for 25 minutes, or until it is very tender. Stir frequently.

2. Spoon 6 tablespoons of the sugar into a heavy saucepan or frying pan and cook over medium heat for 3 minutes, or until the sugar starts to melt, shaking the pan to keep the sugar from burning. Turn the heat to low and cook, stirring, until the sugar is syrupy and dark brown, being careful that it doesn't burn. Spoon the syrup into a pyrex bowl, spinning the bowl around until the sugar syrup evenly coats the sides and bottom. Preheat the oven to 300 degrees.

3. In a bowl, beat the egg yolks with the remaining sugar until they are lemony in color. Remove and discard the lemon rind in the cream-rice mixture. Gradually blend the cream-rice mixture with the egg yolk-sugar mixture. Carefully pour into the bowl coated with the sugar syrup. Set the bowl in a pan of very hot water. The water should come halfway up the side of the bowl. Bake for 35 minutes, or until the flan is set. A knife blade inserted just off center will come out clean. Do not overbake. Cool and refrigerate until ready to serve. Just before serving run a knife blade around the side of the bowl and turn the flan out onto a serving dish with a slightly raised rim.

A Georgia Peach

SERVES 4

1 cup cooked short- or medium-grain rice
3 eggs, beaten
¼ teaspoon salt
⅓ cup sugar
1 teaspoon pure vanilla extract
1 teaspoon grated lemon rind
2½ cups milk
1½ cups sliced fresh peaches, sweetened to taste, or
    drained, canned or frozen sliced peaches
1 teaspoon fresh lemon juice
1 tablespoon brandy
⅔ cup shredded coconut

1. Preheat the oven to 350 degrees.

2. Combine and blend well all the ingredients, except the peaches, lemon juice, brandy, and coconut. Turn into a buttered 1-quart baking dish. Set the dish in a pan of hot water and bake for 45 minutes, or until a knife blade inserted just off center emerges clean. Halfway through the cooking time, use a spoon to stir from the bottom, bringing the rice to the surface.

3. Combine and mix well the peaches, lemon juice, brandy, and coconut. Chill until serving time. Arrange on top of the custard just before serving.

Rice-Coconut Custard

SERVES 6

3 eggs, beaten in a mixing bowl
½ cup sugar
¼ teaspoon salt
2 cups milk
1 cup cooked short- or medium-grain rice
¼ cup raisins
1 teaspoon pure vanilla extract
½ cup shredded coconut
¼ teaspoon ground nutmeg
1 tablespoon butter
¼ cup shredded coconut, toasted until golden

1. Preheat the oven to 350 degrees.
2. Add the sugar and salt to the beaten eggs and blend well. Stir in the milk. Stir in the rice, raisins, vanilla, and the ½ cup of coconut. Pour into a buttered 1½-quart baking dish. Set it in a pan of hot water.
3. Bake for 30 minutes. Stir from the bottom to the top, bringing the rice to the surface as much as possible.
4. Sprinkle with nutmeg and dot with butter. Bake for 30 minutes longer, or until the custard has set.
5. Sprinkle with the toasted coconut just before serving.

Pineapple Pudding

SERVES 6

3 cups cooked short- or medium-grain rice
4 cups milk
⅔ cup sugar
½ teaspoon salt
2 eggs, beaten in a bowl
1 3-ounce package cream cheese, softened
1 teaspoon pure vanilla extract
Pineapple Sauce (see below)

1. Combine and blend well the rice, 3½ cups of the milk, sugar, and salt in a deep saucepan. Cook over low heat, stirring occasionally, until thick and creamy, about 20 minutes.

2. Add the remaining milk and the cheese to the beaten eggs and beat to blend. Stir into the rice mixture in the saucepan. Cook, stirring constantly, for 2 minutes, or until the eggs have set.

3. Stir in the vanilla extract. Spoon into serving dishes.

4. Serve warm or chilled with Pineapple Sauce.

Pineapple Sauce

1 20-ounce can pineapple chunks
1 tablespoon of cornstarch, dissolved in 1 tablespoon
    cold water
1 tablespoon butter
¼ cup firmly packed light brown sugar
⅛ teaspoon salt
½ teaspoon pure vanilla extract

1. Combine and blend well the pineapple with its juice and the cornstarch mixture in a saucepan.

2. Add the butter, brown sugar, and salt and cook over medium-low heat, stirring, until clear and thickened. Stir in the vanilla.

Rice Pudding Glacé

SERVES 6

3 cups cooked short- or medium-grain rice
3 cups milk
½ cup (8 tablespoons) sugar
¼ teaspoon salt
2 teaspoons pure vanilla extract
2 teaspoons grated lemon rind
1 cup sour cream
2 cups mixed fruit, fresh, canned, or frozen, drained

1. In a deep saucepan, combine and blend well the rice, milk, 5 tablespoons of the sugar, and the salt. Cook over low heat, stirring occasionally, until thick and creamy, about 20 minutes. Add 1 teaspoon of the vanilla extract and 1 teaspoon of the lemon rind and blend. Turn into a buttered shallow 1½-quart baking dish. Preheat the broiler.

2. Combine and blend well the sour cream, remaining sugar, vanilla, and lemon rind. Spread over the pudding. Place under a broiler for about 5 minutes to form a glaze. Watch carefully to prevent burning. Serve hot or cold, topped with the mixed fruit.

Orange Rice Ring

SERVES 4 TO 6

3 cups half-and-half
⅔ cup superfine sugar
1½ cups short- or medium-grain rice
1 teaspoon grated lemon rind
2 teaspoons grated orange rind
½ cup freshly squeezed orange juice
½ pint heavy cream, whipped
1½ cups Mandarin orange slices, marinated in Grand
    Marnier to barely cover

1. Bring the half-and-half to a boil in a deep saucepan. Stir in the sugar and then the rice. Turn the heat to the lowest possible setting, permitting the liquid to barely bubble. Cover and cook for 40 minutes, or until the liquid has been absorbed and the rice is tender, stirring occasionally. If the liquid is absorbed before the rice is tender, add a small amount of hot half-and-half or milk, and continue cooking. Remove from the heat and cool.

2. Stir in the lemon and orange rinds and orange juice, blending thoroughly. Fold in the whipped cream.

3. Spoon into a lightly oiled 9-inch ring mold. Refrigerate overnight. Unmold onto a cold serving dish and fill the center with the marinated, well-drained orange slices.

Pudding with Hazelnuts

SERVES 4 TO 6

3½ cups milk plus 2 tablespoons heavy cream (see below)
1½ cups short- or medium-grain rice
¾ cup sugar
½ cup boiling water
¾ cup hazelnuts, toasted, skinned, and ground
½ pint heavy cream, less the 2 tablespoons (used above), whipped and sweetened to taste

1. In a saucepan, bring the milk and cream to a boil. Stir in the rice, turn the heat to the lowest setting, cover, and cook for 25 minutes, or until the rice is tender and the liquid has been absorbed. Stir occasionally. Cool.

2. In a saucepan, over medium-low heat, melt the sugar, stirring, so it doesn't burn, until it is syrupy and brown. Standing back as the combining of the hot sugar and water can cause spattering, stir the water into the syrup and blend. Simmer for 5 minutes. Stir carefully into the cooled rice.

3. With a metal fork, add the ground hazelnuts to the rice, mixing well, lifting the rice as you mix.

4. Fold the whipped cream into the rice and serve cold in dessert glasses.

Creamy Raisin Rice

SERVES 4 TO 6

½ cup short- or medium-grain rice
½ cup water
½ teaspoon salt
2¾ cups milk
½ cup raisins
Dark rum to cover the raisins, warmed
3 tablespoons butter
2 eggs, beaten in a bowl
⅓ cup sugar
½ teaspoon pure vanilla extract

1. In a deep saucepan, combine the rice, water, and salt. Bring to a boil, lower the heat, cover, and cook for about 5 minutes. Stir in 2¼ cups of the milk. Cover and cook over low heat for 1 hour, stirring occasionally.

2. Meanwhile, cover the raisins with the rum; let stand for 15 minutes. Drain in a sieve and set aside.

3. Stir the butter into the hot pudding.

4. Combine and blend well the eggs, sugar, and remaining milk. Add to the pudding mixture, stirring constantly. Cook for 2 to 3 minutes, or until the mixture thickens and the eggs have set. Remove from the heat and stir in the raisins and vanilla extract.

5. Spoon into serving dishes. Serve warm or cold.

Old-Fashioned American Rice Pudding

SERVES 6 TO 8

This is an American classic, born in the South, and the favorite of several Presidents of the United States.

> 3 cups cooked short- or medium-grain rice, thoroughly drained
> 3 eggs, beaten
> 1 cup milk
> 1 cup heavy cream
> ½ cup light brown sugar (without lumps)
> 1 teaspoon pure vanilla extract
> 2 teaspoons fresh orange juice
> ⅛ teaspoon ground mace
> ½ cup golden raisins

1. Preheat the oven to 325 degrees.
2. In a bowl, combine all the ingredients and blend lightly with a metal fork. Spoon into a buttered 8-inch-square by 2-inch-deep baking dish and bake for 15 minutes. Stir and bake for 25 minutes longer, or until set. The pudding can be served either warm or cold.

Strawberry-Rice Custard Pie

SERVES 6

The Rice Custard

2 egg yolks, beaten in a large bowl
½ cup cooked short- or medium-grain rice
½ cup sugar
1 teaspoon grated lemon rind
½ teaspoon pure vanilla extract
Pinch of salt
1½ cups milk
2 egg whites, stiffly beaten
9-inch partially baked pastry shell

The Strawberries

1 quart ripe strawberries, washed, hulled, and
    thoroughly drained
1 cup sugar, mixed with 3 tablespoons cornstarch

1. To prepare the Rice Custard, preheat the oven to 325 degrees. Blend the egg yolks with the rice, sugar, lemon rind, vanilla, salt, and milk. Fold in the egg whites. Pour the mixture into the pastry shell and bake for 40 minutes, or until set. Remove and cool.

2. Select and set aside the most perfect, uniform berries. (They should amount to at least half of the berries.)

3. Mash the remaining berries and push them through a strainer (or process in a food processor) into a 2-cup measuring cup. If you do not have 1½ cups, add water to yield that amount. Pour into a saucepan. Gradually stir in the sugar and cornstarch. Cook over medium heat, stirring, until the mixture simmers and thickens. Simmer for 1 minute, stirring. Cool.

4. Arrange the reserved whole berries attractively on top of the rice custard. Pour the sauce over and chill thoroughly. Decorate with whipped cream, if desired.

Top-of-the-Stove Rice Pudding

SERVES 6

½ cup short- or medium-grain rice
4 tablespoons (½ stick) butter
1 cup water
½ teaspoon salt
4 cups milk
½ cup sugar
2 eggs, beaten
½ cup heavy cream
1 teaspoon pure vanilla extract
½ cup raisins, plumped in port wine and well drained
Ground cinnamon

1. In a saucepan, combine the rice, butter, water, and salt. Bring to a boil, lower the heat, cover, and simmer until all the water has been absorbed.

2. Pour in the milk and bring to a boil. Turn the heat to the lowest setting and simmer, stirring often, for 25 minutes, or until the rice is very tender.

3. Beat the sugar and eggs together. Stir into the cooked rice, stirring constantly until the egg mixture is set. Remove from the heat and blend in the cream, vanilla, and raisins.

4. Spoon into a serving bowl and cool. Refrigerate until serving time. Sprinkle the top lightly with cinnamon before serving.

Rice Tart

SERVES 6 TO 8

We found this one in Parma, that region in Italy that is also famous for remarkable ham, the spicy *culatello,* and superb cheese, *parmigiano-reggiano.*

> *5 cups milk*
> *1 cup granulated sugar*
> *1½ cups short- or medium-grain rice*
> *3 egg yolks*
> *½ cup chopped blanched and toasted almonds*
> *Grated rind (no white) of 1 orange*
> *½ teaspoon pure almond extract*
> *3 egg whites, stiffly beaten*
> *Confectioner's sugar*

1. In a saucepan, bring the milk to a boil. Lower the heat and stir in ½ cup of the granulated sugar and then the rice. Simmer, covered, over the lowest heat for 15 minutes. Stir occasionally. Remove from the heat and cool. Preheat the oven to 325 degrees.

2. In a large bowl beat the egg yolks with the remaining granulated sugar. Blend in the rice and milk, almonds, orange rind, and almond extract. Fold in the egg whites.

3. Pour into a buttered 12-inch-square cake pan with high sides and bake for 50 minutes, or until set.

4. Before serving, sprinkle on the confectioner's sugar. Or sprinkle lightly with *amaretto* and then the sugar.

Raspberry-Rice Mold

SERVES 6 TO 8

3 cups cooked short- or medium-grain rice
3 cups milk
⅓ cup sugar
1 tablespoon butter
¼ teaspoon salt
2 eggs, beaten in a bowl
½ cup golden raisins
½ cup drained crushed pineapple
1 teaspoon pure vanilla extract
⅔ cup raspberry jelly, melted
½ cup chopped pecans

1. In a deep saucepan, combine and blend well the rice, 2½ cups of the milk, sugar, butter, and salt. Cook over low heat until thick and creamy, 20 to 25 minutes, stirring occasionally.

2. Combine and blend well the eggs and the remaining milk. Stir into the rice mixture. Stir in the raisins. Cook, stirring constantly, for about 2 minutes, or until the eggs are set. Stir in the pineapple and vanilla. Spoon into individual molds or one large mold. Cool slightly. Unmold and spoon on the melted raspberry jelly. Sprinkle with the pecans.

Strawberry Rice Crème Brûlée

SERVES 6 TO 8

3 cups cooked short- or medium-grain rice
3 cups milk
⅓ cup granulated sugar
¼ teaspoon salt
2 3-ounce packages cream cheese, softened
1½ teaspoons pure vanilla extract
1 cup heavy cream, whipped
1 pint strawberries, hulled, rinsed, sliced and
        sweetened to taste, or 1 16-ounce package frozen,
        sweetened whole strawberries, thawed, drained,
        and cut into halves
½ cup light brown sugar (without lumps)

1. In a deep saucepan, combine the rice, milk, granulated sugar, and salt. Cook over low heat until thick and creamy, about 20 minutes, stirring occasionally. Remove from the heat. Add the cream cheese, in small pieces, and the vanilla extract, stirring until the cheese has melted. Chill.

2. Fold in the whipped cream and chill thoroughly.

3. Arrange the strawberries on the bottom of a shallow baking dish. Spoon the pudding over the berries. Sprinkle evenly with the brown sugar, smoothing the top. Place under the broiler until the sugar melts forming a glaze. Watch carefully so the sugar does not burn. Serve as soon as the glaze cools and hardens.

Raspberry Parfait

SERVES 6

1½ cups cooked short- or medium-grain rice
1½ cups milk
3 tablespoons sugar
¼ teaspoon salt
1 teaspoon pure vanilla extract
¼ cup toasted sliced almonds
1 cup heavy cream, whipped
1 10-ounce package frozen raspberries (or
    blueberries), thawed

1. Combine and blend well the rice, milk, sugar, and salt in a saucepan. Cook over low heat until thick and creamy, about 20 minutes, stirring occasionally. Remove from the heat and stir in the vanilla. Cool.

2. Fold in the almonds and two thirds of the whipped cream.

3. In parfait glasses, alternate layers of the rice mixture and the fruit, ending with fruit and a dab of the remaining whipped cream. Chill until ready to serve.

INDEX